...elly dancers body on

...lace-up boots, all ca...

...features more define...

...e alone, a loft downto...

...want to be an art...

...t about it, overdre...

...ould seek asylum i...

...htness' of that image...

...l, but especially by...

...ch like hers, older b...

...ying too hard. They...

...on looking for mor...

...vere similar, not sou...

...d at least. In these t...

...time, h... ...em on...

f she's changed. no

huge leather jacke

ke her face, small

ss, emblazoned: lu

onsense baby, if yo

I am in debt, no dou

mmitted, wishing t

. Stunned by the 're

ued by every detai

had a presence m

attractive without i

ad to have them, sel

ly found some that

ut stylishly distress

g, wore them all t

Imaging Desire

Mary Kelly

Imaging Desire

The MIT Press Cambridge, Massachusetts London, England

This book was set in Bembo by Graphic Composition, Inc.

Printed and bound in the United States of America.

Library of Congress Cataloging-in-Publication Data

Kelly, Mary, 1941–

    Imaging desire / Mary Kelly.

      p.   cm.

    Includes bibliographical references and index.

    ISBN 0-262-11214-0 (alk. paper)

    1.Feminism and art—United States.   2. Feminist art criticism—United States.   I. Title.

    N72.F45K46   1997

    704′.042—dc20   96-38867

                                                  CIP

Contents

For Kelly Barrie

Illustrations

III *Postmodern Oppositions*

3.1 Jackson Pollock, *Yellow Islands,* 1952. Collection Tate Gallery, London, Courtesy Art Resource, New York.

3.2 Joseph Kosuth, *Art as Idea as Idea,* 1967, photostat mounted on cardboard, 48 × 48 ins. Photo: Dorothy Zeidman. Courtesy Leo Castelli, New York.

3.3 Robert Morris, *Untitled,* 1966, plywood, 4 × 8 × 8 ft. Courtesy Leo Castelli, New York.

3.4 Gina Pane, *Azione Sentimentale,* Galerie Diagramma, Milan, 1973. Courtesy Anne Marchand, Paris.

3.5 Ulrike Rosenbach, *Salto Mortale,* 1978. Courtesy Haags Gemeentemuseum, The Hague.

3.6 Catalogue, *Beyond the Purloined Image,* Riverside Studios, London, 1983. Cover design by Marie Yates.

3.7 Details, (above) Karen Knorr, Marie Yates, Susan Trangmar, Judith Crowle; (below) Olivier Richon, Ray Barrie, Yve Lomax.

3.8 *Difference: On Representation and Sexuality,* New Museum of Contemporary Art, New York, 1984, installation view, foreground, Silvia Kolbowski, *Model Pleasure,* 1982–84.

3.9 Ray Barrie, *Master-Pieces,* 1981, 6 units, 30 × 30 ins. each, color autone photographs.

3.10 Mary Kelly, working on *Interim,* 1985. Photo: Ray Barrie.

IV *Invisible Bodies*

4.1 Mary Kelly, *Interim,* Part I: "Corpus," 1984–85, installation view, Henry McNeil Gallery, Philadelphia, 1988, photolaminate, silkscreen, and acrylic on plexiglass, 6 of 30 panels, 48 × 36 ins. each.

4.2 Detail, "Corpus."

4.3 J.M. Charcot, "Attitudes passionelles," (Planche XXIII, Extase), *Nouvelle Iconographie Photographie de la Salpêtrière,* vol. 2, Paris, 1878.

4.4 "Obsession," Calvin Klein, *Vogue* (United States), March 1985. Photo: Bruce Weber.

4.5 Edward Kienholz, *The Wait,* 1964–65, Tableau 6 ft. and 8 ins. 12 ft. and 4 ins. × 6 ft. and 6 ins. Gift of The Howard and Jean Lipman

Acknowledgments

With regard to the collective effort required for this publication, I am especially thankful for the research of Judith Mastai, the editorial work of Liz Dalton, the assistance of Elizabeth Cohen, Toby Greenberg, and Klaus Ottmann, and above all, the advice of Ray Barrie throughout this process. I am also grateful to Barbara Kruger for suggesting the idea of the selected writings project and to Roger Conover for undertaking it.

In addition, I would like to thank Emily Apter, Hal Foster, Margaret Iversen, Laura Mulvey, and Paul Smith for permission to reprint conversations which were formative moments in thinking through the implications of my work. Finally, I would like to acknowledge some of those who, through their interest, example, or friendship, have made this endeavor meaningful: Parveen Adams, Alex Alberro, Sally Alexander, Pauline Barrie, Maurice Berger, Homi Bhabha, Victor Burgin, Norman Bryson, Susan Cahan, Juli Carson, Ron Clark, Elizabeth Cowie, Rosalind Delmar, Rosalyn Deutsche, David Diao, Leslie Dick, Gary Dufour, Bonnie Engdahl, Steve Fagin, Ann Gibson, Helen Grace, Renee Green, Hans Haacke, Joanna Isaak, Isaac Julien, Michael Kelly, Silvia Kolbowski, Lucy Lippard, Jan-Erik Lundstrom, Anne Naldrett, Mark Nash, Linda Nochlin, Constance Penley, Griselda Pollock, Yvonne Rainer, Jacqueline Rose, Gertrud Sandqvist, Magda Sawon, Allan Sekula, Terry Smith, Blake Stimson, Abigail Solomon-Godeau, Gayatri Spivak, Mary Anne Staniszewski, Lynne Tillman, Leslie Tonkonow, Marcia Tucker, Anthony Vidler, Kathleen Woodward, Peter Wollen, Jane Weinstock, and the participants of the Whitney Independent Study Program.

Introduction: Remembering, Repeating, and Working-Through[1]

Until recently, I could not even open, much less examine, the contents of a certain folder. It contains reviews that appeared in the tabloid press during the exhibition of *Post-Partum Document* at the Institute of Contemporary Art (ICA) in London, in 1976. Just a glimpse of the insalubrious prose decrying "dirty nappies" was enough to prompt a swift return to the archive where they remained gathering anxious dust for almost twenty years. Now when I look at them, I see a history that for the most part is taken for granted, but that in the making seemed difficult and confrontational, sometimes disconcertingly so. Yet the affective force of that moment and, crucially, its repression interest me, given that, in the course of preparing this volume, I have come to view my "writing" as a form of "acting out," that is, as a transference of the past onto the present situation with its renewed fascination with conceptual art and feminism of the 1970s. It has provided for me, and I hope for the reader, an occasion to work through what might be called the *social trauma,* or at least the difficult experience, of those events euphemistically referred to as the "sexual revolution."

"Resistance" and its "interpretation" in this instance are at once political and psychical. My resistance, in part, has taken the form of forgetting the conflicts I see so sharply at a second glance. Where I wanted to find the unity of feminism or the continuity of an avant-garde, I have discovered instead a rupture: "identity's" unruly content—sexual difference—had divided the field, not only of feminist debate within the movement, but also of critical practice within the institutions of fine art.

Evening Standard, London,
October 14, 1976.

After the Tate's bricks

NAPPY LINE-UP at the ICA Gallery—there are 22 framed exhibits captioned with relative details.

On show at ICA ...dirty nappies!

By Roger Bray

MARY KELLY: "They are

TAXI drivers and other forthright citizens may have a blunt answer for it. But the question, "Are dirty nappies art?" is now demanding a serious reply.

Nappy-liners, to be more precise. Used ones. And all 22 of them to be viewed publicly in their smudged and sepia glory at the Institute of Contemporary Arts in the Mall.

"I know," admits artist Mary Kelly disarmingly, "that it makes people hostile, but I want this to be taken seriously. I am not doing this as a joke."

Mounted

"I am doing it because I have been influenced by the women's movement, because I am an artist and a mother."

The nappy-liners, mounted and framed and captioned with details of the food Mary's baby had been consuming that day, form only part of her exhibition at the ICA's New Gallery.

There is another section covering her child's speech development and Mary's reaction to it, all part of the

she says, to focus attention on the woman's role and the effect of mother and child upon each other.

London's young marrieds, who may feel that they have seen enough dirty nappy-liners to last them a lifetime, may however like to know what emotions all this is supposed to stir.

"It would make people question the function of labour between men and women—the actual effects of a task being exclusively for the mother. I am trying to take three significant events—first the introduction of solid food, then when the child learns to speak, and then when he starts school.

"I already have fantastic interest from other women, particularly women who have some interest in things like this—I don't dare to say Women's Lib."

In psychoanalytic terms, she says "They are visual representations of cathected memory traces," but in laymen's terms "they are art because I say so."

"The important thing about art is that it only exists because it cannot be defined and because it fills that extra need for that which cannot be defined."

an art lecturer married to an artist, sweetly dismisses questions about hygiene, remembers with a grimace the Press reaction to her exhibition in Newcastle, worries about the impact of another news story down here and is coy about her private background.

One visitor to the gallery says he finds it very refreshing.

Warmly

References to the famous Tate Gallery bricks are not greeted warmly. Asked about the motive behind the exhibition, gallery director, Mr Barry Barker, says he doesn't want to get into "that sort of dialogue."

Mary says her "cathected traces" in combination with "the diaries, time-tables and feeding charts constitute what I would call a discourse which 'represents' my lived experience as a mother."

"But they are consciously set up in an antagonistic relationship with the diagrams, logarithms and footnotes constituting another discourse which 'represents' my analysis, as a feminist, of this lived experience."

Evening Standard: Graham Wood

FUNDAMENTAL ART—one of Mary Kelly's exhibits at the Institute of Contemporary Arts. The diet also includes a half-teaspoonful of egg yolk taken at 13.00 hours and six teaspoonsful of apple at 17.30 hours.

charmingly, have no commercial value, but a spot of notoriety, arguably a more stable currency than the shaky £, is not to be sniffed at, and

as they used to say North of Watford," where there's muck there's brass."

Richard Cork's London Art Review . . . Page 22.

Coming next week

The Institute's Arts Centre director Mr Ted Little was today wrestling with the problem of a coming attraction— a show which had been planned for next week involving the display of what you might call "girlie" pictures.

"Photographs from widely-available porn magazines," explained Mr Little, though he was reluctant to elaborate on

"A question has been raised about it," he said mysteriously, "It is internal."

The photographs have been planned as part of an exhibition and performance by a company called Coum.

"It's a show called Prostitution—implying prostitution in its widest sense and divided into four sections, one of which is retrospective of their past work," said Mr Little.

Mary Kelly, *Post-Partum Document,*
Documentation I: Analysed fecal
stains and feeding charts, 1974,
detail 1 of 28, 11 × 14 ins. each.
Collection Art Gallery of Ontario.

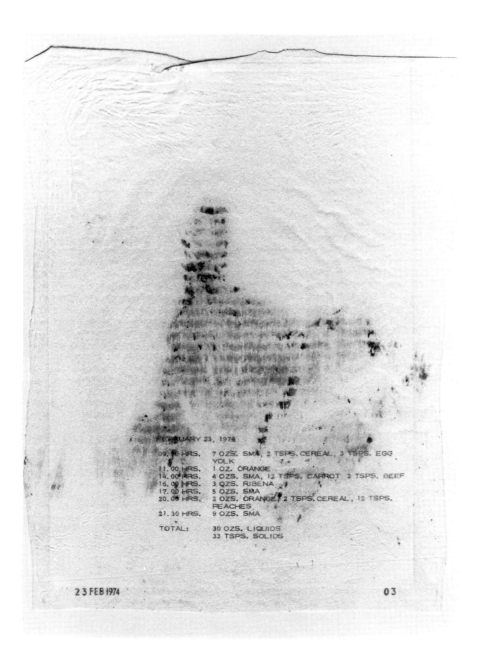

For some women, an account of subjectivity grounded in psychoanalytic theory was problematic then. It questioned the explanatory power of experience that gave the emerging movement ideological as well as organizational cohesion in the form of consciousness-raising groups. In 1970 I joined what was perhaps provocatively called the "History Group," a name indicating that we had set ourselves a somewhat different agenda from the "local" groups: to make the experience of sexuality pass into the historical discourse of feminist politics; in other words, to be "named" in the grand narrative of social change.[2] Clearly, it was an aim informed but not delimited by Marxism. We argued that the psychic economy was regulated in the unconscious by the laws of primary process, and it therefore required a theoretical method appropriate to that object, namely, psychoanalysis—Freud's certainly, but more controversially, Lacan's reading of it. This we initially discovered in the work of Althusser, laboriously pursuing untranslated references, not out of academic interest, but out of a sense of political urgency: to change our lives and what we saw as the iniquitous conditions of "all" women's lives, blatantly enforced in the workplace (the Equal Pay Act was not effective until 1975) and more subtly sustained in the home through the naturalization of the woman's role in child care.

This was the context in which I began *Post-Partum Document* in 1973. The "Introduction" consisted of four framed objects and a brief statement or "footnote."[3] Phrases from it, such as the "ideology of the family" and the "heterosexual imperative" reappeared in those infamous reviews incongruously juxtaposed with inexquisite details of dejecta "scandalously exhibited" within a block of Buckingham Palace. Although *Post-Partum Document* overlapped with and was informed by two other projects, the film *Nightcleaners* (1970–73) and the installation *Women & Work* (1973–75)—both of which were concerned with the social/sexual division of labor—it was the ICA show of the *Document* in 1976 that provoked controversy, perhaps because it focused on the psychic structure of that division. First, it fueled the existing conflict over "male-dominated" theory—that is, the relevance of psychoanalysis for feminism—which had become a movement issue when it was openly debated at the Patriarchy Conference that same year. Second, it drew attention to the question of "women's practice in art," which had been anticipated in the aftermath of conceptualism with the re-

Mary Kelly *Post-Partum Document,*
Introduction, 1973, 4 units,
8 × 10 ins. Photo: David Atkins.

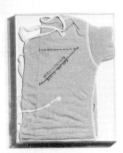

turn of "synthetic propositions" and the imposition of "social purpose."
Finally, it became at least expedient, if not necessary, to acknowledge that
the art world had a second sex. Demands for parity, proposed as early as
1972 by the Women's Workshop of the Artists Union, did not find a public
forum until the conferences Art and Politics in 1977 and The State of British
Art in 1978.[4]

That specific intersection of events incited the "interventions" of chapter
1, and now prompts me to begin the story called "Selected Writings" there;
not because it is historically accurate or inclusive but because, for me, that
moment is so vivid. It has the quality of a "screen memory"—deceptive
perhaps but rich in psychic collateral, and for that reason conducive to the
uncanny work of remembering.

Chapter 2 follows another trajectory through the 1970s, one in which
my writing is inextricably bound to a project-based art form. This has not
been exactly the result of an interdisciplinary move but, as Homi Bhabha
has suggested, a "transdisciplinary" gesture. I began with a "problem," in
this case, how to represent the mother's desire, and accepted the hybrid,

even monstrous solutions that process bred.[5] So what started with the intuitive superimposition of a Lacanian Schema on the soft wool surface of the tiny vests unfolded in the footnotes and diagrams of the *Document's* subsequent six parts with an obsessive intensity that clearly defies their function as explanation. Yet, in retrospect, I have seen the "Experimentum Mentis" sections (written between 1976 and 1979) as a significant chronicle of feminist engagement with psychoanalysis at that time as well as a possible contribution to the specific analysis of maternal femininity, and because of this I have included them separately in this collection.

Initially, of course, "The Footnotes and Bibliography" formed an integral part of the installation; and when the work was first exhibited, they affronted the aesthetic sensibilities of some even more than the fecal stains. The *Evening Standard's* scatological headline, after all, was prefaced with the invocation of another scandal—"after the Tate's bricks . . ." (referring to the Tate Gallery's purchase of a work by Carl Andre)—an expeditious move to cut public spending predictably disguised as an ethical question of appropriate art forms. According to the article, I retorted: "It's art because I say so;" reiterating, however absurdly understated, conceptualism's once provocative assertion that art is a set of analytical and self-referential procedures.

In this respect, *Post-Partum Document* simply followed the metadiscursive dictate of language-based work of the 1960s. But what I had assumed to be inevitable—that interrogating the conditions of existence of the object would necessarily include the question of the subject and sexual difference—was not the case. Although there was a move to extend the analytical method beyond the exclusive parameter of aesthetics (for example, Art and Language in the mid-1970s), it stopped dramatically short of synthesizing the subjective moment into that inquiry.[6]

In fact, the *Document's* procedural emphasis was often viewed as performative. The field was stylistically, if not literally, divided between men and women. The art object's "dematerialization" was effected on the one hand by a systematic displacement of its spatial integrity, and on the other by a substitution of the body as its temporal metaphor. The ephemeral yet emotive presence of a work "performed" subverted phenomenological reduction was well as philosophical ordering by introducing the unpredictable dimension of spectatorial transference. And the body, however rigorously deployed within that representational schema, was signified as feminine. On the part of performance artists (women, and especially dancers), it required a persistent effort to subvert those prevailing gender stereotypes.

As a consequence, much of my writing then was preoccupied with theorizing the strategic absence of the woman's body as iconic sign, questioning the notion of a pregiven or essential femininity, and broaching the topic of female fetishism. These arguments entailed the somewhat daunting task of introducing the subjects of psychoanalysis and semiotics into the discussion of visual arts—an initiative that is summarized in my conversation with Paul Smith (significantly, a literary critic) in 1981. But the initial step was taken earlier when I wrote "Notes on Reading the *Post-Partum Document*" (1977) and "On Femininity" (1979) for *Control Magazine*.[7] The essays were solicited by the editor, conceptual artist Steve Willats, whose main interest was in politically engaged but conceptually oriented art informed by systems and communication theories. Semiotics, which could accommodate the disruptive notion of unconscious processess, was largely ignored (with the exception of Victor Burgin and Dan Graham). Artists whose practices involved an excursion into linguistics, for the most part, took the positivist route.

Alternatively, independent filmmakers and theorists had productively followed and developed that critical apparatus since the 1960s. Their influence is evident in both my visual and written work. My extended collaboration with Laura Mulvey, for example, is documented in a conversation that is included here. In 1979, I joined the editorial board of *Screen,* and over the next three years (together with the editor Mark Nash) I tried to generate a comparable critical writing on what would be rigorously referred to as the "work of art" or the "artistic text" in order to contest the term and therefore the system "painting" as the paradigmatic instance of picturing.

Although developments in France—for example, work by Julia Kristeva, Jean-Louis Schefer, and Hubert Damisch—provided the impetus for this project, all of the contributions to *Screen* moved outside the internal signifying system of the picture toward the semantic field of socially, historically, or discursively constructed meaning (and, in a sense, anticipated the tendency now known as the New Art History). The series included Tim Clark's essay on Manet's *Olympia* and Peter Wollen's response to it, Griselda

Pollock's work on van Gogh that formulates the imbrication of sexual difference and artistic authorship, and finally "Re-Viewing Modernist Criticism," which begins chapter 3. My particular preoccupation at the time of writing it (one shared with Griselda Pollock and enhanced by our frequent discussions) was with the fortuitous transformation of modernism's renunciation of the feminine into postmodernism's marginalization of the feminist.[8] It was shaped, I thought, not exclusively but most forcefully within the field of criticism, and in that article I focused on its function in relation to what I termed the "exhibition and system."

Although I did not take it up then, the problem resided not only in the dominant practices of the museum or the discourses of "great art," but also in the strategies of opposition. Take the all-woman show. For example, in the catalogue for feministische kunst internationaal (The Hague, 1979), the organizers define feminist art as a separate movement, comprising a definite set of conventions and constituting an international style.[9] Or in Lucy Lippard's Issue: Social Strategies by Women Artists (London, 1980), a different precedent was set by posing a united front of politically engaged art against the divisive claims of cultural and socialist feminisms. In The Revolutionary Power of Women's Laughter, curated by Joanna Isaak (New York, 1983), the politics of representation were also foregrounded, but they acknowledged the division between theories of "cultural construction" and so-called essentialism in a way that defined the agenda for art informed by feminism in the 1980s.[10]

My own curatorial effort, Beyond the Purloined Image (London, 1983), took a different tack: one in which the artists (both men and women) participated, through their photographic practices and their predominantly poststructuralist overviews, in defining the exhibition's theme. The intent was to engage polemically with American artists who were attempting to carve out an oppositional space within the institutional frame of postmodernism, which was rapidly being filled by the retro-expressionism of the "transavant-garde." This show also formed the basis for another collaboration with Kate Linker, Jane Weinstock, and Silvia Kolbowski that aimed to cut across both media and gender to emphasize the issue: Difference: On Representation and Sexuality (New York, 1984). Both shows are discussed in this volume.

In a certain respect, however, I see all of these important initiatives as part of a generational resolve to tidy up the cultural confusion of that interim (beginning in 1968 and still lingering) known as the "Seventies." The discourse of periodization, with its repetitive formula for establishing the "representative" practices of pregiven durations, has designated "feminist art" as alternative or marginal. This has taken the stance of a separate history, unique genealogy, definitive style, or thematic rupture. But the question remains: alternative to what? There is a significant absence of the exemplary in the legacy of the 1970s. Rather, it is the irritating, irreducible *heterogeneity* of the means of expression that characterizes that interval.

Likewise, feminism did not generate a unified aesthetic. Nevertheless, it infiltrated or overtly influenced every art- (or un-art-) making process of that moment in distinct and irreversible ways: *notably, by transforming the phenomenological presence of the body into an image of sexual difference, extending the interrogation of the object to include the subjective conditions of its existence, turning political intent into personal accountability, and translating institutional critique into the question of authority.* In this sense, feminism's impact was not marginal but central to the formation of modernism's "post" condition. Moreover, it suggests that the havoc of material uncertainty and discursive complexity wrought upon the institution not only by feminism but by all the social movements of the 1960s has not been easily resolved.

"Desiring Images/Imaging Desire" was written initially in response to the frequent proclamations of *post*feminism in the early 1980s. Since then, however, it has become significant for me in another way, as the pivotal point of an ongoing effort to decipher and critically rework the codes of a "feminine aesthetic." In it, I introduced the question of positioning the woman-as-spectator in a way that was both critical and pleasurable. That possibility had floundered in a theoretical dilemma. Scopophilia had been formulated on the one hand as a fundamental psychic disposition of the subject, and on the other as evidence of the cultural overdetermination of woman's objectification. Film theorists such as Mary Ann Doane had suggested (in her early work) that masquerade solicits the production of femininity as surface effect, and that it has transgressive potential when deployed as a means of conscious acting out; whereas psychoanalysts like Michèle Montrelay had focused on the internalization of those effects, that is, the unconscious organization of the "feminine" drives and their symptomatic consequences. I wanted to take account of both, suggesting that the visualizing process mimes the unconscious invention of precocious femininity, by insisting on the heterogeneity of the sign, and throws its claim to "unrepresentability" into relief as a kind of trompe l'oeil. Seen in this light, the artwork itself is a form of masquerade, an empty space of reflection rather than identification for the viewer that structures, but does not necessarily explain, the anxious proximity of the maternal body.

In "Desiring Images," the scriptovisual practice put forward in "Notes on Reading the *Post-Partum Document*" is recoded as the heterogeneity of the sign, and the notion of "writing" as an aesthetic device moves from stylistic trope to metaphorical invocation of the feminine. This is taken still further in "Re-Presenting the Body," where it signals a strategic shift in the field of vision from "looking" to "listening." Here, I am less concerned with prescribing the absence of the woman's body as image than with problematizing its presence. But increasingly the process of disturbing that presence is displaced onto modes of spectatorship: the fragmentation of the visual field, the imposition of a temporal sequence, the intrusion of peripheral vision, the ephemeral effect of light, and above all the physical presence of the viewer in the installation. "Listening," extended in this way, becomes the more encompassing procedure described in the conversation with Margaret Iversen about the exhibition *Gloria Patri,* as the *narrativization of space*. The body dispersed by desire is invoked in its representational forms first by the hieroglyphic substitute, then by the polysemic sign, and finally, by the spectator's negotiation of its presentified absence.

The collection of articles and interviews in chapter 4 constitutes what I have often referred to as a "parallel discourse," parallel to the exhibition *Interim* (1984–89) not as interpretation, but as another form of engagement that is *debate* rather than site specific. "Re-Presenting the Body," written while working on "Corpus" (*Interim,* Part I, 1984–89), sets out a number of questions concerning not only the status of the body, but also the femininization of hysteria and the politics of psychoanalysis, as these continue to be addressed in relation to specific themes throughout the project's four parts. For instance, in "(P)age 49: On the Subject of History," the aging physical body of "Corpus" transmutes into the senescent body politic of

"Historia" (*Interim,* Part III, 1989). Reflecting on the longevity of the women's movement was also of course an incentive to remember the intense pleasure of "identity formed in the company of other women," and perhaps to repeat it, that is, to act out its loss. But most important, it was a way of working through a moment of political misrecognition that constructed the unquestioned unity of feminism. What emerged in the critical wake of this reflection was the issue of *differences*—social and racial as well as sexual— and how to acknowledge them without reinstating a hierarchy of demands or denying conflict through a hysterical identification with the other.

These questions were addressed at the symposium also entitled On the Subject of History, held in conjunction with the exhibition, *Interim,* at the New Museum of Contemporary Art in New York in 1990. The event also initiated a discussion with Emily Apter, "The Smell of Money," which revolved around the topic of female fetishism. Once the concept was no longer tied so to speak to the clinical context, its unrestricted use, in my view, produced a certain confusion. In the preface to *Post-Partum Document,* I had proposed a version of the Freudian fetish in which the mother's memorabilia functioned as prosthetic substitute for the child-as-phallus. But in retrospect, I have found it useful to distinguish this from the psychic maneuvers of coprophilia and copophobia, where the woman's relation to her "things" is one of inaccessibility and could be described as an archaic scenario of incorporation and expulsion rather than substitution. This also in a sense contaminates the familiar version of commodity fetishism by introducing the dimension of anal eroticism and maintaining that it may have more significance for women than its phallicized and sanitary symbol, *money.* "Pecunia" (*Interim,* Part II, 1989), in its specific materiality, refers to this observation, connecting it with the investment value of the art object and other preoccupations of the 1980s (such as real estate and robbery), and in the realm of theory, with a certain tendency to keep a safe distance from the messy business of experience.

In the exchange with Hal Foster, for instance, my response to his invocation of "the everyday" was, in a way, to distance myself from the ordinary or experiential implication of my work by recasting it in the ethnographic mold of the participant observer. Yet there is something uncomfortable about that formulation now, a significant difference between a European artist participating in the rituals of a "third world" culture and a woman observing the process of her own aging. It is a difference I want to account for not by recourse to an essentialism of the subject, but as a reevaluation of the analysis, as Joan Scott says, of that knowledge we call experience.[11] Not to do so, I believe, simply reinforces the critical caricature of so-called constructionist feminism and the art informed by it as radically disinterested in corporeality or sentience, in effect coprophobic. This, in turn, provokes a reaction formation that valorizes a coprophilic return to the "real" of the body in the form (or *en forme*) of abject art.

The stylistic schism that reaction induces has become, in fact, the visual embodiment of generational dissension in the 1990s; yet it signals, I believe, a far deeper but less visible divide, one that concerns the unexpected consequence of feminism's influence in the public sphere. This is particularly so in the United States, where there is constant talk of breaking the glass ceiling or canvas, for that matter, and finally, the front line in the recent Gulf War. All of these aspirations could be attributed in part to the successful outcome of a struggle for women's rights. When equal access implies the right to kill, however, the logic may be sound, but the ethics of that demand are still a cause for reflection.

The selections in chapter 5 try in different ways to give a visual and discursive shape to that reflection. "On Display," which followed the production of *Gloria Patri,* comments on the media's spectacularization of digitized destruction during the Persian Gulf War and on the installation's attempt to disarm it through parody. Above all, though, it was the promotion of a kind of kick-ass masculinity as support for an aggressive nationalism that dramatized the way certain social pathologies are propped up on the psychic disturbance of sexual difference. Within the military institution, for example, it seems that gender stereotypes are recruited in the service of rank and hierarchy. A demand for equality (by women, gays, and lesbians) in that context is obviously limited, but it is also symptomatic of a more elusive restraint: the unconscious desire to identify with an ideal of masculinity that inevitably entails the denigration of the feminine term.

Theoretically, what interests me is that, in a relation of power, the woman's assumption of the masculine imago describes a psychic structure that radically diverges from that of masquerade. If authority is not encoded primarily as visible effect, then what conceptual devices can be used to track it? Could the concept of display extracted from Lacan's discussion of mimicry and extended to the "female animal" distinguish a gesture of intimidation from the aim of seduction? This is the project undertaken in *"Miming the Master: Boy-Things, Bad Girls, and Femmes Vitales,"* the article that concludes this volume. In it, I also argue that display's maneuvers are institutionally specific. For instance, what the exhibition Bad Girls (New York and Los Angeles, 1994) demonstrates by miming, however ironically, the master discourse of the avant-garde is the persistence of a masculine ideal, institutionalized in the guise of a transgressive femininity and assumed by the "artist" as a form of virile display. Unlike their predecessors, who either denied their gender and tried to pass or wore it on their sleeve and suffered, Bad Girls, according to the curatorial legend, flaunt difference. They do so not out of deference to heroic conquests of the visual turf inspired by feminism in the past, but in defiance of all restraints.[12]

This, then, underlines the deeper disjunction of feminist politics spoken of earlier: in the course of distancing ourselves from the fussy femininity of the postwar era, we have also divided women into "us" and "them," that is, those who, like us, are "liberated" and the others who still live their lives as "women." That rift, insofar as it is socially and economically circumscribed, has deepened. Predictably, this has incited an opposition comprised of more dutiful daughters, good girls disguised as *very* bad girls, who have tried to reclaim, by repeating or acting out, an imagined moment (of utopian) activism in the 1970s. Yet a repetition of the past will not necessarily resolve it. For one thing, what was once a claim to unity—that women shared, at least, the subjective moment of their oppression—now defines the cause for separation, given that subjectivity must account for the internalization of real or imagined forms of empowerment as well. For another, what transpired in the 1970s as a synchronous effort to change the legal system of discrimination and to alter the understanding of its ideological support through theoretical work on representation now expedites political descent.

While "theory" in the 1980s evolved ever more subtle elaborations of the complex and irreducible psychic economy of sexual difference, conservative governments delivered ever more blatant setbacks in civil rights legislation (for example, abortion law and more recently, affirmative action). In such circumstances, the legitimate desire for unity can encourage a reckless certitude in which theory is culpable and activism blameless. Instead, it seems to me, this historical discontinuity might be viewed not as an aberration to be straightened out, but as the very conditions of existence for a feminist politics or an art inflected by such imperatives at the present time. From that perspective, division would be tolerable, perhaps productive, even welcome.

In the end, it has enabled me to retrieve the toxic bundle from my archive and review the obstinance of those memories rather than translate them into an exotic language of the moment. Undoubtedly, there is my desire to be a bad-enough-mother for the current generation of women artists I much admire, and inevitably the recognition of our separation. But I have not configured this separation as "loss." Fredric Jameson has said that "the rewards of historical commemoration do not always take the form of imitation."[13] This I think aptly expresses the aspirations of feminism in relation to modernism and explains the absence of "great movements," as he puts it, in postmodernity. My ambition for this project is much less monumental. It is simply this: to evoke in the reader an impulse to remember, and subdue, in effect, my own compulsion to repeat.

New York City, 1995

Notes

1. Sigmund Freud, "Remembering, Repeating and Working-Through: Further Recommendations on the Technique of Psychoanalysis," 1914, Standard Edition, vol. 12, trans. James Strachey (London: Hogarth Press, 1958).

2. See "Mary Kelly and Laura Mulvey in Conversation," in this volume.

3. "Introduction," 1973, published in Mary Kelly, *Post-Partum Document* (London and Boston: Routledge & Kegan Paul, 1983), p. 1.

4. I was a founding member of the Women's Workshop and the first chairman of the Artists Union, 1972–73. See "Art and Sexual Politics" and "The Crisis in Professionalism," in this volume.

5. "Translator Translated, W. J. T. Mitchell Talks with Homi Bhabha," *Artforum,* XXXIII, no. 7 (March 1995): 80–83, 110–114, 118–119.

6. "Conceptual Art, Subjectivity and the *Post-Partum Document*," Mary Kelly in

conversation with Terry Smith, Chicago Humanities Institute, University of Chicago, March 1995 (unpublished transcript).

7. *Control Magazine,* Issue Ten (1977): 10–12; Issue Eleven (1979): 14–15.

8. See "Mary Kelly and Griselda Pollock in Conversation at the Vancouver Art Gallery, June 1989," ed. Judith Mastai, with an introduction by Margaret Iversen, VAG Documents I, Vancouver Art Gallery 1989; excerpts published in *Parachute* 62 (1991): 24–31.

9. In one way, feministische kunst internationaal could be seen as precedent for the recent Bad Girls exhibition (New York, Los Angeles, 1994) in that both established the communality of artists and viewers by privileging the visual rhetoric of the joke. In another way, it is similar to *The Division of Labor: Women & Work* (New York, Los Angeles, 1995), insofar as it proposed a genealogy for feminist art.

10. A revised version of this exhibition was presented in 1995. *Laughter Ten Years After* (catalogue with essays by Joanna Isaak and Jeanne Silverthorne), Houghton House Gallery, Hobart and William Smith Colleges, Geneva.

11. Joan Scott, "Experience," in *Feminists Theorize the Political,* eds. Judith Butler and Joan Scott (New York and London: Routledge, 1992), p. 37.

12. See "A Conversation on Recent Feminist Art Practice," *October* 71 (Winter 1995): 49–69.

13. Fredric Jameson, "An Unfinished Project." A review of *The Correspondence of Walter Benjamin* 1910–1940, eds. Gershom Scholem and Theodor Adorno (Chicago: University of Chicago, 1994), in *London Review of Books,* August 3, 1995.

I Feminist Interventions

Art and Sexual Politics

First of all, I'd like to make a distinction between "feminist practice" and "the feminist problematic" in art (problematic in the sense that a concept cannot be isolated from the general theoretical or ideological framework in which it is used).[1] One aspect of the problematic is that it points out the absence of a notion of practice in the way the question is currently phrased and most familiarly posed—"What is feminist art?" The question provokes moralistic answers along the lines of "It is this, *not* that." These answers define essences; they are unified, noncontradictory, and exclusive. They are grounded in the classic subject/object structure of knowledge, which implies that through experience the subject recognizes the object in its representation, which in turn implies that art forms represent social classes (the art = ideology equation which we have inherited from the early 1970s). But no ideology, including socialism and feminism, is homogeneous. Rather, the "ideological" is a nonunitary complex of social practices and systems of representation which have political consequences.[2]

This may seem like a hairsplitting distinction, but I think it is crucial to understanding women's practice in art. It is exactly the tendency to homogenize the notion of the revolutionary which relegates feminism to the realms of economically given class positions (bourgeois, middle class, nonrevolutionary). Furthermore, I think that a socialist theoretical practice which does not include a critique of patriarchal (as well as capitalist) social relations has the political consequences of ghettoizing the issue of sexuality. This, in turn, has a determining effect on the ideological forms of feminism. For instance, there is the inversion of patriarchal attitudes in cultural feminism (a tendency within the women's movement) which seeks to identify in the present, excavate from the past, or invent for the future a self-contained set of social practices, in fact, a separate symbolic system altogether, (again unified, noncontradictory, and exclusive). Such inversions merely have the effect of confirming our negative place in political practice, which still ghettoizes women but allows us to misrecognize our position in it. Cultural feminism gives a place to the fantasies of Amazons, matriarchs, and virginal mothers, who contain all good things, including babies, and, of course, the privileged signifier of the patriarchy—the phallus.

(Right now you are probably thinking. Oh no, she's not going to reduce the whole issue to penis envy.) No, not exactly. I think it can only be a reduction if your notion of the subject (human subject, female subject, yourself as subject) is a unified, discrete, ultimately transcendental subject somewhere outside of the social totality but still acting on it. If this subject, who knows through experience, hasn't experienced penis envy, then it doesn't exist. But I would rather think of the subject as dynamic, as socially constituted, and moreover, to think of the speaking subject as fundamentally divided: for example, by the conscious/unconscious split which has operations characteristic of both sides: signifying processes (drives) on the one hand and social constraints such as family structures or modes of production on the other.[3] Why do I say "speaking subject?" Because it is at the moment of our entry into language that we take up a feminine or masculine position in the symbolic structure of our society.

Learning to speak depends upon the ability to conceptualize absence and establish differences. The phallus becomes the privileged signifier in language not simply because society is patriarchal but also because the recognition of the presence or absence of the penis at this moment is infused with the meaning of a whole series of presences and absences which precedes it, for example, the breast, the mother, and all of the child's good objects. I would say that femininity is synonymous with our "negative signification" in the order of language and culture. It begins even before you're born, when you're given your father's name. It is structured at the moment of your entry into language by the castration complex, that is, anxiety concerning the penis for boys and envy of the penis for girls, which underlies the later equation penis = baby. If the phallus (not the penis, but a kind of symbolic plenitude) represents the ability to please the loved object,

Miriam Shapiro, Collaboration Series:
Mary Cassatt and Me, 1976, acrylic
and collage on paper, 22 × 30 ins.
Photo: eeva-inkeri. Courtesy
Steinbaum Krauss Gallery, New York.

originally the mother, then a threat to the phallus is an enormous threat to the child's narcissism (a pleasure-seeking instinct which is later shaped by the ego through various identifications).[4] This is, I would say, of special relevance for women, because it is precisely in trying to make sense of this threatening symbolic "lack" that she carves out the characteristic features of feminine narcissism, which are the need to be loved and the fear of losing her loved objects, in particular, her children. Freud maintains that a person's choice of love object is constituted either according to the dependent or *anaclitic* type (the woman who tends or the man who protects), or according to the feminine or *narcissistic* type (what she herself is, what she once was, what she would like to be, or someone who was once a part of herself).[5] I realize that out of the context of his article on narcissism this might sound vaguely like a horoscope, but since Freud's distinction has a special appeal to women—via narcissism—I would like, at least metaphorically, to relate these positions to various forms/means of signification used in women's art practice now.

1. Female culture (mother art): identification with the woman who tends; that is, the mother who feeds you. She produces milk and therefore all good things. There is a valorization of all her products, her *labors of love:* patchwork quilts, candles, bread, and assorted magic rituals. She is the phallic mother. The uncastrated parthenogenator of the pre-Oedipal instance. But there is also the castrated and (unconsciously) despised mother of the Oedipus complex. Her labor of love is signified as "women's work," a kind of iconography of victimization. It includes installations, and more frequently, performances of obsessive activities such as scrubbing, ironing, and, above all, preparing food, possibly referring to the cannibalistic relationship between mother and child or to the totem meal, in which ingestion of the father signifies appropriating his name and status.

2. Female anatomy (body art): identification with herself, or what herself is. It seems to correspond to the way in which representations of the female genitals recapitulate a kind of primordial autoeroticism. The vagina is documented in film or photograph, or monumentalized as painted or sculpted metaphors. She has chosen as her model not her mother but

Suzanne Santoro, book cover,
Towards New Expression, published by
Rivolta Femminile, 1974.

herself, and loves herself with an intensity comparable to the mother's love for her.

3. Feminine experience (ego art): an identification with an image of what she would like to be underlies the affirmation of "feminine experience" in art, but paradoxically what *she* would like to be is usually what *he* wants her to be, the desired object. Currently in women's art practice, there is a proliferation of forms of signification where the artist's own person, in particular, her body, is given as object, as signifier of the man's desire. As object she is also his symptom, because he is judged through her. (Men exchange women, not vice versa.) she is seen; he is the "look." The literal mirror or video screen as mirror often signifies a narcissistic structure grounded on the return of her image to herself in a moment of pseudo-totalization, or it can signify the alienating function of this misrecognition in the fracturing, fragmenting, or violating of the mirror/video which is often carried out in conjunction with attacks, visible or verbal, on her own person, a kind of exorcism of her negative signification.

But there is also an inversion of this identification with "what she herself would like to be," which negates feminine experience as such. She can explicitly valorize the phallic woman with gun, flag, or scythe in hand, and occasionally with a baby in the other hand or an enemy underfoot; or she can implicitly valorize the phallus, by adopting exclusively and uncritically the dominant forms of signification in the art practice of men.

4. Feminine discourse (Other art): identification with the Other can take up any one of the aforementioned narcissistic positions but is primarily what she herself once was or was once a part of her, because self-analysis in a sense is always retrospective. In her practice she articulates the intersubjective relationships which constitute her as a female subject, not object. She is usually not present, visibly, in the work, or if she is, then some forceful means of distancing is used, such as, for instance, a text (a frequent device in filmmaking). Such work is usually scriptovisual precisely because feminine discourse is trying to articulate the unsaid, the "feminine," the negative signification, in a language which is coincident with the patriarchy; but for this reason her work is always in danger of being subsumed by it.

Hannah Wilke, S.O.S. Starification
Object Series, 1974, 1 of 35 black-
and-white photographs, 5 × 7 ins.
Photo: Less Wollam. Courtesy Ronald
Feldman Fine Arts, New York.

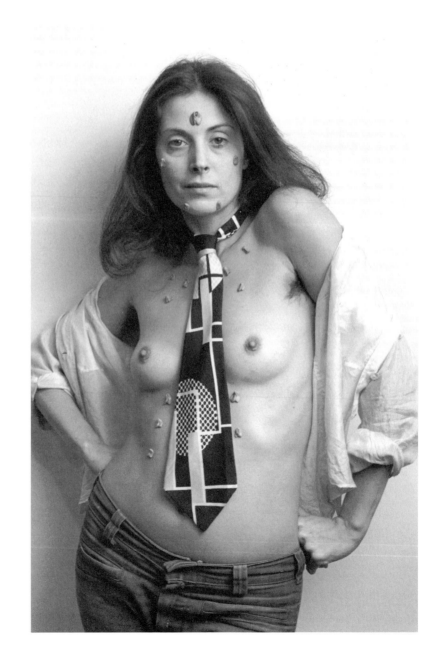

Adrian Piper, *I Embody,* 1975, 8 × 10
ins, oil crayon on paper. Courtesy
John Weber Gallery, New York.

Nancy Spero, *Torture in Chile,* 1974,
printing on paper, 37¾ × 122 ins.
Photo: Diana Church.

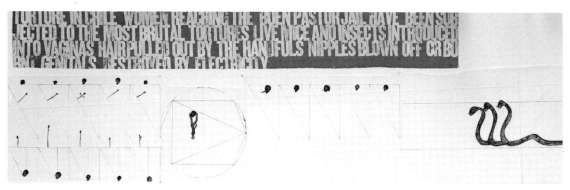

In summary, I think that feminine narcissism is an essential component of the feminist problematic insofar as it includes a symptomatic reading of our visual inscriptions, a reading based as much on absences as on presences; that such a reading suggests the way in which heterogeneous signifying processes underlie and often erupt into a signifying practice; that because of the coincidence of language and patriarchy the "feminine" is set (metaphorically) on the side of the heterogeneous, the unnameable, the unsaid; and that insofar as the feminine is said, or articulated in language, it is profoundly subversive.[6] As for the radical potential of art practice in general and women's art practice in particular, I think that the notion of the problematic resists the prescriptive answers required by the father/daughter duet *"what is revolutionary/feminist art?"* It requires formulating the problem of representation as the product of a practice of signification which will generate questions like *"How do the means of signification in a given art practice function?"* and only then *"What is signified and with what political consequences?"*

Notes

"Art and Sexual Politics," paper presented at the Art and Politics conference, AIR, London, 1977. Published in *Art and Politics,* ed. Brandon Taylor (Hampshire, England: Winchester School of Art Press, 1980), pp. 66–75; and in *Framing Feminism,* eds. Rozsika Parker and Griselda Pollock (London and New York: Pandora, 1987), pp. 303–312.

1. Louis Althusser, *Pour Marx,* trans. Ben Brewster (Allen Lane, 1969), glossary (definition of problematic), p. 53.

2. Paul Q. Hirst, "Althusser's Theory of Ideology," *Economy and Society* 5 (November 1976) on "Representation": 407–411.

3. Julia Kristeva, "The System and the Speaking Subject," *Times Literary Supplement,* October 12, 1973.

4. J. Laplanche and J. B. Pontalis, *The Language of Psychoanalysis* (London: Hogarth Press, 1973) (definition of narcissism), p. 255.

5. Sigmund Freud, "On Narcissism: An Introduction" (1914), *Collected Papers,* vol. IV (London: Hogarth Press, 1971), p. 47.

6. Julia Kristeva, "Signifying Practice and Mode of Production," trans. Geoffrey Nowell-Smith, *Edinburgh Magazine* 1 (1976); see introduction.

The Crisis in Professionalism

I would like to commend Peter Fuller for his very lucid exposition of the historical origins of the present crisis, in particular for the way in which he located "fine art" practice within the "visual tradition as a whole." For me his discussion suggests that the visual tradition, when considered at any given historical moment, is not unified but rather consists of a set of complex, often contradictory "professional practices," in which one system of representation takes up a position of dominance. Currently, as Peter Fuller says, it is the "megavisual" (commercial) system which dominates. These practices and systems of representation constitute a part of what I would call the ideological level or instance of the social formation as a whole. However, I find it necessary to distinguish this level from the economic and political levels in order to clarify for myself what Peter Fuller means by his rather less lucid proposal for dealing with the crisis—"that artists demand the right to act socially." The confusion caused by such an ambiguous formulation is the result of collapsing the political and economic into the ideological instance in such a way that the work of art itself reflects the economic cause of the crisis and, at the same time, has a direct political effect on it. A kind of vicious circle ensues in which Peter Fuller's "moment of visual becoming" simply couldn't happen.

Change can occur precisely because there are necessary noncorrespondences and contradictions between the levels. For instance, it is evident to anyone who attended the exhibition at the Hayward Gallery on surrealism that an artist's political intentions cannot be "read off" from the work itself. On the contrary, one notes that a variety of forms and means of representation are used by artists who share a common political commitment. This emphasis is placed on the importance of the political analysis or "reading" which the artist/viewer/critic brings to the work. This in turn stresses the autonomy of the political level and suggests that perhaps artists have been "acting socially" in ways which are necessarily excluded by Peter Fuller's particular reading of recent events.

It has been ten years now since the American black militant Bobby Seale first raised the slogan "Seize the time." The time seized not only by the black movement but also by the women's movement, the antiwar movement, and student movements everywhere. These events had a profound influence on shaping a generation of artists in this country who have attempted to "take their standards from a possible future" (as Peter Fuller puts it) not only in their individual practices as artists but also in their collective efforts to organize themselves as artists in groups ranging from the Artists Union, the Women's Collective, the Artists for Democracy, the Artists Placement Group, the Women's Art Alliance, the Free University, to name just a few. (Perhaps it is the critics and not the artists, who have only recently begun to seize the time.)

I feel that Peter Fuller did not seize the time in 1972 when he wrote an article for *Art and Artists* in which he advised the newly formed Artists Union to abandon their project to establish a trade union and create instead a group of "like-minded artists who perceived their ambiguous situation and knew the only way forward was ideological *not* economic struggle."[1] However, the Artists Union's proposed code of practice shows that the issues involved are not at all ambiguous and that they certainly affect more than "like-minded artists." For instance, there should be restrictions on the amount of commission a private gallery can take on the sale of artists' work. Currently it is 50 percent and sometimes as high as 70 percent. Furthermore a contract should be required which specifies the minimum conditions for insurance, transport, and display of artists' work for all exhibition contexts. Reserved rights and sale agreements on the reproduction or resale of artists' work should be legally enforced. There are already such legal protections in Belgium, Holland, Luxembourg, France, and Italy, and the Common Market executive commission wants the application of these laws to be generalized throughout the EEC. They also recommended tax allowances and a possible wages scheme for writers, painters, and sculptors, maintaining that "creative workers are entitled to a living wage for their endeavours."

With regard to publicly funded galleries, there should be a guaranteed minimum fee paid for the exhibition over and above contributions towards expenses involved in installation. Hundreds of artists exhibit in London and Regional Arts Council galleries throughout the year. The work is shown for at least a month and is seen sometimes by thousands of visitors during that time. Why are the artists the last ones, if paid at all, to be paid? It is assumed that recognition for one's work is enough. I sympathize with the striking fireman who said "Conscience doesn't pay for food and rent."

Moreover, even at the level of ideological struggle which Peter Fuller has designated as a priority, he didn't seize the time again in 1977, when he stated that "there are also secondary signs of the ataraxy (stoical indifference) in the British art sector: *i.e.,* the women's art movement remains rudimentary and ineffective." Far from being rudimentary, I would say it is possibly the most theoretically advanced group in that sector. The women's movement has given the subject of ideological practices an entirely new perspective by raising the issues of subjectivity and the unconscious, by questioning the formation of "masculinity" and "femininity," and, most crucially, by examining the patriarchal relations which shape every social practice and underlie the "visual tradition as a whole."

This perspective has significantly influenced the work of male artists in what Peter Fuller calls the "theoretical-left tendency," and it has profoundly affected performance art, the area in which most younger women artists are now working. That their work has remained relatively unknown is not because, as I have often heard men say, there are no good women artists in this country, but because they are simply not getting the recognition they deserve. There are no English equivalents of Lucy Lippard. Women's issues are taken up briefly and then dropped in favor of other topics. Shouldn't gender and race as well as class be vital and continuing areas of concern? Ironically, the women's art movement is still considered politically marginal at a time when most male practitioners of "social purpose art" are political voyeurs, while most women artists have shared a grassroots involvement in the women's movement, have felt their political commitments deeply, and have fought for them daily in their personal lives.

But thinking about it further, about the difficulty of intervention, I came to the conclusion that this weekend debate is something like the revolt of the sons against the father, and that it cannot possibly include us at the moment. The form that this revolt has taken, or the way this debate has divided between a kind of formalism, on the one hand, and a reductionist, undialectical materialism, on the other, means that we have not been able to locate the way in which the authors' or the artists' reworking of those ideologies produces new meaning in the text. But the possibility does exist for a very vigorous form of black and women's art to intervene not simply as an alternative, but as a revitalization of the mainstream.

Nevertheless, I should like to conclude by saying that the so-called social critics must be defended ultimately because (to twist yet another phrase of Peter Fuller's) "any hope for 'critical' truthfulness lies with them."

Note

Paper delivered at the conference entitled The State of British Art: A Debate, ICA, London, February 10–12, 1978, organized by Peter Fuller, Andrew Brighton, Richard Cork, and John Tagg. Proceedings published in *Studio International,* no. 2 (1978). "The Crisis in Professionalism" was the title of a paper by Peter Fuller to which panel members responded. In it, Fuller suggests that the modern professional fine art tradition emerged in Britain in the mid-eighteenth century when the "open market" for pictures was established. This gave rise to professional organizations (for example, the Royal Academy) which trained artists. But contemporary professional practice is in crisis because the prevailing ideology in art colleges is that art cannot be taught. The crisis in capitalism, he argues, has produced this view because the market economy advances the "megavisual" system in which the novelty and entertainment value of art dominates at the expense of the "tradition as a whole." (Here, in effect, he is combining John Berger's thesis in *Ways of Seeing* with Perry Anderson's "Origins of the Present Crisis," *New Left Review,* no. 23.) In conclusion, Fuller urges artists to defend and preserve traditional art practices, in particular, painting, and to reject "arid formalism and postmodernist antics alike." The paper ends with the injunction, ironic in my view, to "seize the time."

1. Peter Fuller, "United Artists?" *Art and Artists* 7 no. 4, issue 76 (1972).

Feminist Art: Assessing the 1970s and Raising Issues for the 1980s

In the 1970s we saw the rise of the "women's art movement." It was stylistically and strategically heterogeneous but nevertheless recognizable as a consistent attempt to give a positive place to the work of women artists within a wide configuration of art world institutions.

Until the Whitney Museum was picketed and threatened with human rights legislation in 1970, very few, if any, women artists were included in major public exhibitions of contemporary art. As a direct result of this action, the Whitney raised its quota of women by 20 percent, indirectly affecting later events such as the Paris Biennale of 1975, which included twenty-five women, and the Hayward Annual of 1978, where all the organizers and a majority of the exhibitors were women. Although this represented a significant advance, some feminist art critics caricatured the results as "getting a piece of the rotten pie" (Rozsika Parker, *Spare Rib,* September 1978, after Lucy Lippard, *From the Centre,* 1976). The implicit moral of "rotten pie-ism" in turn suggested the notion of an alternative approach, though the alternative, in this case, was relative to a specific pie: the all-woman show, Kunstlerinnen International, Berlin, 1977, was an alternative to mixed exhibitions; the feminist exhibition, feministische kunst internationaal, The Hague, 1979, was an alternative to general women's shows. Open submission shows were also proposed as alternatives to selected exhibitions, and women's arts and crafts were put forward as alternatives to fine art, and so on. Other feminist critics pointed out the danger of merely embracing the separate sphere to which we have already been consigned by art critics, historians, and organizations (Griselda Pollock, *Feminist Review,* no.

Catalogue cover, *feministische kunst
internationaal,* 1979. Collection Haags
Gemeentemuseum, The Hague.

2, 1979). The danger here, they suggested, was in embracing a theory of feminist politics in which "the feminine" was once again viewed as marginal, incorruptible, and different.

The 1970s saw the emergence of women's galleries such as AIR in New York, and the Women's Free Art Alliance in London, which were run as feminist cooperatives. Some private commercial galleries directed by women also promoted feminist art, such as de Appel in Amsterdam. Ambitious projects like the organization of museum shows and the survival of many other exhibition spaces were dependent on public or private financial assistance. Less conspicuous, but perhaps even more important for us, was the effect of attitudes in publishing—newspapers, magazines, art books, and catalogues—and whether or not the art critic encouraged, ignored, debated, or debunked the issue of women artists and the intervention of feminist art.

With respect to criticism, one strategy for women was to take over an established art journal and produce a special issue on women artists (e.g., *Art News,* 1971; *Art and Artists,* 1973; *Art Press,* 1977; *Studio International,* 1977; *Kunstform,* 1978). Another was to start their own magazines (e.g., *Womenspace, Feminist Art Journal, Heresies*). Feminist art historians (notably Linda Nochlin) initiated one of the crucial debates of the decade by asking the questions: why have there been no great women artists? and, have there been art forms unique to women? On the one hand, the answers insisted that there was a recognizable feminine sensibility in the work of most women artists and that there had been many great women artists merely forgotten or excluded (Karen Petersen and J. J. Wilson, *Women Artists,* Women's Press, 1978); on the other hand, that women had not been excluded but had occupied and spoken from a different place in a dominant culture, concluding that if feminine sensibility was culturally rather than biologically determined, then it could not be recognized in the work of women artists.

During the 1970s, feminist artists consciously attempted to transform the existing representations of women. Some adopted forms of classical realism and either replaced the conventional image of women with muscle-bound, fist-clenched militants or inverted the artist's role by painting the male nude. Others subscribed to an abstract formalism with an assumed feminine

Hayward Annual 1978, The Hayward
Gallery, London. Mary Kelly leading a
seminar on *Post-Partum Document.*

content. "Central imagery" cut across a number of different media—painting (Judy Chicago), sculpture (Harmony Hammond), photography (Suzanne Santoro)—but in spite of the variety of forms, it remained reducible to a single metaphor: female genitals = feminine essence.

Alternatively, many women were drawn to performance art and other multimedia experiments which consistently used the artist's own body or its image. Often the video was used as a mirror, either exploring the narcissism implied in the image (Hannah Wilke, Ulrike Rosenbach, Tina Keane) or presenting it in an alienated role—fractured and fragmented. In some works the artist violated herself visually or verbally as an exorcism (Renata Bertelmann, Adrian Piper, Gina Pane).

At the same time the 1970s produced feminist artists who emphasized feminine subjectivity not as part of their nature but as part of tradition, ritual, and behavior. The figure of the artist was seldom present in such work, which often incorporated writing (Nancy Spero, Annette Messager). A new emphasis on narrative emerged from concern with political debate, and attempted to provoke critical awareness in the viewer (Martha Rosler, Nil Yalter, Sarah McCarthy).

Developments in feminist art theory and practice in the 1970s raise several crucial issues for artists in the 1980s. First, it became clear that politics could not simply be seen as the content of an artwork but as part of its specific construction of meaning. Second, that the cultural was itself political and not merely the reflection of something else. Finally, that the politics of a work of art could only be constructed in the context of its reading. Within the broader frame of social purpose in the 1970s, it was art informed by feminism that pioneered the now constant reexamination of our identities and our politics.

Note

"Feminist Art: Assessing the Seventies and Raising Issues for the Eighties," *Studio International* 195 (no. 991/2 1981): 40–41. Revised version of a collective paper, "Representation vs Communication," which included sections on literature (Jacqueline Rose and Cora Kaplan), film (Claire Johnston and Elizabeth Cowie), and visual arts (Marie Yates and myself), presented at the National Conference of Socialist Feminists, London, 1978.

Notes on Reading the Post-Partum Document

The Discourse of the Women's Movement

The *Post-Partum Document* is located within the theoretical and political practice of the woman's movement, a practice which foregrounds the issues of subjectivity and ideological oppression. More specifically, the *Document* is identified with the tendency that bases the notion of ideological oppression on a psychoanalytic theory of subjectivity, that is, the unconscious.[1] Freud's discovery of the unconscious had crucial implications for theorizing the process by which human subjects become constituted in ideology. If there is no ideology except in practice and by a subject, then ideological oppression is not merely false consciousness. The ideological refers not only to systems of representation but also to a nonunitary complex of social practices which have political consequences. Moreover, these consequences are not given as the direct effect of the means of signification employed in a practice. They depend on a political analysis of what is signified.[2]

For the purposes of such an analysis, the *Post-Partum Document* is the product of a practice of signification, and as such, it does not reflect but reworks the feminist ideology in which it was founded. This is primarily the ideology of consciousness-raising groups that still form a major part of the women's movement. The *Document* reiterates, at one level, the unique contribution that consciousness-raising made to political practice in general by emphasizing the subjective moment of women's oppression.[3] But, at another level, it argues against the supposed self-sufficiency of lived experience and for a theoretical elaboration of the social relations in which femininity is formed. In this sense, the *Post-Partum Document* functions as part of an ongoing debate over the relevance of psychoanalysis to the theory and practice of both Marxism and feminism. Furthermore, the debate includes a

Mary Kelly, *Post-Partum Document,*
Documentation III: Analysed markings and
diary perspective schema, 1975, 10 units,
14 × 11 ins. each, pencil, crayon on paper.
Collection Tate Gallery, London.

Detail, *Post-Partum Document,*
Documentation III.

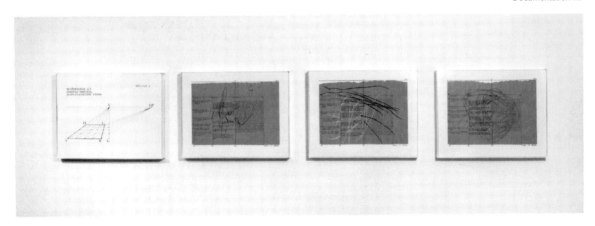

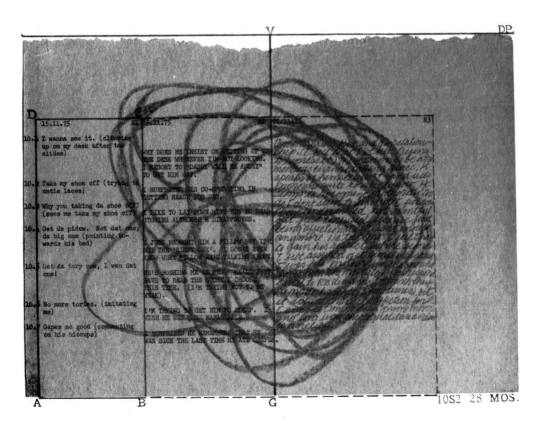

critique of the patriarchal bias underlying some of the theoretical assumptions on which the *Document* is based.[4]

The Discourse of the Mother-Child Relationship

The *Post-Partum Document* describes the subjective moment of the mother-child relationship. An analysis of this relationship is crucial to an understanding of the way in which ideology functions in/by the material practices of childbirth and child care. Feeding or dressing a child depends as much on the interchange of a system of signs as teaching him/her to speak or write. In a sense, even the unconscious discourse of these moments is "structured like a language."[5] This underlines the fact that intersubjective relationships are fundamentally social. More precisely, every social practice offers a specific expression of a general social law and this law is the symbolic dimension which is given in language.[6]

In patriarchy, the phallus becomes the privileged signifier of this symbolic dimension.[7] Although the subject is constituted in a relation of "lack" at the moment of his/her entry into language, it is possible to speak specifically of the woman's "negative place" in the general process of significations or social practices that reproduce patriarchal relations within a given social formation. In childbirth, the mother's negative place is misrecognized insofar as the child is the phallus for her.[8] This imaginary relation is lived through, at the level of ideology and in the social practice of child care, as proof of the natural capacity for maternity and the inevitability of the sexual division of labor.[9]

The documentations of specific moments such as weaning from the breast, learning to speak, and entering a nursery demonstrate the reciprocity of the process of socialization, that is, the intersubjective discourse through which not only the child but also the mother is constituted as subject.

The Discourse of Women's Practice in Art

The *Post-Partum Document* forms part of the "problematic" of women's practice in art. The problematic includes a symptomatic reading of the visual inscriptions of women artists. Such a reading, based as much on absences as presences, suggests the way in which the realm of "the feminine" is bounded by negative signification in the order of language and culture.

Because of this coincidence of language and patriarchy, the feminine is, metaphorically, set on the side of the heterogeneous, the unnameable, the unsaid. But the radical potential of women's art practice lies precisely in this coincidence, since, insofar as the feminine is said, it is profoundly subversive.[10]

However, the *Post-Partum Document* is not an excavation of female culture, or a valorization of the female body or of feminine experience as such. it is an attempt to articulate the feminine as discourse, and therefore places the emphasis on the intersubjective relationships which constitute the female subject.[11] Currently in women's art practice, there is a proliferation of forms of signification where the artist's own person, in particular her body, is given as a signifier, that is, as object. In the *Document,* as a means of distantiation, the figure of the mother is not visibly present. Although it is a self-documentation of the mother–child relationship, here between myself and my son, the *Post-Partum Document* does not describe the unified, transcendental subject of autobiography, but rather, the decentered, socially constituted subject of a mutual discourse. Moreover, this subject is fundamentally divided. There is a conscious/unconscious split which has operations characteristic of both sides: the signifying processes or drives on the one hand, and the social constraints such as family structures or modes of production on the other.[12] The means of signification used in the *Document* are scriptovisual in order to articulate the gap left by this split, that is, to show how the unconscious processes irrupt into a signifying practice and cut across the systematic order of language and, also, to show the difficulty of the symbolic order for women.

In the *Post-Partum Document,* the art objects are used as *fetish objects,* explicitly to displace the potential fetishization of the child and implicitly to expose the typically fetishistic function of representation.[13] The stained liners, folded vests, child's markings, and word imprints have a minimum sign value in relation to the commodity status of representational art, but they have a maximum affective value in relation to the libidinal economy of the unconscious. They are "representations," in the psychoanalytic sense, of cathected memory traces.[14] These traces, in combination with the diaries, speech events, and feeding charts, construct the discourse of the mother's lived experience. At the same time, they are set up in an antagonistic relationship with the diagrams, algorithms, and footnotes which construct the discourse of feminist analysis. In the context of an installation, this analysis is not meant to definitively theorize the *Post-Partum* moment, but rather to describe a process of secondary revision. In a sense, this text is also included in that process not as a topology of intention, but as a rewriting of the discourse of the *Document* which is at once a repression and a reactivation of its consequences.

Notes

"Notes on Reading Post-Partum Document," *Control Magazine,* Issue Ten (1977): 10–12. Prepared for a seminar entitled Psychoanalysis and Feminism, ICA, London, 1976, that was held during the exhibition of *Post-Partum Document (PPD) I-III.*

1. The *Post-Partum Document* is most closely associated with the debate that surfaced after the publication in 1974 of Juliet Mitchell's book, *Psychoanalysis and Feminism,* and in particular with a Lacanian reading of Freud, which was in strong evidence as a theoretical tendency at the Patriarchy Conference in London in May 1976. A seminar entitled Psychoanalysis and Feminism was organized during the showing of the *Post-Partum Document* at the ICA New Gallery in October 1976. The relevance of psychoanalysis to ideology, feminine psychology, and art practice was discussed by a panel on which I was a participant along with Parveen Adams, lecturer in psychology, Brunel University, Susan Lipshitz, psychologist, The Tavistock, film-maker Laura Mulvey, and writer Rosalind Delmar.

2. Paul Q. Hirst, "Althusser's Theory of Ideology," *Economy and Society* 5 (November 1976): 396; see also section on "Representation," pp. 407–411.

3. Rosalind Coward, "Sexuality and Psychoanalysis," unpublished paper, 1977.

4. For a useful outline of the debate see the Editorial Collective's article on "Psychology, Ideology, and the Human Subject" in *Ideology and Consciousness* 1(May 1977): 5–56. The critique concerns Lacan's acceptance of the "universality of language," c.f. Luce Irigaray, *Speculum de l'Autre Femme* (Paris: Editions de Minuit, 1974). See also "Women's Exile: An Interview with Luce Irigaray," trans. Couze Penn, *Ideology and Consciousness* 1 (May 1977), pp. 62–76.

5. See Jacques Lacan, "The Insistence of the Letter in the Unconscious," in *Structuralism* (New York: Anchor Books, 1970), pp. 287–323.

6. Julia Kristeva, "The System and the Speaking Subject," *Times Literary Supplement,* October 12, 1973.

7. For an elaboration of the consequences in terms of sexual difference, see Jacques Lacan, "La Signification du phallus," *Ecrits* (Paris: Editions du Seuil, 1966), pp. 685–695.

8. Misrecognition here refers specifically to Lacan's sense of the term as in "the function of misrecognition which characterizes the ego in all its structures," and not to ideological "misrecognition." See Jacques Lacan, "The Mirror Phase as Formative of the Function of the I," *New Left Review,* no. 5, vol. 47–52 (1968): 71–77.

9. The sexual division of labor is not a symmetrically structured system of women inside the home, men outside it, but rather an intricate, most often asymmetrical, delegation of tasks which aims to provide a structural imperative to heterosexuality. Mary Kelly, *Post-Partum Document,* "Footnotes and Bibliography," p. 1, ICA New Gallery, 1976.

10. See Julia Kristeva, "Signifying Practice and Mode of Production" in *La Traversée des Signes* (Paris: 1975), Editions du Seuil, trans. and intro. Geoffery Nowel-Smith, *Edinburgh Magazine* 1 (1976).

11. In "Art and Sexual Politics" I defined the forms/means of signification employed in women's art practice in terms of the underlying structures of "feminine narcissism," based metaphorically on Freud's description of narcissistic object choice in "On Narcissism: An Introduction" (1914), Collected Papers, vol. 4 p. 47. See also "Women's Practice in Art," Susan Hiller and Mary Kelly in conversation, *Audio Arts* 3 (no. 3, 1977), and "Women and Art," *Studio International,* no. 3 (1977).

12. Julia Kristeva, "The System and the Speaking Subject," *Times Literary Supplement,* October 12, 1973, c.f. the splitting of the subject, Marcelin Pleynet, "de Pictura," trans. Stephen Bann, *20th Century Studies,* December 1977.

13. See Stephen Heath on fetishism and "representation" in classic cinema and popular photography, "Lessons from Brecht," *Screen* 15 (summer 1974); see also Laura Mulvey, "Visual Pleasure and Narrative Cinema," *Screen* 16 (autumn 1975).

14. J. Laplanche and J. B. Pontalis, *The Language of the Self* (London: Hogarth Press, 1973), p. 200. For Freud, the idea/presentation/representation is to be understood as what comes from the object and is registered in mnemic systems, and not as the act of presenting an object to consciousness; op. cit., p. 247, memory trace/mnemic trace is used by Freud to denote the way in which events are inscribed upon the memory, they are deposited in different systems and reactivated only once they have been cathected; op. cit., p. 62, cathexis is an economic concept pertaining to the fact that a certain amount of psychical energy is attached to an idea or group of ideas, a part of the body, or an object.

II Unspeakable Subjects

Mary Kelly and Laura Mulvey in Conversation

Laura Mulvey: One of the most important things about the *Post-Partum Document* is the way in which it encapsulates the interface between psycho-analysis, feminist theory, feminist politics, and art, and brings these areas together in an exemplary manner. As my own work has been concerned with the same kind of issues, *Post-Partum Document* has particular meaning for me. Over the past ten years, we have been working within a similar in-tellectual and political climate or dialogue, so it's rather satisfying to find ourselves literally in dialogue now, facing each other.

Although this conversation marks the publication of *Post-Partum Docu-ment,* the work has been exhibited frequently, in stages, since 1973 when it was first initiated. In 1975, Part I was shown in Newcastle; in 1976, Parts I, II, and III were shown in London at the ICA; in 1977, Parts I–V were shown at the MOMA in Oxford; in 1979, Part VI was shown on its own in the "issues" exhibition, again at the ICA; and then all the sections were brought together in the exhibition The Critical Eye/I at the Yale Center for British Art in 1984. The work, in its own body and its own shape, represents the preoccupation of feminist film criticism, *sorry,* aesthetics, with psychoanalysis in a way that has been theoretically productive, but also has a particular relationship with the spectator's own fantasies. It gives rise to reverie, makes you stop and think and dream around the issues that it raises. In the end, it brings up a lot of questions that are relevant now and for the future direction of this kind of theory and practice. You look as though you wanted to comment on that, Mary.

Mary Kelly: It's very hard to sit here and listen without commenting because I keep reminiscing about all the things that you and I have taken part in in the past. When you said feminist film theory, for instance, and it sounded like a slip, I was thinking, no, that's exactly right, because in fact it was the context of feminist film theory that actually gave more impetus to the way the ideas developed in my work than perhaps the fine art context. I was thinking in particular of *Penthesilea,* the film based on Kleist's version of the Amazon myth, that you and Peter (Wollen) made in 1974. I remember how it was divided into sequences and I thought at the time, why can't you expect that much from an artwork? Why can't an artwork be like a film, why can't it be drawn out, perhaps serialized, and the spectator be drawn into it in a way that creates the space for a critical reading?

LM: You mean the film concept of montage, which we used with long takes, rather than the assembly of shots associated with montage, to juxtapose ideas and engage the spectator with the process of making meaning and sense of the argument.So you're saying that you felt you, too, could use a kind of montage in your work as an artist, give it that kind of heterogeneity and produce ideas out of juxtaposition.

MK: Not exactly, I remember writing a review of *Penthesilea* in *Spare Rib,* do you remember that? In it, I compared your work with Straub-Huillet's *Othon.* What fascinated me in both their film and yours was the way the long take could be so emotionally appealing and at the same time analytical. This was an effect that I attempted to get by dividing the document into sections, that is, to create a kind of expectation of narrative development, but one that's never resolved.

LM: I think you're talking about something rather different now—the use of real time, the long take as a method of documentation, rather than the long take as montage theater.

MK: I was purposely emphasizing the point about real time because I think that in fact it was much more important in forming my work. At the time it seemed like the use of montage as juxtaposition had become such an obvious strategy for static works. In *Riddles of the Sphinx,* where you do this wonderful 360-degree pan, it's almost like fulfilling the prophecy of the long take, but the way you use that to talk about maternity or maternal femininity also makes it emblematic. This, too, was rather coincident with the way I was thinking about my work—using repetition of units to under-line the replay of separation and loss in the mother-child relationship. Sig-nificantly, you and Peter then incorporated some of *Post-Partum Document* in *Riddles.* When you came to see the show at the ICA, I remember Peter saying something about levels of diegesis in the work, making a kind of analysis of the work in filmic terms.

LM: When you say the levels of diegesis, you are talking about different formal levels or different narrative levels?

MK: Both, but primarily I was referring to heterogeneity of discourse, that is, to the different ways that you're drawn into the work. There's the experi-ential narrative, which is the mother's voice; there's the kind of empirical or pseudoacademic discourse that frames the work in some kind of social sense; and there's the psychoanalytic reading, which you could consider almost as another level of the way those events were experienced. You could say, on the one hand, the footnotes to the *Document* paralleled feminist debates at the time, but you could bring in another kind of psychoanalytic reading of them as secondary revision, that is, the way the mother, or I myself, worked through a very intense personal experience.

LM: Mary, you're bringing up so much now, I'm going to have to stop you. In a way you're running too far ahead, and I thought it might be interesting if we could take these points more chronologically and simply, and go back perhaps again to our relationship over the years. In 1970, we were in the same women's reading group, which we called the "History Group." It was then that we started reading Freud and thinking about psy-choanalysis. I wanted to introduce the subject of psychoanalysis, which in-fluenced us and other people working at the time through the context of the reading group. And I wanted to say also that the group was of enormous importance to me, personally as well as intellectually. The project of collective reading made it possible to question and be in command of the "grand ideas of great men." As a part of a group, one suddenly found the confidence to ask questions from a political point of view, which as an individual student, as an isolated person struggling with difficult works, had always been impossible (for me at any rate). It was only from being in that group that it became possible to read, and then subsequently to write. The first thing I wrote, in fact, was in the *Shrew* on the "Miss World Demonstration." You edited it and laid it out, didn't you?

MK: I remember doing the article on "National Liberation and Women's Liberation" in that issue.

LM: I think you did the layout too.

MK: Perhaps I did.

LM: Anyway, reading Freud, for all of us, was the most fundamental event of the whole group experience. It had an enormous impact and then also led to the group splitting up and turning into a much more specific study of psychoanalysis and Lacan.

MK: Juliet Mitchell wrote the piece on Freud in that issue, too, which was one of the first things she did on psychoanalysis, wasn't it?

LM: Yes, it must have been 1971. But I wanted to place our discovery of psychoanalysis in a political context and then go back to your comments about film, your interest in film, real time, and documentation, and I wanted you to say something about your work with the film *Nightcleaners*. I remember being very impressed with the rigorous way that you approached film time, particularly in the sense of recording what the cleaners actually had to do. If they were cleaning a lavatory, for example, the film would actually record that entire process. It was a work about actions and time as well as a document of film, and I think that has some implications for what you were saying about film and your subsequent work.

Stills from *Nightcleaners,* Part I, 90
mins., 16mm black-and-white film,
1975. Berwick Street Film Collective
(Mark Karlin, James Scott, Humphrey
Trevelyn, Mary Kelly).

MK: The film initially started as a documentation of the campaign to unionize women cleaners, which, as you remember, was even prior to the implementation of equal pay, and so the question of low-paid work was a very important issue. It was coincident with the kind of discussions and ideas in the women's movement at that time, which were still very much focused on the question of the sexual division of labor, particularly on the question of domestic labor and the effects that had in the so-called services sector. This was also the focus of another collective project that I was involved in from 1973 to 1975, the exhibition Women & Work: A Document on the Division of Labor in Industry. But what I think is interesting, historically, about the way the film was made is that it attempted to document not only the campaign and the cleaners' work, but also the filmmaking process itself.

In the Berwick Street Film Collective, everyone participated in schooling, editing, and so on. Consequently, it was very time consuming, but it was productive in terms of debate within the group and also in terms of our relationship to the campaign. It was the result of a certain historical imperative for political art, I mean, the tendency to look at the so-called new media as though they were somehow inherently more progressive; that is to say, film and photography were more suited to representing social issues than something like painting or sculpture. But I think I have a very different perspective on that now.

LM: Perhaps at this point you might talk about the influence of conceptualism and, importantly, your break with it.

MK: Well, when *Post-Partum Document* was shown at the ICA in 1976, the program of exhibitions included work by artists like Bernard Venet, Dan Graham, Victor Burgin, Larry Weiner, Art and Language—the kind of work that had been defined as conceptual—but the historical emphasis was already being placed on a critical practice in art much earlier. What I felt or hoped that I was doing, in the context of showing the work then, was implementing a shift at the level of content and saying, perhaps it's possible to put the so-called synthetic proposition back on the agenda, that is, to reverse Kosuth's dictum that art is an analytical proposition, and to say art

Women & Work: A Document on the Division of Labor in Industry, 1975. Kay Fido, Margaret Harrison, Mary Kelly. Installation view, South London Art Gallery. Photo: Ray Barrie.

Women & Work, Portrait of metal box workers, 134 black-and-white photographs, 8 × 8 ins. each.

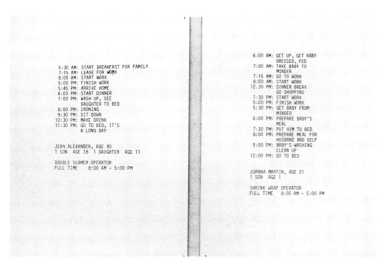 

Women & Work, Daily Schedules,
series of 14, 16 × 20 ins. each, detail,
Shrink-Wrap Operator.

Mary Kelly, *Post-Partum Document,*
Documentation II: Analysed utterances and
related speech events, 1975, detail, 1 of 23
units, 8 × 10 ins., wood rebate, rubber,
ink. Collection Art Gallery of Ontario.

isn't confined to speaking about art; it can refer to things outside itself, it can have what you could call "social purpose." And I think if we're going to talk about an oppositional postmodernism, then some of the most fundamental tenets of modernism still haven't been challenged. First, there is the question of medium. When the means of visualization are absolutely dictated by the primacy of *content,* then the critical work of art can't be defined according to the strategic role of medium alone. Second, there is the question of authorship, that is, when we question the centrality of the artistic subject and undermine the modernist notion of expression, then I don't think we can do this without also posing the problem of sexual identity, and that comes back to the crucial relationship between feminism and postmodernism.

LM: So that was a little chain, a linked chain beginning with feminism and the way you wanted to shift the center of art, the avant-garde theory of art, out of art itself into what you call "social purpose." That brought up questions of the artist, and then with that you come back to the question of

Recording session for Documentation
II, 1975.

sexual identity—the artist as male or female—and this brings you back once again to feminism and to the shift that takes place between your film and *Post-Partum Document.*

MK: *Post-Partum Document,* I think, brought those issues into clearer focus for me as an artist. For instance, medium; was it necessarily film or photography that could answer the kind of questions I was asking: What is maternal femininity? How is it constructed in the context of the mother–child relationship? I looked at what I called the feminine psychology of the woman and the process of socialization in the first few years of life, but in fact as the work developed, what you see is a shift that paralleled psychoanalytic work in the women's movement, a shift from the question of sexual division to one of sexual difference, that is, the sexual positioning of the subject within a very specific discourse and even a very specific moment like the mother-child relationship. So to emphasize this, I decided not to use anything that actually gave the impression of being a "slice of life," not to say, that's the function of photography; rather I wanted to avoid that interpretation in order to talk about the construction of maternal femininity in terms of the mother's fantasies. This is where heterogeneity in terms of the visual sign system comes in, not just the heterogeneity of discourse that we mentioned before. Here we have a configuration of objects and texts where the so-called representational image of the woman may be absent but her presence is traced or felt or visualized in a way that will convey the sense, the implication, of her desire in that relationship.

LM: Visualization is a word that you use a lot, for instance, that the work is a visualization of the relationship between the mother and child. But now you're also saying that the visualization allowed the representation of a theoretical argument within the work, out of the formal device of heterogeneity, which also allowed the representation of fantasy. It is as though the absence of the actual image of the mother, as absence of the iconic, allowed both theory and fantasy to appear. Is that what you're saying? I didn't completely understand something you said earlier as well, about the shift from a concept of division to a concept of difference. Could you say a little more about that?

MK: First, I want to say that "the image" is not reducible to the iconic sign, that indexical signs like found objects or symbolic signs such as writing can be used to invoke the nonspecular in the visual field. Second, that it is necessary to do this in order to release the "female" spectator from her identification with the "male" voyeur and to create a certain kind of pleasure in recognizing and *losing* her sense of femininity as something archaic, essential, unrepresentable.

Now, for the bit on sexual difference. When you and I first put forward the possibility of using psychoanalysis in the context of an artwork at the ICA in 1976, I remember how I backed out during the discussion and retreated to the safe idea that, yes, it was the sexual division of labor really and all we needed to do was to get fathers involved in child care. The way I see it, we were still struggling at that point with ways of transforming the notion "the personal is the political." Some of us were trying to change the emphasis from ideological oppression to what we called the "subjective moment" of women's oppression, since this would allow us to say that Freud's theory of the unconscious has some very crucial implications for the way we understand ideology. It would shift from the old concept of false consciousness to one concerned with systems of representation produced by many different, often contradictory, social practices. Consequently, the artwork would occupy a much more politically strategic place, because it would be assumed that you actually made things that reinforced or changed existing definitions of women. What the psychoanalytic view did, in my opinion, was to give another dimension to that notion of representation by shifting it away from the analysis of images and toward a theory of sexuality, that is, to speak about the representation of the drives in terms of aims and objects. Once we started to talk about masculinity and femininity in terms of "active" or "passive" aims, it was no longer possible to see sexual identity merely as a consequence of the social division of labor. So, we began to speak more specifically about the psychic construction of sexual difference, but that's not to say there's no need to theorize how femininity is formed in certain social relations.

LM: You nearly said patriarchy . . .

MK: Hang on. If I could just suggest what I think the outcome of that trajectory of the personal and the political has been. Well, it's not a question of either/or; that is, the psychic isn't outside of the social or the truth of the social. It's simply another level of the social inscription of subjects, but one which may require or construct an autonomous object of discourse. I ask that question rhetorically at the end of the preface to the book.

LM: Let's leave that to one side for the time being. What might be helpful at this point is to put what you've just been saying in the specific context of, why motherhood? Could you talk about it perhaps from a personal point of view, how the work started and also how it illustrates that relationship between the psychic and the social you were talking about just now.

MK: Through my own experience of the mother-child relationship, I began to feel that all these little activities like feeding or dressing a child were just as dependent the system of signs as written and spoken language. I think, initially, I was very attracted to Julia Kristeva's idea that all social practices were expressions of general social law or symbolic dimension, as she put it. So I thought the work should attempt to look at the structure of those events, perhaps as an interface between feeling and articulated language.

LM: On the one hand, it seems to me that the work gives a language, a symbolic representation, to an area particularly marked by lack of language and lack of presence within culture. On the other hand, the mother-child relationship has its own language, particularly in early infancy. You could almost say that the fact that the mother and child can't actually speak to each other is a literal representation of the way that it is not available to language. I think what you're doing in giving a representation, or language, to the mother-child relationship is much more radical than what you seem to imply, which is that it supplies imagery for a gap or absence. I don't think that language exits unless other people can read it too. I mean, what you're doing is taking an idiolect and putting it into a system of representation, making it available.

MK: Yes, but in this respect, I didn't consider my way of theorizing the experience of motherhood to be so different. It was very intimately related to those events. That's why I left the footnotes unaltered, because they paralleled the moments of separation, gave meaning to things like weaning from the breast, learning to speak, starting school. All of these were worked through in a way that changed in relation to the debates in the women's movement at the time, and I consider all of that—our history, our politics—to be a necessary part of the representation of women as mothers. So in my work I was trying to challenge the notion that motherhood represents some kind of unspeakable otherness. I wanted to make it apparent that this experience is very much within the order of language in the widest sense of the term.

LM: Can I interrupt you for a second? I think there are experiences—like falling in love—that are in a sense unspeakable, beyond words. But poetry throughout the ages, and art, representation, everything has tried to capture and express that particular case of the inexpressible, while the mother-child relationship, which is just as inexpressible, just as intense, erotic, and overwhelmingly personal, has never been spoken by culture. Of course, there is the image of Virgin and Child in Christian iconography, but that closes off more than it opens up. So, while poetry and art are there to speak the unspeakable, this area of unspeakability has been conspicuous by its absence—until you came along.

MK: After that, Laura, what can I say?

Note

"Mary Kelly in Conversation with Laura Mulvey," *Afterimage,* no. 8 (1986). Transcript of the seminar held in conjunction with the publication of *Post-Partum Document* (London and Boston: Routledge and Kegan Paul, 1983), London, 1983, Institute of Contemporary Art.

Preface and Footnotes to the Post-Partum Document

Post-Partum Document was conceived as an ongoing process of analysis and visualization of the mother-child relationship. It was born as an installation in six consecutive sections, comprising in all one hundred thirty-five small units. It grew up as an exhibition, adapted to a variety of genres (some realizing my desire for it to be what I wanted it to be, others resisting, transgressing), and finally reproduced itself in the form of a book.

But why invoke the metaphor of procreation to describe a project which explicitly refutes any attempt to naturalize the discourse of women's practice in art? First, I want to acknowledge the way in which every artistic text is punctuated with an unconscious significance that cuts across the constraints of medium or intentionality. Second, I would like to underline one of the central and perhaps most controversial questions this particular work poses in relation to the mother's desire: the possibility of female fetishism.

Sexual identity is said to be the outcome of a precarious passage called the Oedipus complex; a passage which is in a certain sense completed by the acceptance of symbolic castration. But castration is also inscribed at the level of the imaginary, that is, in fantasy, and this is where the fetishistic scenario originates and is continually replayed. The child's recognition of difference between the mother and the father is above all an admission that the mother does not have the phallus. In this case, seeing is not necessarily believing since what is at stake for the child is really the question of his or her own relation to having or being. Hence the fetishist, conventionally assumed to be male, postpones that moment of recognition, although certainly he has made the passage—he knows the difference, but denies it. In terms of representation, this denial is associated with a definite iconography

Post-Partum Document, 1973–79,
installation view, Anna Leonowens
Gallery, Nova Scotia College of
Art and Design, 1981. Photo:
Robert Bean.

of pornographic images where the man is reassured by the woman's possession of some form of phallic substitute or alternatively by the shape, the complete arrangement of her body. Yet the woman, insofar as the outcome of the oedipal moment has involved at some point a heterosexual object choice (that is, she has identified with her mother and has taken her father as a love object), will also postpone the recognition of lack in view of the promise of having the child. In having the child, in a sense she has the phallus. So the loss of the child is the loss of that symbolic plenitude—more exactly the ability to represent lack.

According to Freud, castration anxiety for the man is often expressed in fantasy as the loss of arms, legs, hair, teeth, eyes, or the penis itself. When he describes castration fears for the woman, this imaginary scenario takes the form of losing her loved objects, especially her children; the child is going to grow up, leave her, reject her, perhaps die. In order to delay, disavow, the separation that she has already in a way acknowledged, the woman tends to fetishize the child: by dressing him up, by continuing to feed him no matter how old he gets, or simply by having another "little one." So perhaps in place of the more familiar notion of pornography, it is possible to talk about the mother's memorabilia—the way she saves things—first shoes, photographs, locks of hair, or school reports. My work proceeds from this site; instead of first shoes, first words set out in type, stained liners, hand imprints, comforter fragments, drawings, writings, or even the plants and insects that were his gifts; all of these are intended to be seen as transitional objects, not in Winnicott's sense of surrogates but rather in Lacan's terms as *emblems* of desire. In one way, I have attempted to displace the potential fetishization of the child onto the work of art; but I have also tried to make it explicit in a way which would question the fetishistic nature of representation itself.

Now the publication of *Post-Partum Document* prompts another question: What is the difference between them—the "original" exhibition and its bookish offspring; what loss is sustained by their inevitable separation?

As an installation within a traditional gallery space, the work subscribes to certain modes of presentation; the framing, for example, parodies a familiar type of museum display insofar as it allows my archaeology of everyday life to slip unannounced into the great hall and ask impertinent questions of its keepers. This reading relies very heavily on the viewer's *affective* relation to the visual configuration of objects and texts. There will obviously be a loss of that kind of material specificity in viewing black and white reproductions, but what I have tried to retain, in place of an accurate record or photographic substitute for the "real object," is a certain texture, a sensibility associated with its function as *mnemic* trace. In this context, it made sense to lose the frames altogether, letting them slide toward the edge of the page, becoming the size and shape of the book itself, defined by different institutions, referred to other limits (I noted that an odd size is known in the trade as a "bastard").

Indeed an exhibition may not appear to be a legitimate parent for a book. The authority of that work is so often grounded in academic discourses which define themselves precisely by their difference from artistic practices; by definite objects reliable sources, and logical sequences; by being read from beginning to end. An exhibition takes place, but never so completely, not from cover to cover, except in the catalogue, which is exactly why the exhibition as a system (i.e., including its associated field of publications) should be the object of art criticism rather than the utopian notion of the individual tableau. Although it is subject to the constraints of a particular site, the exhibition as an intertextual system is potentially self-reflexive.

As an exhibition, the *Post-Partum Document* is intended to construct several readings or ways through the work, indicated by the juxtaposition of found objects and commentary with a series of diagrams. These diagrams, in turn, refer the viewer to another text entitled "Footnotes and Bibliography," where the framed material is reworked in order to create a space for critical reflection rather than explanation as such. In book form, however, the footnotes are interspersed with the illustrations in a way which tends to close that gap, to pull the visible more firmly into the space of the readable. Typographical variation was one way of attempting to avert that kind of closure, of trying to maintain the heterogeneity and openness of the "original" (mother?). I wanted to avoid setting up an opposition between image and text. Ideally, each should hold the possibility of becoming the other, or perhaps the same, that is, "writing."

Initially the reader will be caught up in the mother's story. The first-person narrative describes particular events in my own relationship with my son, from birth until age five. Events such as weaning from the breast, learning to speak, starting school, writing; but *Post-Partum Document* is not simply about child development. It is an effort to articulate the mother's fantasies, her desire, her stake in that project called "motherhood." In this sense, too, it is not a traditional narrative; a problem is continually posed but no resolution is reached. There is only a replay of moments of separation and loss, perhaps because desire has no end, resists normalization, ignores biology, disperses the body.

Perhaps this is also why it seemed crucial, not in the sense of a moral imperative, but as a historical strategy, to avoid the literal figuration of mother and child, to avoid any means of representation which risked recuperation as "a slice of life." To use the body of the woman, her image, or person is not impossible but problematic for feminism. In my work I have tried to cut across the predominant representation of woman as the object of the look in order to question the notion of femininity as a pregiven entity and to foreground instead its social construction as a representation of sexual difference within specific discourses. For me, this is not a new form of

Post-Partum Document, installation
view, Footnotes and Bibliography,
Diagrams, and Documentation I.
Photo: Robert Bean.

iconoclasm but a shared aspiration (truly postmodernist?) to "picture" the woman as subject of her own desire.

Although the mother's story is my story, *Post-Partum Document* is not an autobiography (nor do I think of this book as an artist's monograph). It suggests an interplay of voices—the mother's experience, feminist analysis, academic discussion, political debate. For instance, in the "Documentation" and "Experimentum Mentis" sections, the mode of address shifts to the third person. Here the Mother (she) is no longer so accessible, so replete (not someone who is like you, like you once were or would like to be). For the reader this implies a moment of separation (for some, perhaps an uncomfortable confrontation with the Father) or at least a "breathing space" in the text.

The "Documentation" notes began as an attempt to explain the empirical procedures adopted in individual works and probably ended up saying more about the inadequacy of those descriptive systems. One motive for appropriating a certain pseudoscientific language in this section was to counter the assumption that child care is based on the woman's natural and instinctive understanding of the role of mothering.

This so-called antiessentialist position is taken up (with a vengeance?) in the "Experimentum Mentis" section where maternal femininity is drawn from the perspective of Freudian and Lacanian psychoanalysis. Some readers will undoubtedly ask, why Freud, why Lacan? Why endorse their "patriarchal" authority? In one way, for me these texts are a means of working through a difficult experience—secondary revision, in the psychoanalytic sense. This is not exactly a recourse to rationality as authority. It expresses a more fundamental desire to know and to master.

Even, or especially, when I use something as eccentric as the Lacanian diagrams, they are first of all images, representations of the difficulty of the symbolic order for women; the difficulty of representing lack, of accepting castration, of not having the phallus, of not being the Phallic Mother (which is finally as significant in that order as the Dead Father). They are like blazons of a love-hate relationship with the Father (Phallic Mother?) cathected as much, perhaps more, than the memorabilia.

At the same time, I realize that these texts have other implications. They are metadiscursive. They assume a certain knowledge based on readings of and debates around specific articles. The writing is not explicitly polemical and the sources may seem somewhat ambiguous, but the reader will find that they are sited in the reference section with a key indicating the relevant "Documentation" or "Experimentum Mentis" section.

Freud's 1914 essay, "On Narcissism: An Introduction," together with my reading of Lacan's "Signification of the Phallus," determined the *Document's* central concern with the mother's desire as desire for the child to be the phallus, and the coincident trajectory of narcissistic identification through which her imaginary stake is articulated. Lacan's exposition of the two end points of the mirror phase was crucial to my understanding of the events referred to in the first two sections: "Weaning from the Breast" and "Weaning from the Holophrase." The third section, "Weaning from the Dyad" relied especially on Maud Mannoni's view of the importance of the mother's words (that is, above all, her reference to the father) in *The Child, His Illness and the Others.* Sections IV and V, "On Femininity" and "On the Order of Things," were centrally concerned with the representation of loss, not only as loss of the child but also as loss of the material body, and were profoundly influenced by Michèle Montrelay's "Inquiry into Femininity." In the final section, "On the Insistence of the Letter," an analysis of the child's prewriting posed certain problems concerning the phonocentric (perhaps even logocentric) bias underlying notions of language derived from Jakobson's linguistics, and prompted me to consider ideas which were more tangential to Lacan's, for instance Klein's essay on "The Early Stages of the Oedipus Complex." Once again there is a progression but no resolution, a theoretical elaboration but not necessarily a consistent argument (a Symbolic but "full of holes"); and here the reader will undoubtedly discover that another story unfolds, not simply my story, or the mother's story, but a kind of chronicle of feminist debate within the women's movement in Great Britain during the 1970s. The terms of my analysis are those of definite tendencies at particular moments in that history.

At the time of writing the "introduction" to the *Post-Partum Document,* in 1973, the problem of "the feminine psychology of the mother" seemed to be posed as if it were an effect of the sexual division of labor; but there was also an insistence on the "reciprocity of the process of socialization," which suggested that the notion of "subjectivity," especially one founded on Freud's theory of the unconscious, might displace the more familiar rhetoric of "ideological oppression" as indeed it eventually did. Juliet Mitchell introduced that position in *Women's Estate* and consolidated it with *Psychoanalysis and Feminism*. By the time "Experimentum Mentis I, II, and III" were written in 1976, the Lacanian rereading of Freud was under way. The Patriarchy Conference in London that same year clearly indicated that the debate had shifted from the terms of sexual division to the question of sexual difference. Some readers will regard such formulations as "negative entry" or "negative place" with skepticism (or perhaps nostalgia?), but will recall the context and our first attempts to articulate a different relation to language (and to castration) for women without subscribing to the essentialist notions of a separate symbolic order altogether. In "Experimentum Mentis IV and V," 1977, those terms (and the arguments which implied that "the feminine" position was ultimately transgressive), as well as the problematic concept of patriarchy itself, were abandoned. (Significantly, that year the feminist journal *m/f* was founded in order to take up and extend such debates.)

Instead the question of representation was foregrounded. On the one hand, it referred to the ideological, that is, "femininity" understood as the representation of difference produced within specific discourses or social practices; on the other, it was used in the psychoanalytic sense as the representation of the drives with respect to aims and objects, that is, "the feminine" understood as the subject's position in language, symbolic castration defined as the representation of loss.

But at this point, certain feminists began to worry about another kind of loss—losing sight of the "social," in the end, failing to understand the political relevance of the personal. Were we suggesting in some way that the psychic was the truth of the social? Could psychoanalysis simply become another political orthodoxy? By 1979, when the last part of the *Document* was completed, the movement's founding slogan, "the personal is political," had been through the theoretical mill, first formulated as the subjective moment of women's oppression, then dispersed as the question of positionality in language, and finally making a reappearance in the form of the "relation between the psychic and the social." The notes to "Documentation VI" attempted to address this problem by describing the construction of the agency of the mother/housewife within the institution of the school. Yet the psychoanalytic discourse of "Experimentum Mentis VI" was unable to articulate exactly what, for instance, "social deprivation" meant in terms of the psychic economy of the mother. Perhaps, there is no "relation," only "the social." If the psychic is neither outside of it nor the truth of it, but simply another level of the social inscription of subjects, then is it one which necessarily constitutes an autonomous object of discourse? Problems remain. The debate continues. The *Post-Partum Document* tells that story. For this reason I left the notes as they were originally written: to allow the gaps and inconsistencies as well as the insights to describe a process of reworking, which was, at the same time, a shared history and to let it speak, in a certain way, for our desire to understand and change our lives.

Experimentum Mentis I: Weaning from the Breast

During the antepartum period (gestation inside the mother's body) and continuing during the breast-feeding phase of early postpartum, the mother's negative place in the patriarchal order—more precisely the Symbolic—can be "misrecognized" because in a sense the child is the phallus for her. Until birth the child is part of the mother's body, and later comes to her as an object which was once a part of herself. Thus feminine narcissism is reinforced because she can produce complete object love without relinquishing a narcissistic object choice. The mother's "misrecognition" of her negative place at this moment is not necessarily a captation in the Imaginary, as this would indicate psychosis, but rather a confrontation between the Real and the Imaginary which is already grounded within the Symbolic and is ultimately resolved when the primacy of the Symbolic structure is asserted. The specificity of the postpartum confrontation for individual mothers is related to the way in which initial Oedipal conflicts are reenacted at this moment and as such is the terrain of psychoanalytic therapy. But, in general, the difficulty of the Symbolic order for women is precisely the difficulty of resolving Oedipal castration when the privileged signifier of that order is the phallus.

Weaning from the breast is a significant discovery of absence not only for the child but also for the mother. Insofar as it is a real separation (can be specularized), it does not provoke a "recognition" of castration, but it does rupture the symbiosis of the biologically determined mother–child unit.

Weaning from the breast, taken literally, does not only imply the termination of breast-feeding (as this varies) but also the inevitable end of an exclusively liquid diet and the introduction of solid food. This transition has usually taken place by the infant's sixth month. It has a psychical parallel in that around the age of six to eight months the child enters a phase of identification, a transformation takes place in him when assuming an image (as in the example of an image in the mirror). It is this identificatory movement of the child toward an ideal which mediates his anaclitic and primary relationship to the mother (or a part of her body) and consequently inscribes a sense of lack in her because it threatens her own Imaginary identification with the child as *someone who was once a part of her.*

There is also at this moment, for the child, a splitting of object love and identification love so that his objectal movement toward the mother, that is, his desire to be what she wants him to be, now complements the mother's desire that the child be the phallus for her. In the early postpartum period, what the mother wants the child to be is primarily, "healthy." The normal feces is not only an index of the infant's health but also within the patriarchy it is appropriated as proof of the female's natural capacity for maternity and child care. But the impending absence of plenitude is expressed in her words, "What have I done wrong?" The child is the mother's symptom insofar as she is judged through him. But the child's symptom, as, for example, in the lack of correlation between the nutritional data and the diarrheal stain, undermines the ideological notion of "natural capacity" and queries the expediency of the sexual division of labor through which the mother's secondary social status is confirmed.

Experimentum Mentis II: Weaning from the Holophrase

Because the acquisition of language is founded on a discovery of absence which is Imaginary, not Real, it is not only the constitutive instance in the formation of the child's castration complex, but it is also the pivotal moment in the mother's "rerecognition" of castration and of her own negative entry into language and culture. During the period of prepatterned speech (i.e., prior to syntax), a unique process of signification develops within the specific relation of intersubjectivity between mother and child. The child's single-word utterance is thought by the mother as a holophrase, that is, a conceptually complete sentence. Consequently, it is the moment of the child's emerging syntax (i.e., patterned speech) of "weaning" from the holophrase, which reiterates the lack of object (i.e., child as phallus) for the mother. Specifically, it is the enigmatic pivot, /weh/ which provokes the maternal utterance, "Why don't I understand?" and once again demonstrates the contingency of the "natural capacity" for maternity. Insofar as the pivot is always combined with another utterance, it anticipates the child's capacity for expressing himself grammatically and eventually being understood without the mediation of the *maternal signified*.

Significantly, the moment of emerging syntax coincides with the termination of the mirror phase, around eighteen months. By then the child's projected image of himself can be returned and internalized, allowing him to situate an Imaginary and libidinal relation to the mother "in the world." This ultimately "weans" the mother from the Other *who was once part of her* since she is no longer identified as the child's mirror, returning his image in her own look or returning his word with her own meaning. Thus the mother must reconstitute her narcissistic object choice along the lines of an identification with the child as *what she would like to be*.

For the child, the Imaginary Other of the mirror phase also includes an Imaginary identification with the *imago* of the father. This initiates an ambivalent rivalry whereby the child desires to be in the father's place as the Other of the mother's desire and simultaneously in the mother's place as signifier of the father's desire. The former is complemented by the father's desire to be in the child's place insofar as the child is the signifier of the mother's desire, and in the latter by the mother's desire to be in the father's place because he is the Other of the child's desire. The conflicts which characterize the formation of the Oedipus complex are only resolved, if ever, when the child takes up a masculine or feminine position in language.

Experimentum Mentis III: Weaning from the Dyad

For both the mother and the child, the crucial moment of "weaning" is constituted by the intervention of a *third term* (i.e., the father), thus consolidating the Oedipal triad and undermining the Imaginary dyad which determined the intersubjectivity of the pre-Oedipal instance. This intervention situates the Imaginary *third term* of the primordial triangle (the child as phallus) and the paternal *imago* of the mirror phase within the dominance of the Symbolic structure through the Word of the father—that is, the mother's words referring to the authority of the "father" to which the real father may or may not conform. When she calls upon him to bear witness to the child's indiscretions, she is conclusively reinstated in her negative place precisely because, in order to be what she herself would like to be, the child must be handed over to the Symbolic father, the figure of the Law. In this way, the "cutting out" of the child's ego leaves what is lacking in the mother's ego, that is, her lack of the privileged signifier of the Symbolic. The consequent denigration of the mother for this lack posits her insufficiency as an ego-ideal for the child, and this reinforces the initial depletion of her own ego.

This critical moment is overdetermined by the child's entry into an extra-familial process of socialization (the school). It is ultimately here that the child masters the finite system of language and sublimates the absence on which it is founded through the infinite fabrications (marks, songs, rhymes) of his autonomous desire. The Oedipal child learns that being what the mother wants him to be is what he wants to be but cannot be. Consequently, the mother's sense of lack is lived through as the repetitious transgressing, by the child, of her narcissistic aim. This provokes her question, "Why is he/she like that?" For the boy it is because he is like his father, a projection which reinforces the maternal separation; but for the girl, inevitably, it is because she is like her mother, an introjection which recapitulates the ambivalence of the Oedipal moment for the female subject.

Experimentum Mentis IV: On Femininity

At the Oedipal moment, the mother, father, and child inhabit a closed field of desire. But for the mother, the distancing function of the father uncovers the source of narcissistic satisfaction which is sustained by her Imaginary object, the child as phallus. This is the pleasure of *maternal femininity.* The site of this excavation is precisely the corporeal reality of the child's body (the soft, round, perfectly formed body of her baby), because the pleasure she derives from it must be relinquished. This loss is preordained on the one hand by the natural process of maturation, and, on the other, by the prohibitions of the Father and the Law. The Oedipal melodrama is staged as a maternal version of the Fort/Da game, "How grown up you are"/ "You're still my baby" or elided as in "You're not a baby, but a grown-up boy" (i.e., "I wish you were still my baby but . . .").

This moment is decisive if her child is a boy since the prohibition to incest is insured by the threat of castration. However, the mother-daughter relationship is more ambivalent because the girl enters the Oedipal situation in retreat rather than in confrontation, in hope of receiving the phallus from her father, eventually in the form of a child. To achieve this end, she must identify herself with her own mother and take up a position of lack. This process of identification with the ideal type of her sex makes it possible for a woman to see herself as desirable, to enter into a sexual relationship with a man, and to satisfy the needs of the child produced by this relationship; but it also introduces her to the pleasure of having the mother's body, cathecting her own body as that of her mother (or of another woman). Beyond the pleasure of the real of the child's body lies the pleasure of the maternal body experienced as real through it; the loss of this pleasure constitutes the ultimate threat to the mother's narcissism. Her "memorabilia" and the child's "transitional objects" are emblems which testify to the threatened loss of mutual enjoyment, but the desire in which they are grounded can only be caused in the unconscious by the specific structure of fantasy.

When the mother anxiously poses the question, "What do you want?(!)" in response to her child's whining, aggressive, or clinging complaints, she is essentially asking herself "What does he want of me?" The child's demand constitutes the mother as the Other who has the privilege of satisfying his needs and, at the same time, the whimsical power of depriving him of this satisfaction. To a certain extent the mother recognizes the unconditional element of demand as a demand for love. It is this recognition which under-lies her feeling of "ultimate responsibility" for the child even when the sexual division of labor in child care is radically altered to include the father.

But there is another cause for this asymmetry which is not necessarily given at the level of consciousness. This is the mother's desire to remain the privileged Other of the pre-Oedipal instance, insofar as the child's demands are the guarantee of her *maternal femininity.* Thus, she transforms the child's gifts into proofs of love and his indiscretions into denials. In this situation it is difficult for the child to locate his desire. Finally, it is the Law, of which the Father is the original representative, that intervenes to insure the autonomous status of desire, that is, to substitute for the unconditional element in the demand for love, the absolute condition of desire. Paradoxically this implies a detachment which is the minimum condition for the Oedipal child's unsolicited expression, "I love you, Mummy." Through the child's words, "the real" of the mother's body is represented as signifier of the Real Other in the register of the Symbolic.

Experimentum Mentis V: On the Order of Things

The mother's relation to castration, to the Father and the Law, is called into question by the sexual researches of her child. These researches are crucial in structuring the castration complex. The consequences of this moment determine the child's sexual identity and his future choice of love object. For the mother this moment necessitates the representation of a double loss—the child as phallus and the body as *feminine.*

Castration privileges the phallus as signifier of desire. The desire of the mother is the phallus; the child wants to be the phallus. Because desire is always the desire of the Other, it includes the desire to know. To know the mother's body is to test the desire of the Other. When the child asks a question concerning the presence/absence of the penis, such as "Where is your willy Mummy?," it is not definitive simply because he hears or sees the mother's answer. He must acknowledge the fact that she does not have what it is that he is looking for. However, taking up this position requires a sacrifice for both the mother and the child. At first he denies the mother's lack. He searches with voyeuristic intensity for the evidence which will confirm the imaginary dominance of the phallic attribute. This search is motivated by his newly discovered pleasure in masturbation. Even the mother's bodily processes, such as micturition and defecation, are subject to the child's scrutiny. But she exhibits nothing. Moreover, she denies nothing. Her silence is imposed by the child's insistent misrecognition.

When the child repeatedly asks, "What's that?," he already knows the answer is "A breast"; but what he does not know, and why he continues to ask, is what he himself is. For the child, at this moment, the mother still has the power to determine his relation to the signifier; to have or to be the phallus. In turn she asks herself the crucial yet unspoken question, "What am I?" It is unspoken because "I" is not the subject of a sentence but a place, the unconscious. In this place she is designated as *feminine* by a complex of archaic oral, anal, and vaginal drives, which recede from the site of speaking the more she tries to speak. It is the lacunae in the mother's answers to the child's questions that ultimately censor his research.

The child's spontaneous scopophilia provokes the mother's sense of "shame." This does not happen conspicuously at the level of these lived events but at the level of the unconscious, as an effect of the re-presentation of the castrated image of her own mother.

Nevertheless, there is a reprieve at the founding moment of castration, that is, the Father's promise. This promise is reiterated in the child's valorization of the mother's body which he sees as having the phallus in the form of a baby, when he says, "Why can't I have a baby?" In pregnancy, the mother presents herself to herself in the mirror image of repletion and plenitude. However, the anatomy of fantasy is fragile and always entails the fear of falling back in disarray. It is the drive for self-mastery which underlies the illusion of unity. In this respect the mother is like her child. For him, the figure of the Phallic Mother is frightening, seductive, and ultimately castrating. In part, this is because she is the one who first aroused the child's genital feelings by the constant and intimate care of his body. The mother's susceptibility to guilt for excessively gratifying or restricting her child (often in fantasy) is reinforced by pedagogy which urges her to take a "friendly but not indulgent" attitude toward his erotic activities. The child's displays of exhibitionism and "cruelty" are met with inhibition and compassion from the mother. Her dread of violence is motivated by a vicarious identification with the castration fears of her child (if he is a boy), her sexual partner, and, above all, her father. For the child, the threatening "badmen" mark the intervention of the Law. Thus "I will give you a baby . . ." becomes "I can't give you a baby . . ." and subsequently introduces the theories about where babies come from, as in "Do babies come from bottoms?"

The mother's shame, inhibition, compassion, and dread of violence are also intimately linked to her initial discovery of "the mystery of birth." It is precisely the effect of her mother's words with regard to childbirth and sexual intercourse which constitutes the locus of her fear of pain, evisceration, rape, and, in fact, of vaginal castration insofar as she represents to herself the motive of her fear—the loss of the body's "feminine interface." But the fear of *femininity,* in the sense of "feminine drives," remains a source of anxiety because it appears to be unrepressed, anarchic, archaic, and utterly unrepresentable. It is only represented, if ever, in the symbolic castration of the sexual act. This is also why the mother protects the child from witnessing the "violence" of "making love"; insofar as she desires to be the phallus for the Other (sexual partner), the mother's *femininity* is lost in the castrating moment of her enjoyment. For the child, accepting the mother's castration is often marked by symptomatic consequences, notably the fear of snakes, spiders, ghosts. But when he finally concedes that she does not have the phallus, the child takes up a masculine position in relation to the signifier, that is, to have the phallus, as implied in the heterosexual imperative of "Men don't dance with mens . . . they dance with womans." Thus theories about the birth of babies are turned into inquiries about sexual difference and these eventually give way, under the weight of repression, to questions about origins and the order of things.

Experimentum Mentis VI: On the Insistence of the Letter

Prewriting emerges as postscript to the Oedipus complex and as preface to the moment of latency. Insofar as the child's sexual researches are repressed by the Law and the Father, they are sublimated in the body of the *letter;* but it is the mother who first censors the look, who wipes the slate clean with her silence and prepares the site of inscription. For the mother, the child's text is a fetish object; it desires her. The polymorphous perversity of the letter explores the body beyond the limit of the look. The breast (e), the hook (r), the lack (c), the eye (i), the snake (s); forbidden anatomies, incestuous morphologies; the child's alphabet is an anagram of the maternal body. For the child, the grapheme-as-body-in-the-position-of-the-signifier plays with difference, not the difference of the founding moment of castration, the ultimatum of being or having, but rather a replay of differences and separations already sanctioned in the structuring and dissolution of the Oedipus complex. A cross (x), a round (o), an up and a down (n, m), a straight and a round (p, b, d, q); pairs of graphemic oppositions designate the symbolic function of presence and absence in a double movement of memory and forgetting. Feces, mark, imprint, utterance—a residue of corporality subtends the letter and overflows the text. The gift unfolds the child's desire to-be-what-she-wants-him-to-be; but the letter constructs the cannot-be of his autonomy and instigates the unexpected pleasure of deferment.

With the inscription of his proper name, the child is instituted as the author of his text. Each purposeful stroke disfigures the anagram, dismembers the body. The mother is dispossessed of the phallic attributes of the pre-Oedipal instance, but only as if retracing a vague figure of repletion on a distant screen. Fading, forgetting—she cannot remember although "it seems like only yesterday." This wound to her narcissism is now a caricature: a tearful bliss, a simulated ecstasy, a veritable stigmata in the Name-of-the-Father. With the child's insistent repetition of the Name, he appropriates the status of the Father, the dead Father, the absent Father, the precondition of the "word." The incestuous meaning of the letter is ciphered by the paternal metaphor. But at the same time, this introduces the possibility of "truth," the truth of the mother—that is, the fiction of the "real mother," not the Madonna, but the Pieta, dispelling imputations of guilt with patience, self-sacrifice, long-suffering, and resignation. Resignation punctuated with protests: "he is too little . . . he is too young . . . they are too rough . . . it is too far." In fantasy, the mother endures an endless series of threats to the child's well-being; sickness, accident, death. Her castration fears take the form of losing her loved objects, primarily her children; but underlying this is the fear of losing love, that is, the fear of being unable to reconstitute her narcissistic aim, of being unable to see herself as infinitely good and unconditionally loved. Ultimately, it is the fear of her mother's death and of her own death as the imaginary stake in the representation of that loss. This negation is constituted by a recognition of unbearable dependence; but it is also an affirmation of life since the child's independence is implicated in the renunciation he imposes on her desire.

The effects of repressing Oedipal pleasure for both the mother and the child are evaded through sublimation, that is, through their mutual inscription in an order of extrafamilial discourse and social practice. But the very movement toward a nonparental ideal that prompts the child's creative initiatives or indiscretions and constructs the representation of his social place returns the mother to the site of the family, to the parental ideal of her own mother and of the representation of *maternal femininity*. Such a circuitous passage is problematic; being the phallus, she cannot have it; not having it, she cannot represent herself as subject of desire. She finds it difficult to assume responsibility for her pleasure without guilt; to provoke her sexual partner, to slight her child. Fearing failure, she is distracted from the projects which interest her most. There is a reprieve; another child, the fullness of the dyad, the sweetness of that imaginary encapsulation which reduces the outside world to absurdity. But there is also the inevitable moment of separation reiterating a lack always already inscribed and impossible to efface. She asks herself, "What will I do? . . . when he starts school . . . when he grows up . . . when he leaves home . . . when he leaves me . . ." This moment signifies more than separation; it articulates a rupture, a rent, a gap, and a confrontation—a confrontation not only because of the way in which her desire, as desire for the child to-be-what-she-wants-him-to-be, is produced within a field of social and economic constraints, but also because of the way in which the dialectic of desire, the movement of subject and object with its insistence on bisexuality, continually transgresses the system of representation in which it is founded. The construction of femininity as essentially natural and maternal is never finally fixed but forever unsettled in the process of articulating her difference, her loss. And it is precisely at such moments that it is possible to desire to speak and to dare to change.

Note

"Preface" and "Experimentum Mentis" sections from *Post-Partum Document* by Mary Kelly (London and Boston: Routledge and Kegan Paul 1983). The book documents a six-part installation begun in 1973 and completed in 1979.

On Femininity

The *Post-Partum Document* is based on the theoretical assumption that femininity is not a pregiven entity, but a representation of difference constructed within specific discourses. In "Documentation IV," the discourse of the mother-child relationship constructs the representation of femininity as essentially maternal. This is not to say there is an essential femininity and that it is maternal, but rather that this feminine identity is a position the subject occupies in language, as signifier for another signifier (the Other as mother for the child). Meaning is not prior to language but is produced by it. In the same sense, there is no preexisting sexuality to be represented. Difference is only ever the difference between signifiers.[1] This reiterates the importance of Freud's concept of bisexuality and his insistence on the notion that there is only one libido—masculine—insofar as it designates that the sexual drive is always active.[2] In regard to desire, there is no quantitative difference between men and women and this is what makes the outcome of the Oedipal moment so problematic for the woman—the impossibility of being both subject and object of desire. According to Lacan, the subject is constituted emphatically in a relation of "lack"—lack in the signifying chain, lack in the Other, and lack in the subject itself which emerges as desire.[3] For both the boy and the girl, the first love object is the mother. The recognition of her lack, the acceptance of symbolic castration, structures the Oedipal moment by making it possible for the child to take up a position as sexed subject—being or having the phallus. Because of the place it occupies in the field of the Other and in the structure of difference, the phallus becomes the privileged signifier of desire. Consequently, the representation of femi-

Mary Kelly, *Post-Partum Document,*
Documentation IV: Transitional
objects, diary, and diagram, 1976,
detail, 1 of 8 units, 11 × 14 ins.,
plaster, cotton, ink. Collection Zurich
Museum, Switzerland.

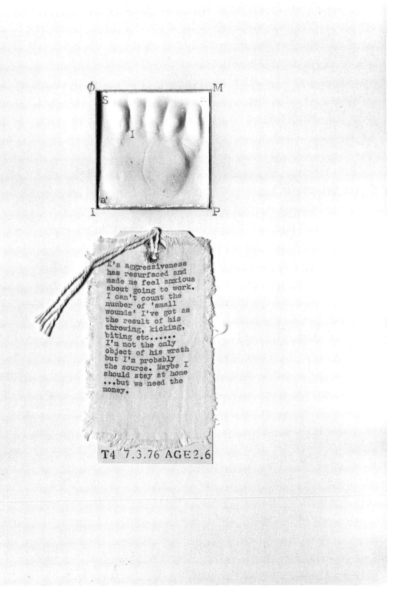

Study for Documentation IV.

ninity becomes intimately bound up with the masquerade of *being the phallus* and prolifically inscribed in the dominant codes of the *image as fetish.*

In "Documentation IV," to refuse to signify the mother through her image, photographic or otherwise, is not to erase her presence from the scene, but rather to locate her desire precisely in the field of the Other through the presence of the child. The "transitional objects"—the hand imprints, the comforter fragments—are the emblems which testify to that desire, to the representation of a pleasure now sublimated, lost. There is an endless redoubling of the child in his surrogate image. At one level this sets up the metaphorical equation, gift=child=phallus, but at another level the gradual effacement of the image by the superimposition of the diagram poses the question of exactly what loss is being represented beyond the pleasure of the child's body. The footnotes to this section, "Experimentum Mentis IV," maintain that it is the pleasure of *having* the mother's body through *being like her* which is at stake. This, then, raises a number of problems concerning the woman's relation to castration, the status of the phallus, and the body in psychoanalytic theory.[4]

Although the figure of the mother is not present in the work, this absence does not suggest that the representation of femininity can escape the corruption, the fetishistic implications, of conventional codes by evacuating the image. In the *Post-Partum Document,* the realism which is repressed in the realm of the look returns in the form of the diary text. This narrative capture is both confirmed and undermined by the diagrammatic representations which intervene to locate other readings of these events. For example, in "Documentation IV," Leonardo's drawing introduces a certain mechanistic scientific discourse on perception which is accompanied in the "Footnotes" by a description of the empirical procedures adopted in the work.[5] This in turn is displaced by Lacan's Schema R, which places specularity within the context of a psychoanalytic discourse of the Imaginary and which refers to a specific moment in the mother-child relationship.[6] These operations of displacement (ultimately summed up by the algorithms) are crucial in forestalling a condition of closure in the text which could otherwise be seen metaphorically as a recapitulation of maternal plenitude.

Finally, the work does not reproduce a struggle in the signifying process between a specifically feminine discourse on the one hand (represented by the memorabilia and the diaries, by feeling, by consciousness-raising or the unconscious) and a specifically masculine discourse on the other (represented by the diagrams and algorithms, by the voices of theory, of distantiation and political intervention); rather, it tries to imbricate image, verbal inscription, and theoretical reworking in the production of meaning. An intertextual practice that resists the division of form and content can encourage, although it cannot guarantee, a reading which refutes the notion of essential femininity and returns the question of sexual difference to the field of language and representation.[7]

Notes

"On Femininity," *Control Magazine,* Issue Eleven (1979): 14–15.

1. Parveen Adams, "Representation and Sexuality," *m/f,* no. 1 (1978): 71–73.

2. Cf. Sigmund Freud, "Three Essays on Sexuality," 1905, Standard Edition, vol. 7, and "Femininity," lecture 33, *The New Introductory Lectures,* 1933, Standard Edition, vol. 11.

3. Cf. Jacques Lacan, "The Function and Field of Speech and Analysis" and "The Significance of the Phallus," *Ecrits: A Selection,* trans. A. Sheridan, (London: Tavistock, 1977).

4. Cf. Michèle Montrelay, "Femininity," trans. P. Adams, *m/f,* no. 1 (1978): 83–101.

5. As regards all visible objects, three things must be considered. These are the position of the eye which sees (b), that of the object seen (a), and the position of the light which illuminates the object (c). I. A. Richter, *Selections from the Notebooks of Leonardo da Vinci* (Oxford: Oxford University press, 1952), p. 130. Quoted in Mary Kelly, "Footnotes and Bibliography." *Post-Partum Document,* Museum of Modern Art, Oxford, 1977, pp. 8–9.

6. In 1966 Lacan explained that Schema R is to be read in three dimensions. J. A. Miller adds the following comments in *Les Cahiers de l'Analyse,* nos. 1–2: The surface R is to be taken as the flattening out of the figure obtained by joining "i" to "I" and "m" to "M," that is, by the twisting which characterizes the Möbius strip. The presentation of the schema in two dimensions is thus related to the cut which enables the strip to be laid out flat. It will be realized that the line IM cannot refer to the relationship of the subject to the object of desire: the subject is only the

cutting of the strip, and what falls out of it is called "the object a." A. Wilden, *The Language of the Self* (Baltimore: Johns Hopkins University Press, 1968), p. 29.

7. For discussion of feminist art practice, see *Representation vs Communication* (Elizabeth Cowie, Claire Johnston, Cora Kaplan, Mary Kelly, Jacqueline Rose, Marie Yates) National Conference of Socialist Feminists, London, 1978.

No Essential Femininity: A Conversation between Mary Kelly and Paul Smith

Paul Smith: Would you begin by describing your *Post-Partum Document?*

Mary Kelly: Speaking quite generally, it's an extended documentation which I began in 1973 of the mother-child relationship. It took about six years to complete and is divided into six sections including, in all, about one hundred thirty-five pieces. I suppose I should also say that it was conceived as a piece for the conventional gallery space; that is, specific modes of presentation are employed. The plastic frames, for instance, parody the whole iconography of the museum "display"—not just the art museum but something like the natural history museum as well (which I've always thought of as a vast metaphor for the exploration of the mother's body). I wanted to put this archeology of everyday life into that kind of framed space—an unexpected place—which would set up certain conditions for a critical reading. I felt it was crucial to consider how the work intervened in a particular institutionalized context. So, in a sense, the way it looks in the gallery is an important consideration. On the one hand, it appears to be a record of external events, but on the other, it doesn't function in that space as simply a document; the installation is intended to construct several readings or ways through the text. These are indicated first by the objects and the narrative texts which accompany them; second, by a series of diagrams which refer elsewhere to a kind of explication of the empirical procedures in the work; and third, by another set of diagrams which refer specifically to the work of Lacan and which suggest another possible reading based on psychoanalysis.

Mary Kelly, *Post-Partum Document,*
Documentation VI: Pre-writing
alphabet, exergue and diary, 1978,
15 units, resin and slate, 11 × 14 ins.
each. Collection Arts Council of
Great Britain.

So, at one level the spectator is caught up, as it were, in a first-person narrative which traces the events specifically related to moments in the child's—that is, my son's—relationship with me: for instance, weaning from the breast, learning to speak, starting school, the first questions about sexuality, and finally, learning to write. Each one of these moments "develops" in an empirical sense, and this might indicate that the piece had a definite beginning and end; but, of course, at another level, the space of the diagrams that refer to the Lacanian readings places much less emphasis on a literal document or on a notion of, say, developmental stages, than on the construction of the relationship in terms of the mother's fantasies.

PS: I'd like to pick up on a lot of those points, but would you start by talking about the notion of narrative here? As I see it, the story of the mother-child relationship *is* specifically a story, chronological and linear, working on the level of traditional narrative in the sense that there's a problem posed and a resolution reached (which, here, is the final imposition of the social and symbolic upon the child). And also, isn't the spectator obliged to move around the work in the linear way that narrative traditionally entails?

MK: Certainly I didn't see it as a narrative in the traditional sense. I suppose that the diaries give a place to the mother in terms of the subject "I"; she speaks in the first person. But that's displaced by the metadiscursive style, which enters by way of the footnotes and which uses the third person as the dominant mode of address. So I'm not really privileging the autobiographical discourse—I'm always attempting to disrupt it.

As to what you say about a sort of development and resolution: I think that movement is thwarted in the work as well. In a traditional narrative one would perhaps expect a central point at which the heroine makes the decisions which produce a certain effect or dictate her fate. That's not the case here. The diaries just prolong and extend the description of events at the same level; so that when you talk about a resolution, I'd reply that resolution refers in a much more general way to the theoretical implications of the work, which are presented in the footnotes. That's to say, when I describe the mother-child relationship in the postpartum period as a confrontation between the Real and the Imaginary which is always structured within the *primacy* of the Symbolic, that can be referred to in a certain sense as a resolution. It's less to do, though, with the narrative structure of the work and more with the theoretical perspective, which always sees the positioning of the subject and the construction of femininity as framed within the limits of language and culture. Some feminists, I know, might not agree. But then you have to ask yourself a question: if you don't subscribe to that notion of the universality of language, if you say that men and women don't enter into the same order of language and culture and that it's essentially different for the woman, that she can discover something outside, as it were, in opposition to that order, then doesn't that also effect a kind of closure—perhaps one that's even more dangerous in its implications for feminism? In its most extreme form, it would imply that femininity is tied to essential biological differences; or, alternatively, it would place emphasis on the experience of the pre-Oedipal moment as privileged for the woman, maintaining that the passage she makes through the Oedipus complex is somehow incomplete, or that she occupies a position "outside" in relation to representation. This would ultimately suggest that all women are in some sense neurotic as the necessary effect of their psychic positioning within the Symbolic.

PS: I suppose that, traditionally, one of the most effective ways of imposing a closure through a visual means of representation is to use the biographical or autobiographical image, always given as a wholeness. You've very deliberately left out of the *Post-Partum Document* your own body, your own image. What's involved in foregoing that temptation, and what kind of image of yourself do you think finally emerges from the work?

MK: When I placed emphasis on the fact that the work wasn't a reiteration of child development but an attempt to give a place to the mother's fantasies, this was also relevant in terms of the modes or forms of representation which I chose for underlining that decision. For me it was very important not to use filmic or photographic means—that is, nothing which would suggest the notion of documentation as a "slice of life"—not because that's actually the function of film or photography but rather, strategically, it was important to avoid any implication of that sort. The decision was also crucial because I feel that when the image of the woman is used in a work of art, that is, when her body or person is given as signifier, it becomes extremely problematic. Most women artists who have presented themselves in some way, visibly, in their work have been unable to find the kind of distancing devices which would cut across the predominant representations of woman as object of the look, or that would question the notion of femininity as a pregiven entity. I'm not exactly an iconoclast, but perhaps historically, just at the moment, a method needs to be employed which foregrounds the construction of femininity as a representation of difference within a specific discourse.

In the *Post-Partum Document* I'm concerned to see how femininity, within the discourse of the mother-child relationship, is produced as natural and maternal. Of course, the practices that are implied in that process, such as feeding or dressing a child, are as dependent on a system of signs as are writing or speaking. In a sense, I see all social practices as expressions of a general social law (of a symbolic dimension, as Kristeva puts it), which is given in language. This means that the formal emphasis on written and spoken words in my work simply stresses the fact that the production of the subject is primarily a question of positionality in language.

But I'm also aware of another implication: what I've evacuated at the level of the look (or the representational image) has returned in the form of my diary narrative. A kind of capture of the viewer occurs within the first-person narrative of the diary texts. For me, it's also absolutely crucial that this kind of pleasure in the text, in the objects themselves, should engage the viewer, because there's no point at which anything can become a deconstructed critical engagement if the viewer is not first—immediately and affectively—drawn into the work. I also think that narrative can function differently in an artwork because it is unexpected and controversial in that space.

PS: Working in this manner, you're cutting across a certain type of women's art practice which, in the last ten or so years, has been concerned to alter woman's given image by exactly the opposite mode you've chosen. I wonder if there's not something important going on in such work, which treats the woman as the object of the look but where she is redefined in some way.

MK: I suppose I'd like to broaden the question into a consideration of how the construction of femininity is viewed within differing art practices by women artists. Since the early seventies you could probably point to at least four different categories of work.

First, we have what we think of as cultural feminism, an attempt to excavate a separate order of language and culture for women. This work usually inscribes itself as either an appropriation of earlier forms of traditional women's crafts or as a reinvention and exploration of those means in terms of a contemporary practice—say, for instance, the emphasis on pattern painting in New York. Perhaps the most important example of that tendency was the early work of Judy Chicago and the project *Womenhouse,* and more recently is triumphant finale, as it were, with *The Dinner Party.* Chicago suggests that his valorization of women from the past is taking place precisely because history has tended, as she puts it, "to devour women." There, interestingly, you have a kind of inversion of the totem-meal: what's forbidden on the one hand—the devouring of the mother—is permitted on this one ritual occasion where the historical mother figures are put in the position of the father, their name and status ingested, as in the totem-meal, by the female viewers of this visual feast.

Second, you have work which actually uses the body itself, such as Suzanne Şantoro's well-known book, *Towards New Expression.* Here, exploration of the female genitals becomes a means of appropriating a specifically feminine relation to language, which is given in the body. Theoretically, I imagine, the most effective exposition of that position would be in the work of Luce Irigaray: she talks very poetically about the female sex as two lips kissing one another. For her, any kind of intervention in that primal auto-eroticism is seen as a sort of violence against the woman.

Then there's a more varied third category which revolves around what could be loosely described as feminine experience. These women artists feel that there is, not necessarily a biologically determined femininity, but an essentially feminine experience of the body, or rules under which women are dominated by *representations* of the body. This is the case with most performance work. Hannah Wilke, for instance, refers to the eroticism of the woman's body. She presents herself very typically as the object of the look, and in doing so I suppose she is acting out the feminine position—the position of being the phallus for the other. But there is a contradiction. That image of totalization, the mirror image as it were, is always subject to fragmentation, disarray, or disavowal. So you have with Gina Pane, for example, the signs of self-mutilation that could be interpreted as the other side of the mirror image, or Adrian Piper, in her *Guerrilla Theatre,* where she makes herself as despicable as possible—a kind of inversion of what she sees as the stereotypical desired object.

What I think emerges as a kind of underlying contradiction is that, while the woman sees her experience in terms of the "feminine" position as the object of the look, she also has to deal with the fact that she's the subject of desire, or that she is, as artist, in the masculine position as subject of the look. The difficulty she finds in being in those two places at once seems to me to demonstrate through the actual practice something about the insistent bisexuality of the drives. You find this in the practice of most of the women artists right through these categories; you find there's some way in which a fundamental negation of the notion of an essential femininity nonetheless appears. Even in work which is overtly derived from the female body you can find a kind of superimposition of phallocentric and concentric imagery—Louise Bourgeois's sculpture is an interesting example. I could go on endlessly citing examples, but the point I'm trying to make in general is that the work itself, in spite of what women say about it, demonstrates that masculine and feminine positions are never fixed.

The question of sexuality which I feel is emerging (partly as a consequence of that other work) is posed neither in terms of a reduction to the body nor in terms of an essential feminine experience, but precisely in the realm of the social construction of masculine or feminine identities. This new tendency is by no means homogeneous. It turns, on the one hand, toward a kind of economic determinism in, say, the work of Martha Rosler, or perhaps, on the other hand, toward a theory of subjectivity—I might use my own work as an example, but I would say that the emphasis should be placed on the intersection of those two instances, the social and the psychic, as they meet in constructing the sexed subject.

PS: You're talking somewhat in psychoanalytical terms and you've also indirectly brought up the question of Marxism. Maybe this is the place to propose my sense of your work as characteristically European, insofar as one of the firm bases of North American feminism has been exactly a repudiation of Freud, a refusal to accept certain of his ideas and, in some cases, a foreclosure of the very idea of the unconscious. This hasn't been true in Europe, so do you see your work at all in that dialectical opposition to such a tendency in North America?

MK: Certainly one of the conspicuous differences in the European women's movement is that socialist feminism has remained alive and well. In America the development of the movement seems to have been circumscribed by radical feminism on the one hand and traditional Marxism on the other; only very recently has there been any real attempt to mediate these positions in terms of art practices. Lucy Lippard's organization of the exhibition Issue at the ICA in London last year was the first real initiative of that kind. But one could still sense there in most of the work by American artists that any emphasis on the "personal" appeared to detract from what they would consider "wider social issues."

Now, in the way that much European feminist work has developed, I don't think that's been the case—the social and the psychic haven't been seen as necessarily antagonistic or contradictory. But one would have to add that within the socialist feminist groupings, say in Britain, it's only a smaller tendency that's been involved in work on psychoanalysis. Certainly the debates around psychoanalysis and Marxism in the movement have been very productive, although the intended marriage of the two never took place. The outcome has been more on the order of discovering that one can only use certain methods of analysis in relation to their specific objects: there's no single theoretical discourse which is going to offer us an explanation for all forms of social relations or for every mode of political practice.

The *Post-Partum Document* found its inspiration, if you can call it that, within the socialist feminist tendency of the women's movement in Britain. I identify very much with those who have been doing work in the field of psychoanalysis—initially the History Group, then the Lacan reading group, and more recently the journal *m/f.* In 1976 there was an important conference on the topic of patriarchy where the issues of psychoanalysis were raised within a wider context. There were workshops discussing Lacan's re-reading of Freud. It was very controversial but nevertheless it was debated within the movement; that hasn't been the case in North America. My work grows directly out of those debates and is almost concurrent with their every stage. I started out with an emphasis on the psychology, the feminine psychology of the mother being sealed in the division of labor and child care—a position which one could say is reflected in Mitchell's book *Woman's Estate,* which I then modified and reworked so that by the last section of the *Post-Partum Document* in 1979 I wasn't talking so much about patriarchy in terms of the division of labor, but rather with reference to the construction of sexual difference.

PS: Implied there, and in those debates, is the necessity of inserting into political considerations a theory of the speaking subject: your work does seem to me to highlight one of the problems that much of this kind of work has had to face, namely, that it can be accused of a certain patriarchal bias because of its reliance on Lacan and his definition of woman in relation to the phallus. Also, there is in your work a sort of recourse to rational structures (diagrams, graphs, theoretical discourse, etc.) which I'd characterize here as patriarchal, as male. Do you accept, on the one hand, that there is this recourse to rationality as an authority in your work, and, on the other hand, do you accept this view of Lacan as being irredeemably patriarchal?

MK: Taking up your question in relation to the art practice itself, one would have to see the theoretical work primarily as "writing" or as a mode of representation rather than as any form of final explication. When I employ something like the Lacanian diagrams, they, too, are cathected as images of the difficulty of the Symbolic, or perhaps as emblems of a kind of love-hate relationship with the father—which is not exactly a recourse to rationality as authority. At one level you could say the work itself, particularly the reworking of that experience of maternity in the footnotes, expresses a fundamental desire to know and to master. Now, in regard to the actual theoretical examples cited—say the articles by Lacan which I used to analyze the various moments of separation—another level of questioning is raised about whether I should be using any kind of "male discourse" as some feminist might say—why Freud, why Lacan? I must admit that I did really want to find alternatives in the beginning. I read Maud Mannoni, Françoise Dalto, Melanie Klein; but Lacan's work, particularly his notion of the two end points of the mirror phase, was crucial for my first three works, "Weaning from the Breast," "Weaning from the Holphrase," and "Weaning from the Dyad"; that material required a rather more complicated analysis of separation and entry into the order of language than could be afforded by either Klein (who pushes the Oedipal moment so far back that we can't get a clear picture of those early distinctions) or Dalto (who places it too schematically, at two-and-a-half years old). But in sections IV and V ("On Femininity" and "On the Order of Things") which are centrally concerned with the representation of loss, not only as loss of the child but also as loss of the maternal body, I rely very heavily on Montrelay's reading of Lacan, her definition of the "feminine" unconscious as the imposition of *concentricity,* an archaic oral-anal schema, upon the phallocentric organization of the drives. Then in the final section, "On the Insistence of the Letter," a definite theoretical shift takes place, initiated by the analysis of the child's prewriting, which raises questions concerning the phonocentric and perhaps logocentric bias of Lacan's position. (By that I mean his dependence on Jakobson's linguistics.)

PS: For me, though, one of the most interesting parts of the whole work is its double inscription of fetishism; on the one hand, the mother fetishizing the child as phallus, and on the other, the sense that the work itself, once installed, becomes a further fetish, replacing the dangers of the fetishization of the child. Underneath that, however, is a discomfort arising from the idea that fetishism is always a surrender to the law of the father, to patriarchal order—and Freud, of course, ascribes fetishism specifically to the masculine domain. So what is fetishism for a woman, and how does it work?

MK: In fantasy, castration anxiety for the man is often represented as the loss of the penis, the arms, the legs, or some other bodily substitute. When

Detail, *Post-Partum Document,*
Documentation VI.

(age 3.6) O IS FOR ORANGE. When he
writes O, he says "a round and an O". It seems
to be set up in opposition to X which is
not round, not closed, not orange and not
eatable. O is for oriface for pleasure, for
fullness and forever not enough. O IS FOR
ALLIGATORS ORDERING OATMEAL. O IS
FOR A OPTICIAN GIVING AN EYE TEST TO AN
OWL. OLGA OPHELIA OWL. GOODNIGHT LITTLE O.

February 8, 1977: Today Kelly jumped off everything,
bumped into everyone, fell over constantly, wouldn't
sing songs and generally embarrassed me. He got jealous
when I helped other children and he expected me to
protect him from a little boy who was trying to take
away his yellow truck. When I wouldn't do it, he went
into a rage and kicked over a chair. I was humiliated.
I asked the supervisor if he did that when I wasn't
there. She said no, but was preoccupied with one of the
twins who was crying hysterically. She was shouting
at her which I didn't think would help and I was
relieved when she finally decided to comfort her.
I took Kelly out of the room and gave him a good-
talking-to. I thought to myself why can't he be like
that good, clever darling little girl that all the
supervisors love.

Casting process, Documentation VI.

we talk about this imaginary scenario for the woman, we say that her castration fears take the form of losing her loved objects, especially her children. They are going to grow up and leave her, reject her, perhaps die. To delay, disavow the separation she has already in a sense acknowledged, she tends to fetishize the child in some way: for example, by dressing him up, by continuing to feed him no matter how old he gets, or simply by having another one. Perhaps then, in relation to pornography, we could talk about the mother's memorabilia: the way she saves things, like the first shoes, photographs, locks of hair, and so on. My work takes off from that point. In place of the first shoes, we have the stained liners or the first words set out in actual typeface. When I used something like the plaster imprints of the child's hands, the fragments of his comforter, or the objects like insects of plants that were his gifts, they are intended to be read as transitional objects, but not in Winnicott's sense of surrogates, rather in Lacan's terms as, say, emblems of desire.

So I've displaced the fetishization of the child at one level onto the artwork. But I've made it explicit in the work so that I think this also functions at another level which questions the fetishistic nature of representation itself. All the objects are framed and fixed in a way which defines them as precious objects, things to be seen or sold. Yet they're commonplace or ordinary. What's more, because they're found objects, they're not properly invested with creative subjectivity, in other words, with the kind of authenticating mark, or authorship, which is so essential to the art market.

But the question of fetishism gets us into some difficulties about the work. One of the clinical definitions of fetishism is that it doesn't concern any specific object: it's simply a question of how the original cathexis is displaced from one idea or object or part of the body to something often totally unrelated. As Freud points out, art is a kind of nonneurotic variation on the theme of fetishism, so there's a sense in which we're not actually talking about the same thing in *Post-Partum Document,* because it's something which is sublimated in a socially acceptable form and therefore generalizable as a discourse and as a practice. But the work is also a case history—it is *my* experience of those events. It has sometimes been frightening, but I don't think the implications of this are really accessible to me for analysis.

PS: I'd like to ask you about writing and language in the work. Because you're overlaying different types of discourse, mapping out various linguistic terrains, and adding one voice to others, there seems to me to be implicitly some kind of hierarchy of discourse established at certain points. This perhaps comes out of my sense that the discourse of psychoanalysis is being privileged, but also on a more local level (as in "Documentation III" where you have your voice, your inner speech, and the child's original discourse all inscribed over the child's scribblings), there does seem to be some sense of a hierarchy pointing to some position of power and suggesting that someone somewhere could be using the "right" language: this brings up the question for the whole work as to what kind of language you're aspiring toward.

MK: Hopefully, the work is a continual displacement rather than a hierarchization of certain forms of language. The way it works through different levels of language is certainly seen to be unraveling the sense in which representation is always a representation of loss. The piece that illustrates this most clearly is "Documentation IV," where the imprints of the child's hands disappear and a diagrammatic representation of the relationship appears. Throughout the work, while I'm speaking about it and trying to understand it, I'm also in the process of recognizing that something has already been lost. So in that particular part, where I talk about the pleasure of the child's body and the problem of the incest taboo for the mother, I'm also trying to see what's at stake beyond the representation of the child's body itself. What emerges, I think, is (as usual) the mother's body. By saying that the representation of femininity is constructed as maternal, I mean that in this relationship the woman experiences that closeness to the mother's body which she imagined in those first identifications with her own mother. In that sense, too, when I use the writing on the slates in "Documentation VI," I'm referring to the child's marks as a kind of anagram of the maternal body. The whole project, not only the visible artwork but the process itself, is about the relation of writing to the mother's body. But this has been said often enough. What I've emphasized in that relation is a moment of transgression where separation threatens the woman's representation of herself as essentially and naturally maternal and creates a kind of chasm which resounds with questions. The woman questions the socially given meanings for the feminine. So I guess the kind of language I'm aspiring to is one which will prolong that rupture.

PS: In some way, you've just answered the question I'm about to ask. If that transgressional moment of loss does open up a new space, it might nonetheless still be read with a certain pessimism regarding women's condition since, even though it gives the impulse to change and to make different things happen, it can surely be a moment that's repeatable only at certain junctures in your life (and for most women not very often at that). Doesn't it suggest finally that the symbolic realm imposed and reimposed upon us is constricting and unchangeable?

MK: On the contrary, I see it as very optimistic because it shows exactly that the symbolic realm is not really fixed and homogeneous, but that it's riddled with contradictions. Precisely because what we call "ideology" is a complex arrangement of social practices and systems of representations which are always inscribing their difference from one another, we can find a space for change. It's the totalizing view of culture that leads to pessimism. When you say either that we're absolutely constrained by patriarchy or that it's only a matter of false consciousness to be shaken off, *that,* for me, is when you come up with a much more constricting view. I think that what's discovered in working through the *Post-Partum Document* is that there is no preexisting sexuality, no *essential* femininity, and that to look at the processes of their construction is also to see the possibility of deconstructing the dominant forms of representing difference and justifying subordination in our social order.

Note

"No Essential Femininity A Conversation between Mary Kelly and Paul Smith," *Parachute,* no. 26 (1982): 31–35. Initiated during the exhibition of *Post-Partum Document* at the Anna Leonowens Gallery, Nova Scotia College of Art and Design, Halifax, 1981.

III Postmodern Oppositions

Re-Viewing Modernist Criticism

Although the phenomenon of the temporary exhibition first made its appearance in the nineteenth century, it was only in the postwar period that it became the most prominent form of entertainment and tuition in the visual arts. The ascendancy of the temporary exhibition, notably the annuals, biennials, theme shows, and historical surveys, indicated a significant shift in the system of patronage from the private sector to institutions funded by the state. This change coincided with an expansion in the art publishing industry, renewed emphasis on the practice of reviewing, and the sanctioning of art criticism as an academic discipline. These occurrences, their points of intersection and divergence, establish the framework for an analysis of the effects and limitations of modernist criticism in particular. In this article, modernism is defined as a determinant discursive field with reference to critical writing since 1945. It is maintained that modernist discourse is produced at the level of the statement, by the specific practices of art criticism, by the art activities implicated in the critic/author's formulations, and by the institutions which disseminate and disperse the formulations as events. An analysis of the formation and transformation of statements in this field is very much needed, but it is beyond the scope of the introductory issues being raised here. However, it is hoped that by identifying the persistent themes of that discourse, pointing out its diversions, describing the process of its modification at a particular moment, and making proposals for the construction of a different object in the domain of criticism at the present time, a space will be opened for future work.

The Pictorial Paradigm

In a note to the article "Photography and Aesthetics," Peter Wollen remarks, "The category of 'modernism' has increasingly been captured by those who see twentieth-century art primarily in terms of reflexivity and ontological exploration."[1] If it is possible to define this capture in other terms as the predominance of a particular discourse within the hierarchy of discourses which constitute modernism as a discursive field, then the effectivity of that discourse can be described more exactly as the production of a norm for pictorial representation which does not necessarily correspond to definite pictures, but rather to a set of general assumptions concerning "modern art." Further, if these assumptions are not seen to be based on the consensus of a homogeneous mass audience of art viewers, but formed within calculated practices of reviewing, publishing, and exhibiting art for a specific public, then the reading of artistic texts is always in some sense subjected to the determining conditions of these practices, crucially those of criticism. Here, at least two preliminary points can be made about the way in which modernist criticism functions as a practice, that is, the rules it deploys in forming these general assumptions as a network of themes which construct definite objects and a system of strategic choices which also permit their modification.

First, the normalization of a mode of representation always entails the marginalization of an alternative set of practices and discourses; for instance, Sam Hunter, hailing the rise of abstract expressionism in *Art since 1945,* claimed that almost every other art practice at that time—geometric abstraction as well as romantic realism and surrealism—was an "exception rather than the rule."[2] But marginalization is not simply a matter of chronological displacement or exclusion. It can also be effected by incorporation. In a passage written later, in 1968, for an exhibition entitled New Directions in American Painting, Hunter referred an even wider area of emergent artistic practices back to the ontological norm:

> When the contemporary artist moves towards the object, the world of packaged mass culture or even towards formal purification, critical problems of artistic choice remain and compromise his most apparently

anonymous productions. The idea of the work of art as an uncertain and problematic act of continual creation, filtered through a temperature and retaining evidence in its final form of that passage, was one of the central contributions of Abstract Expressionism.[3]

The modernist discourse constructs the category of the artistic text. It must demonstrate pictoriality without radical purification, retain the evidence of a passage without imposing the problem of interpretation, filter a temperament without reference to social constraints. *It is preeminently "expressive" and primarily given at the level of the "picture."* Those practices, particularly those anonymous productions which do not in some sense conform to the unity, the homogeneity of the pictorial paradigm, and express the essential creativity of the artistic subject, are not merely marginal; they are not art!

Second, despite incompatible practices or divisions in the discourse, modernism's central themes persist. The current revival of painting (neo-expressionism, New Imagism, Energism) and the coincident dispersal of narrative, conceptual, and social purpose art give some indication of the political consequences of artistic choices founded on a reappropriation of modernist themes. Such trends also imply that the designations "avant-garde" and more recently "postmovement" "postmodernist," and "trans-avant-garde" express nothing more than a desire to break through the circuitous logic of a discourse which demands experiment but nevertheless compels repetition. They reiterate the attempt to find a possible position, although it may be represented as a forbidden place, at the limit of the discourse.

Within the specific institutions and discourses of fine art, the category of "modern art" occupies a place comparable in its centrality to that of the classic narrative film in the domain of cinema. This suggests it is not possible to pose the problem of realism unilaterally across the entire range of representational practices, from film, video, and photography to diverse forms of painting, sculpture, and performance art. The discursive operations which inform them are determined by different historical circumstances.

As Wollen also points out, one of the responses to the advances in photographic techniques was for painting to embrace a Kantian perspective and emphasize the subjective and the intuitive.[4] This response linked photographic history with the apparatus and associated technological progress with the evolutionary perfection of seeing. In contrast, it claimed that art was invented with the first graphic expression of the human hand and that artistic production concerned a timeless refinement of feeling in the field of the look. This representation of essential differences, between sight and insight, between the filmed event and the painted mark, has also produced, at the level of concrete practices, a radical asymmetry in their respective modes of address. What is unfeasible for the narrative film is practicable, indeed, imperative for modernist painting, that is, the subjective image. While in the former the cinematic apparatus is employed to remove the traces of its own steps, in the latter the painterly signifier is manipulated precisely to trace a passage, to give evidence of an essentially human action, to mark the subjectivity of the artist in the image itself. It is above all the artistic gesture which constitutes, at least metaphorically, the imaginary signifier of "modern art."

Why gesture? Of all the painterly signifiers, why is gesture the privileged term of the pictorial paradigm? If signifying function is a property of figure, then color, for instance, is too elusive; it never really accedes to the signifier but remains, as Schefer insists "the difference in the field where 'it' is found."[5]

Gesture, on the other hand, even the most minimal action, retains a certain residue of figuration. The play of presence and absence within the pictorial space turns on gesture; its materialization sustaining texture, matter; its dematerialization transporting color, light, to the field of the signifier. Modernist painting, expressive abstraction, in particular, foregrounds precisely this production of the signifier, but it would be unfounded, consequently, to suppose that this practice implies a deconstruction, a violation, or a transgression of the pictorial space. Clement Greenberg referred to Jackson Pollock's overall paintings as the "domestication of wild things," what he called the "look of accident" and the "look of the void." Thus gesture, however agitated, excessive, or evasive, is immobilized and mastered by the frame, brought to heel by the authority of that inevitable edge. Moreover, abstraction's apparent liberation of gesture from the figurative constraints of perspectival representation renders even more exactly the imaginary effect of a transcendental *chiaroscuro* whereby the spectator recognizes, in the mark of the enouncing subject, an essential humanness,

Jackson Pollock, *Yellow Islands,* 1952.
Collection Tate Gallery, London,
courtesy Art Resource, New York.

smoothly eliding the look of the artist, that unique vision, with his own, assuming in that image an essential creativity which authenticates his experience as aesthetic and validates the object as art.

Gesture is the term which the proponents of modernism cannot afford (literally in the financial sense) to efface. In the 1960s, when the avant-garde expelled gesture, denied expression, contested the notion of an essential creativity, the spectator was called upon to sustain a certain loss: the presence (or rather, presentified absence) of the artistic subject. The dealer, too, was threatened with a deficit: the authenticating mark which figures so prominently in the art market's peculiar structure of desire and exchange. It is not only a particular work of art which is purchased (the title), but also "something" by a unique individual which is possessed (the name). That "something," the object's investment with artistic subjectivity, is secured by gesture, or more explicitly, a signature.

The legal subject, according to Edelman (in Hirst and Kingdom's exposition), is presupposed as possessor of itself.[6] In terms of the law, man's freedom follows from his self-possession, thus he has the right to acquire property; moreover he is his own property. For the artist to sell his painterly property (products) or his labor (as in performance) is merely a confirmation of his freedom. The legal interpolation of the creative subject coincides dramatically with its "imaginary" construction in the critical discourses of modernism. One is reminded again of Hunter writing on the abstract expressionists: "They argue that only the artistic self which is certain of its identity, since it knows that its existence can be proved through an act of creation, is able to be free."[7] At one level it could be said that what is bought in the form of the art object is a commodity; but because, as Hirst and Kingdom put it, the law posits the subject in the form of a commodity, that is, man's freedom consists of putting himself in circulation, at another level, it could be suggested that what is desired and exchanged is an originary creativity and above all an exemplary act of human freedom. It is necessary to include in the modernist determinants of the efficacious artistic text not only self-definition, but also, crucially, the self-possession of the artistic subject. Thus the work of art, filtered through the institutions and discourses that determine its specific conditions of existence, produces artistic authorship in the fundamental form of the bourgeois subject: creative, autonomous, and proprietorial. In a sense there is no "alternative" to that passage; for the very moment that the work of art enters into circulation, it is sanctioned by law as the property of a creative subject (but not to enter into such contract would be to forfeit even the possibility that the artistic text, in the process of its construction of meaning, could indeed interrogate that form).

It is relevant here to point to Edelman's "paradox of photography" for the law of property in the nineteenth century, which ascertained that the image could only be property to the extent that it was mixed with subject, that is, represented and transformed through his creative labor.[8] Although it can now be legally maintained that "a creative subject and his purpose is installed behind the camera," this does not mean that it is generally sanctioned within the traditional institutions and discourses of fine art. Artistic practices, employing film or photography as well as those using found objects, processes, or systems where creative labor is apparently absent, continue to problematize the transcendental imperatives which predominate in critical and historical literature on art.

Criticism's function is to initiate that work which art history eventually accomplishes in the form of the "biographic narrative" that is, as Griselda Pollock describes it, "the production of an artistic subject for works of art."[9] The critic's dilemma is the production of artistic subjects for works of art at a time when their authenticity (and market value) are still tentative. Modernist criticism became particularly precarious when it concerned the installation of creative purposes behind objects which were recalcitrant to such efforts or even, in the case of some conceptual work, absent altogether.

The Crisis of Artistic Authorship

Greenberg's writing is often cited as the apodictic core of modernist criticism; but it is far from coherent. Rather, it marks a point of diffraction, of incoherence, in that discourse. His particular attention to the materiality of the object allowed a divergence from the ontological norm which was furthered by developments of art practice and which, consequently, required a restatement of modernism's central themes at a moment when the vacuity of that project was keenly perceived in contrast to the aims and intentions of some of the artists to whom he referred.

In "Photography, Phantasy, Function," Victor Burgin summarizes Greenberg's definition of modernism as "the tendency of an art practice toward self-reference by means of a foregrounding of: the tradition of the practice; the difference of the practice from other (visual arts) practices: the 'cardinal norms' of the practice; the material substrate, or 'medium' of the practice."[10] At first, Greenberg appears to be ignoring the ontological imperative to self-expression by insisting on a self-referential art, and at the same time avoiding the pictorial constraints of that discourse by emphasizing the specificity and diversity of art forms. But, in fact, his proposal for a scientific, neo-Kantian aesthetics of the art object is founded exclusively on the practice of painting. Sculpture's requisite three-dimensionality, for instance, is forever haunted by the specter of resemblance to ordinary things. With respect to photography, Burgin points out Greenberg's dilemma: to insist on the materiality of the print would be to undermine its founding attribute, that of illusion. Even painting, if it is illusionistic, according to Greenberg only uses art to conceal art. Hence it is not simply painting, but abstraction in particular, which is purely pictorial, essentially optical, uniquely flat, and capable of complete self-reference.

In "Modernist Painting," Greenberg claimed that "visual art should confine itself to what is given in visual experience and make no reference to any other orders of experience."[11] But when the canons of self-criticism, self-definition, and self-reference were rigorously applied in so-called minimal art, Greenberg rejected their implications. The aesthetics of "utter flatness" had gone too far; it was verging on a kind of existential recumbency, tending toward a condition of "non-art." For instance, where the catalogue *The Art of the Real* stated, "The art of today's real makes no direct appeal to the emotions, nor is it involved with uplift, but instead offers itself in the form of the irreducible, irrefutable object,"[12] it meant that the pictorial space was threatened with extinction by the encroachment of shapefulness and impending "objecthood." Consequently, Greenberg made a significant qualification. In "After Abstract Expressionism," he said, "The question now asked . . . is no longer what constitutes art or the art of painting, but what irreducibly constitutes good art as such."[13]

Thus Greenberg's attempt to establish the objective purposiveness of the art object, to define its particular forms of adaptation to definite ends in terms of material substrate, is continually undermined by the exigencies of a subjective judgment of *taste*. And here an altogether different order of purpose emerges. The only necessary condition for *judging* good art is common sense, but for *producing* good art, genius is required. With reference to Kant's *Critique of Judgement,* genius is the mental disposition (*ingenium*) through which nature gives the rule to art. No definite rule can be given for the products of genius, hence originality is its first property.[14] At this point the modernist discourse emerges as the site of an insistent contradiction which is indicated in Greenberg's criticism and repeated in the opposing strategies of the institutions of education on the one hand and those of entertainment and art patronage on the other. The former exacts a formal field of knowledge about art, an empirical domain of teachable crafts, while the latter requires a transcendental field of aesthetic experience and reflection founded on the unteachable tenets of genius and originality. During the 1960s artistic practices attempted to repudiate the notions of genius, originality, and taste by introducing material processes, series, systems, and ideas in place of an art based on self-expression. Some artists maintained that it was necessary to purge the modernist program of such obsolete philosophical presumptions in order to refine its fundamental argument for an exclusively self-referential art. Joseph Kosuth, for instance, following Greenberg's initiative and taking up Kant's distinction between analytic and synthetic propositions, insisted that works of art were analytic propositions: "The propositions of art are not factual, but linguistic in character, that is, they do not describe the behavior of physical or even mental objects: they express definitions of art, or the formal consequences of definitions of art."[15]

The limitations of proposing the linguistic analogy are numerous but primarily concern the fact that images, unlike words, are not doubly articulated. Verbal language is the only signifying system which has the ability to analyze itself. Hence the work of art, with reference to its internal structure, does not possess the means of defining itself as art. This is not to say that unless the artistic text includes a written message it inhabits a realm of extradiscursive, "purely visual" determinations, rather, that the text is informed by discursive operations at the level of its conception, production, and reception in a way which is neither prior to, nor derived from, but coincident with, language. However, this suggests an area of investigation

Joseph Kosuth, *Art as Idea as Idea,*
1967, photostat mounted on
cardboard, 48 × 48 ins. Photo:
Dorothy Zeidman. Courtesy Leo
Castelli, New York.

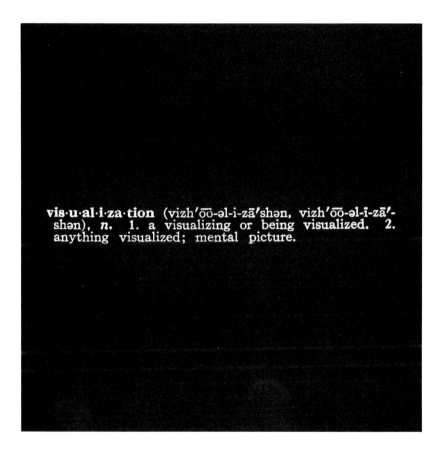

which Kosuth's positivism does not allow. The significance of this refinement of formalism lies in the problem it poses in the domain of aesthetic
judgment. In place of the ever-widening spiral of connotations imposed by
taste, the linguistic analogy proposes the denotative reading of artistic texts.
Artistic practices which are based on such assumptions, however Edenic (as
Barthes describes the desire for a radically objective or innocent image),
nevertheless contest the unique identity, the authorial status, of the art object. Critical discourse, on the contrary, continually shifts to recuperate its
lost investment in the transcendental field, namely, artistic subjectivity.

When, in "Art and Objecthood" Michael Fried maintained that a successful painting was capable of "compelling conviction," he took Greenberg's commonsense notion of "good art" and elevated it from the realm of
opinion to that of faith (art which is compatible with the morality of the
viewer?).[16] Conviction, however, demands more than a self-defining art object, more than the mechanical product of genius; it requires a level of
artistic decision, of choice. Fried insisted that the task of the modernist
painter was to discover those conventions which at a given moment alone
were capable of establishing his work's identity as painting (he writes,
"What constitutes the art of painting and what constitutes good painting
are no longer separable"). The rule of art (material substrate) and the rule
of nature (genius) are reconciled within the modernist discourse, as in the
Kantian dialectic, by positing a supersensible substrate of artistic freedom.

With minimalism's eradication of the painterly signifier, exactly how did
the modernist critic establish an authentic presence for specific works of art?
First, there was the phenomenological insistence on the pure act of perception, an attempt to rescue authenticity as a kind of mechanical aftereffect of
the gestalt. Fried suggested that presence could be conferred by size or by
"the look of non-art." The look of non-art was precisely the pictorial frame,
extended to include the entire situation-variables of the object, light, space,
and crucially, the spectator's body. Awareness of size or scale, as Robert
Morris maintained, was a function of the comparison made between one's
body size and the object—and again according to Fried, this process of
comparison extorted a special complicity from the viewer. "Something is
said to have presence when it demands that the beholder take it into ac-

count, that he take it seriously—and when the fulfillment of that demand consists simply in being aware of it."[17]

Second, establishing the identity, the authorial status of the art object, became increasingly dependent on an extended documentation of the installation or of the artist-at-work, and on critical commentary including statements by the artist. What cannot be reduced to pictures on the gallery wall can nevertheless be reproduced as pictures in the pages of a book.

Although Fried referred to the minimal object as having "stage presence," in effect it remained no more than a prop without the intervention of the actor/artist and his script. Ultimately, it became both necessary and expedient for the artist to stage himself; necessary because it was logically bound up with the interrogation of the object, and expedient because at the same time it rescued a semblance of propriety for ephemeral art forms.

The unity, the homogeneity of the pictorial space, was disrupted by an insistence on temporality and by the intrusion of non-self-referential contents (the return of the repressed synthetic proposition); but what was evacuated at the level of the signifying substance of creative labor (gesture, matter, color)—signifiers of a unique artistic presence—reappeared in the figure of the artist; his person, his image, his gestures. As early as 1965, Rudolf Schwarzkogler stated that his performances, "Aktionen," made their appearance "in place of pictures executed by hand." The insertion of the artist's body within this new pictorial space had nothing to do with the traditional constraints of the artistic nude represented as information or spectacle but, as Schwarzkogler insisted, it concerned the "total nude . . . [a transcendental nudity?] which places itself above the senses through the various possibilities of its repetitive gestures and its repetitive presence."[18] In performance work it is no longer a question of investing the object with an artistic presence: the artist *is* present and creative subjectivity is given as the effect of an essential self-possession, that is, of the artist's body and his inherent right of disposition over it.

Furthermore, there is what could be described as the peculiar paradox of photography for the precarious art practices of the late 1960s and early 1970s. That is to say, what remains of performance, with its temporality, its specific relation of audience and event impossible to trace, is the film or the

Robert Morris, *Untitled*, 1966, plywood, 4 × 8 × 8 feet. Courtesy Leo Castelli, New York.

photograph. What is lost in *that* image, insofar as it can no longer be emphatically marked as the property of the creative subject, is gained to the extent that it is, precisely, a photograph of the artist and as the possessive subject (in law) he has "the right of the photographer" over the disposal of his own image. More importantly, what is taken away from the pictorial text—the painterly signifier of bodily gesture—is given back in photographic form as the visible body, its peculiar gestures acceding to the status of the signifier in another space, that of pictorial quotation.

Benjamin's "aura" may wither away in the age of mechanical reproduction but authenticity remains. What is made more explicit, more transparent, by the so-called dematerialization of the object, is that *the production of authenticity requires more than an author for the object; it exacts the "truth" of the authorial discourse.*

By putting himself in circulation, the performance artist parodied the commercial exchange and distribution of an artistic personality in the form of a commodity. Nevertheless, for criticism, performance art initiated an appropriate synthesis of the disparate elements that had fractured the modernist discourse. On the one hand, it provided the empirical domain with a universal object—the body—and on the other, to the transcendental field, it brought the incontestable authenticity of the artist's experience of his own body.

With Lea Vergine's account of "body art," *Il Corpo Come Linguaggio,* criticism seems to subside once again in the direction of ontology. She speaks of the individual obsessed by the obligation to exhibit himself in order to be.[19] But she is anxious to point out that this move is more than a revival of expressionism. The use of the body in art is not simply a return to origins—"the individual is led back to a specific mode of existence." Moreover, these activities or "phenomena," as she puts it, also document a style of living that remains "outside of art." The critic finds in the analysis of the artist's actual experience the third term which metaphorically grounds the experience of nature (the body) and art (the culture). In *Art Povera,* Germano Celant's artist-alchemist mixes himself with environment: "he has chosen to live within direct experience, no longer the representative, he aspires to live, not see."[20] According to Michel Foucault, modern thought is a radical contestation of both positivism and eschatology: it searches for a discourse neither in the order of a reduction nor in the order of a promise. It is precisely a discourse which constitutes the subject as the locus of a knowledge empirically acquired but always referred back to what makes it possible, and finds in the analysis of actual experience a third term in which both the experience of the body and of the culture can be seen to be grounded.[21]

Throughout the 1970s, the critics who identified their project with the avant-garde effectively modernized Greenberg's archaic classicism. Significantly, Vergine quotes not Kant but Husserl:

> Among the bodies of this nature that is reduced to what belongs to me, I discover my own body. It can be distinguished from all other bodies because of but a single particular: it is the only body that is not simply a body, but also my body: It is the only body that exists inside the strata of abstraction that I have chiseled into the world in which, in accordance with experience, I coordinate fields of sensation in various ways.[22]

Similarly, the authenticity of body art cannot be inscribed at the level of a particular morphology; it must be chiseled into the world in accordance with direct experience. The discourse of the body in art is more than a repetition of the eschatological voices of abstract expressionism; the actual experience of the body fulfills the prophecy of the painted mark. It is also more than a confirmation of the positivist aspirations of *The Art of the Real*. The art of the "real body" does not pertain to the truth of a visible form, but refers back to its essential content: the irreducible, irrefutable experience of pain. The body, as artistic text, bears the authenticating imprint of pain like a signature; Vergine insists, "the experiences we are dealing with are authentic, and they are consequently cruel and painful. Those who are in pain will tell you that they have the right to be taken seriously."[23] (It is no longer a question of good art, but of serious artists.)

Here, it is relevant to note Judith Barry and Sandy Flitterman's observations with regard to the performances of Gina Pane. They maintain that by counterposing an "aesthetics of pain" to one of pleasure, the artist merely reinforces the dualistic bias of Western metaphysics and that particularly, by practicing self-mutilation in her art, a woman invokes the traditional

Gina Pane, *Azione Sentimentale,*
Galerie Diagramma, Milan, 1973.
Courtesy Anne Marchand, Paris.

representation of female masochism.[24] Quite rightly, they point out that this type of art practice is not necessarily in opposition to the dominant discourse of art. However, it seems to be more a matter of phenomenology than metaphysics: an aesthetics of lived experience, rather than pain specifically, is being counterposed to that of the object, and not to pleasure as such. In this case, pain is not opposed to pleasure but becomes a privileged signifier in the field of sensations which the artist coordinates in the name of self-expression. Pane's art addresses not the sexual body but the Husserlian body, discovered as what belongs to me, my body, the body of the self-possessing artistic subject whose guarantee of truth is grounded in the painful state.

Alternatively, the specific contribution of feminists in the field of performance has been to pose the question of sexual difference across the discourse of the body in a way which focuses on the construction not of the individual but of the sexed subject. The body is not perceived as the repository of an artistic essence; it is seen as a kind of hermeneutic image. The so-called enigma of femininity is formulated as the problem of representation (images of women, how to change them) and then resolved by the discovery of a true identity behind the patriarchal facade. This true identity is "the essence in women" according to Ulrike Rosenbach, who defines feminist art as "the elucidation of the woman-artist's identity; of her body, of her psyche, her feelings, her position in society."[25]

Clearly the question of the body and the question of sexuality do not necessarily intersect.[26] When they do, for instance in this particular discourse, the body is decentered and it is radically split; positioned; not simply my body, but *his* body, *her* body. Here, no third term emerges to salvage a transcendental sameness for aesthetic reflection. Within this system of representation, actual experience merely confirms an irrevocable difference in the field of the other.

Partially because of this intransigence, feminist art has been problematic for criticism; how does the critic authenticate the work of art when the author is sexed and "his" truth no longer universal? Consequently, most of this work has been marginalized by or excluded from the so-called mainstream even when the critic's concerns have included areas such as psychoanalysis (Vergine's book is an obvious case in point). Moreover the

Ulrike Rosenbach, *Salto Mortale,*
1978. Courtesy Haags
Gemeentemuseum, The Hague.

predominant forms of feminist writing on art continue to counterpose a visible form to a hidden content, excavating a different, but similarly fundamental order of truth—the truth of the woman, her original feminine identity. But in practice what persistently emerges as a result of foregrounding the question of representation, particularly the image, is more in the order of an underlying contradiction than an essential content. The woman artist sees her experience as a woman, particularly in terms of the "feminine position," as object of the look, but she must also account for the "feeling" she experiences as the artist occupying the "masculine position" as subject of the look. The former she defines as the socially prescribed position of the woman, one to be questioned, exorcised, or overthrown (note Rosenbach), while the implications of the latter (that there can be only one position with regard to active looking and that is masculine) cannot be acknowledged and is construed instead as a kind of psychic truth—a natural, instinctual, preexistent, and essential femininity. Frequently, in the process of its production, the feminist text repudiates its own essentialism and testifies instead to the insistent bisexuality of the drives. It would seem to be a relevant project for feminist criticism to take this further—to examine how that contradiction (the crisis of positionality) is articulated in particular practices and to what extent it demonstrates that masculine and feminine positions are never finally fixed—for the artist, her work, or her public.

In contrast, Vergine's phenomenology constructs the body as empirically given yet impossible to know, a body which is radically divided among the discourses and practices of individual artists (literally the pages of her book), but nevertheless unified by a certain psychological insight; she proposes: "at the basis of 'body art' and all other operations presented in this book, one can discover the unsatisfied need for a love." [27] The question of desire in relation to the representation of pain and to the spectator's pleasure would indeed be pertinent here, but she does not finally address these issues. Instead, the iconography of the art object is merely displaced by a symptomatology of the artist (she gives a canonical list of neuroses). The subject suffers, is "alienated," even sexed, but still remains the unified and coherent center of the signifying system of the artistic text.

Following the paradoxical logic of modernism's demand for objective purposes as well as transcendental truths, avant-garde practices between

1965 and the mid-1970s initiated areas of work that divided the very field of which they were an effect. The potential of that divergence has not been completely realized. First, the materiality of the practice: initially defined in terms of the constraints of a particular medium, it must now be redefined as a specific production of meaning. Second, sociality, raised as the question of context, is the gallery system (inside versus outside), and the commodification of art (object versus process, action, idea, etc.). This must be reconsidered as the question of institutions, of the conditions which determine the reading of artistic texts and the strategies which would be appropriate for interventions (rather than "alternatives") in that context. Third, sexuality, posed as the problem of images of women and how to change them, must be reformulated as a concern with positionality, with the production of readers as well as authors for artistic texts and crucially, with the sexual overdetermination of meaning which takes place in that process.

The dominant critical practices of that same period have, however, so consistently converged on the traditional vanishing point of the artistic subject, self-possessed and essentially creative, that it is not surprising now to find a certain consolidation of that position in artistic practices themselves, in the return of painterly signifiers and their privileged site—the classical pictorial text.[28] Finally, a further question is raised—why theoretical criticism, with a very different history from that discussed so far, was also unable to sustain the discontinuities in the modernist discourse and develop an accessible critique.

Exhibition and System

Critical writing on art which places emphasis on the analysis of signifying practice, rather than on the exhortation or description of artistic auteurs, generally acknowledges that art forms are inscribed within the social context that gives rise to them. Nevertheless, there is a problematic tendency to constitute the pictorial text as the paradigmatic insistence of that inscription in a way which forecloses the question of its institutional placing. The pictorial paradigm constructs the artistic text as both essentially singular and as centrally concerned with the practice of painting, but, as Hubert Damisch has pointed out, when painting is considered at the semiotic level, that is, with reference to its internal system, it functions as an epistemological obstacle, an obstacle never surmounted, only prodded by an endless redefinition of the sign or averted altogether by taking the semantic route.[29] Perhaps to some extent this accounts for what appears to be a certain impasse in the area of art criticism when compared, for instance, with developments in film theory.

Critical texts have focused either on analysis of the individual tableau (sometimes an individual artist's oeuvre) or on the construction of general cultural categories and typologies of art. This work has been both necessary and important. The arguments outlined here are not so much against such contributions as for a reconsideration of what might constitute appropriate terms for the analysis of current practices in art. This reconsideration is prompted first by developments within particular practices. Feminist art, for instance, cannot be posed in terms of cultural categories, typologies, or even certain insular forms of textual analysis, precisely because it entails the assessment of political interventions, campaigns, and commitments as well as artistic strategies. In this instance, interpretation is not simply a matter of what can be discovered at the interior of a composition. Second, a reconsideration of critical methods is required if one takes account of the specific conditions which determine the organization of artistic texts and their readings at the present time: that is, *the temporary exhibition and its associated field of publications—the catalogue, the art book, and the magazine.* From this point of view, "art" is never given in the form of individual works but is constructed as a category in relation to a complex configuration of texts.

In terms of analysis, the exhibition system marks a crucial intersection of discourses, practices, and sites which define the institutions of art within a definite social formation. Moreover, it is exactly here, within this intertextual, interdiscursive network, that the work of art is produced as text.

Rather schematically, it can be said that at one level an exhibition is a discursive practice involving the selection, organization, and evaluation of artistic texts according to a particular genre (the one-person show, the group show, the theme exhibition, the historical survey, the annual and biennial, etc.), displayed in certain types of institutions (museums, galleries), within specific legal structures (contractual agreements, fees, insurance), and preserved by definite material techniques in a number of ways (catalogues, art books, magazines). At another level, an exhibition is a system of meanings, a discourse, which, taken as a complex unit or enunciative field, can be said to constitute a group of statements: the individual works comprising fragments of imaged discourse or utterances which are anchored by the exhibition's titles, subheadings, and commentary, but at the same time unsettled, exceeded, or dispersed in the process of their articulation as events.

An exhibition takes place; its spatiotemporal disposition, conventions of display, codes of architecture construct a certain passage, not the continuous progression of images unfolding on the cinema screen, but the flickering, fragmented frames of the editing machine; a passage very much at the disposal of the spectator to stop frame, rewind, push forward; it displays discernible openness, a radical potential for self-reflexivity. There is nevertheless a logic of that passage, of partition and naming, and in a sense there is a narrative organization of what is seen in the exhibition catalogue; its written (editorial/critical) commentary fixes the floating meaning, erodes the apparent polysemy of the exhibition's imaged discourse. Within a specific order of the book, the catalogue confers an authorship, an authority, on the exhibition events. In it, positions and statuses are assigned for "agents" defined as artists, organizers, critics, and "the public." The authors/organizers impose a declarative order on the exhibition's evasive discursivity (artists, it should be noted, are often the subjects of exhibition statements, but rarely the authors of their formulation). The catalogue constructs a specific reading, opens the space of a possible reworking or perhaps effects a closure, but it always has definite political consequences. This suggests that the catalogue is also an important site for interventions. Catalogue and exhibition constitute what could be called a *diatext,* that is, two separate signifying systems which function together; more precisely, it is at the point of their intersection and crucially in their difference that the production of a certain knowledge takes place.

The exhibition has a definite substantive duration. In its phenomenal form, the installation is subject to the constraints of a definite site; it is only reproducible in a limited sense, but the catalogue remains. It is infinitely reproducible and, moreover, it constitutes the determinant means of institutional control over the continued distribution of works of art. In this context, the absence of a catalogue also becomes significant. Artists generally maintain that the catalogue is more important than the exhibition itself. It gives a particular permanence to temporary events, an authenticity in the form of historical testimony. Together with art books and magazines, exhibition catalogues constitute the predominant forms of receiving and, in a certain sense, possessing images of art. The exhibition remains the privileged mode of reception in terms of the viewer's access to the "original" work, but far more often the reader's knowledge of art is based on reproductions in books and magazines. Critical theories of art founded on the notion of artisanal production fail to recognize that these historically specific means of organization, circulation, distribution, not only determine the reception— reading, viewing, reviewing, reworking—of artistic texts, but also have an effect on the signifying practices themselves. The phenomenon of artists' books, together with the emergence of specialist publishers, is now well known; this is often commented on, but rarely analyzed in terms of the particular relations of representation it prescribes.

How is the work of art, reproduced as photographic image, *produced* as the artistic text within the system of the book? What kind of readers and authors are positioned there? Obviously, there is the loss of material specificity—problems of black-and-white reproduction, aspect ratios, and so on —the characteristic homogenizing tendency of the book; but the difference between the reproduction in the catalogue and the original in the exhibition is not merely a question of photographic techniques. It is a question of particular practices of writing, of the gaps, omissions, and points of emphasis through which certain images are outlined and others erased. The authorial discourse (organizer, critic, or artist) constructs a pictorial textuality which pertains more to the readable than to the visible.

In this sense it would be appropriate to speak of quoting rather than illustrating artistic texts (although this is not to say they are essentially quotable). At one level the signifying structure of the pictorial quotation has something in common with the press photograph insofar as it presumes to "record" the exhibition events or to identify the object to which the reproduction supposedly refers. This process of identification appears to be immediately fixed by the denominative function of the linguistic text which accompanies it: name, title, dimensions, medium. More crucially, however, it depends on a certain cultural knowledge, as Barthes suggested, a body of techniques and practices already read as art.[30] This reading is grounded in the academic discourse of fine art and circumscribed by the limits of its traditional regimes: architecture, painting, and sculpture.

The quotation subscribes to a form of pictorial rhetoric which defines those regimes (and the varied practices they subsume) in terms of medium: thus painting's pictorial quality, its one-dimensionality, is signified by the correspondence of frame to edge of photograph; video by the framing edge of the monitor and the "grain" of an electronically transmitted image; sculpture's three-dimensionality by lighting or architectural setting; performance, similarly, by an establishing shot (i.e., performer in context of audience, camera, etc.). Photography also relies on an installation shot or the repetition of units to signify its fine art context. But the pictorial quotation seems to be subject to a double imperative which repeats the dilemma of modernist criticism; while identifying the art object in terms of medium, at the same time, it must establish the unique and individuating style of a particular artist's work. Hence there is also the "artistic photograph": the detail, the interesting composition which displaces the record. It gives the appearance of transgression, but effectively it is a fragment, a metonymy, enveloped by the all-pervasive pictorial metaphor, addressing the reader with continued reference to the grand regime of painting.

However, if the work of art is extracted from the discursive system in which it is established as statement, as event, then it is possible not only to construct a rather utopian view of the pictorial text as essentially concerned with a single picture, but also to assume, as Raymond Bellour does in "The Unattainable Text," that unlike the filmic text "the pictorial text is in fact a quotable text."[31] The concept of pictorial quotability suppresses the diversity of artistic practices insofar as it foregrounds a particular system of representation, the painting. Moreover, when he adds, "From the critical point of view it has one advantage that only painting possesses: one can see and take in the work at one glance," another problem is posed: Precisely what forms of painting possess this advantage of being taken in at a glance? Here Bellour's perceptual emphasis implicates his arguments with those of modernist criticism by constructing a similar object, namely, the purely visual, uniquely flat, abstractionist painting which illustrates Greenberg's pictorial paradigm.

Consequently, even if, at the center of that paradigm, it is not the truth of an author but that of the signifier itself which is sought, as long as the site of that search is designated as the object or even the system "painting," a problem remains. On the one hand the pictorial text, with reference to the object, is too easily attained—taken in at a glance; on the other hand, as Damisch presents it, pictorial textuality is constituted in a divergence between the register of the visible and that of the readable, "a divergence by way of which it is appropriate, in relation to the system Painting to pose the question of the signifier." But since the signifier cannot be produced or even recognized by way of a position of exteriority, the effect of painting, like that of the dream-work, is created "outside any relation of interpretation."[32] The truth of painting, like that of the signifier, is the impossibility of knowing it. And the pictorial text remains in a certain sense unknowable, impossible, unattainable. That is why it now seems more appropriate, in relation to the signifying system of the artistic text, to pose not the question of the signifier but that of the statement: as Foucault suggests, "to situate these meaningful units in a space in which they breed and multiply."[33]

Notes

"Reviewing Modernist Criticism," *Screen* 22, no. 23 (1981): 41–62. Reprinted in *Art After Modernism: Rethinking Representation,* ed. Brian Wallis (New York: 1984) The New Museum of Contemporary Art in association with David R. Godine, Publisher, Inc. Boston, pp. 86–103.

1. Peter Wollen, "Photography and Aesthetics," *Screen* 19, no. 4 (Winter 1978–1979):27, note 22. However, in the context of this article, it would be more problematic to follow Wollen's suggestion that "the category 'avant-garde' is best reserved for works which prolong and deepen the historic rupture of Cubism," since, regardless of oppositional intentions, works are continually being recaptured by a reflexive criticism. It would be maintained here that the "rupture of Cubism" does not constitute a continuous discourse, that is, a set of persistent themes and objects in transformation. It is relative to a particular instance; consequently, contemporary art practices cannot prolong it. They must reinvent it.

2. Sam Hunter, chapter on "The United States" in *Art since 1945* (New York: Harry N. Abrams, 1958).

3. Sam Hunter, from the catalogue of the exhibition *New Directions in American Painting* (Waltham, MA: Poses Institute of Fine Arts, Brandeis University, 1963).

4. Wollen, "Photography and Aesthetics," p. 10.

5. See Jean-Louis Schefer, "Split colour/blur," trans. Paul Smith, *20th Century Studies,* nos. 15–16 (December 1976): 82–100, special issue on Visual Poetics.

6. Paul Hirst and Elizabeth Kingdom, "On Edelman's 'Ownership of the Image,'" *Screen* 20, nos. 3–4 (winter 1979–80): 135–140.

7. Hunter, *Art since 1945,* p. 362.

8. See Bernard Edelman, *Ownership of the Image: Elements for a Marxist Theory of Law,* trans. Elizabeth Kingdom, introduction Paul Q. Hirst (London: Routledge and Kegan Paul, 1979). It is also relevant to note here that the position of artists in Great Britain under the present 1956 copyright act (amended in 1971) is not much improved. For example, a sculptor or equivalent can only get protection under the law if he or she can prove that the production of the work involves "craftsmanship" and constitutes more than "machining of parts." See Richard Mann, "British Copyright Council," *Artists Union Journal* (August 1980).

9. Griselda Pollock, "Artists, Mythologies and Media—Genius, Madness and Art History," *Screen* 21, no. 3 (fall 1980): 57–96.

10. Victor Burgin, "Photography, Phantasy, Function," *Screen* 21, no. 1 (spring 1980): 73. See also Burgin's critique of Greenberg in "Modernism in the Work of Art," *20th Century Studies,* nos. 15–16 (December 1976): 34–55.

11. Clement Greenberg, "Modernist Painting," *Arts Yearbook,* no. 4 (1961), reprinted in *The New Art,* ed. Gregory Battcock (New York: E. P. Dutton, 1973), p. 74.

12. See the cover of the catalogue for the exhibition *The Art of the Real: American Painting and Sculpture 1948–1968* (New York: The Museum of Modern Art, 1968; London: The Tate Gallery, 1969).

13. Clement Greenberg, "After Abstract Expressionism," *Art International* 6, no. 8 (October 1962):30.

14. Immanuel Kant, *Critique of Judgement,* trans. J. H. Bernard, First Part, Second Book, "Analytic of the Sublime" (New York: Hafner, 1951), pp. 150–153.

15. Joseph Kosuth, "Art After Philosophy I & II," *Studio International* (October and November 1969), reprinted in *Idea Art,* ed. Gregory Battcock (New York: E. P. Dutton, 1973), p. 84. Cf. Theirry Kuntzel and Bernar Venet, *Lecture de Représentation graphique de la fonction y = −x2/4* (Paris: Arthur Hubschmid, 1975). They also em-

phasize the linguistic character of art, not as an analogy but as an alternative practice. Using Jacques Bertin's semiology, they propose a denotative art based on the graphic image (monosemy) in place of the pervading ambiguity (polysemy) of pictorial representation.

16. Michael Fried, "Art and Objecthood," *Artforum* 5, no. 10 (June 1967); reprinted in *Minimal Art: A Critical Anthology,* ed. Gregory Battcock (New York: E. P. Dutton, 1968), pp. 143–146.

17. Ibid., p. 124.

18. Rudolf Schwarzkogler, "Panorama Manifesto I/II: The Total Nude, 1965," in Lea Vergine, *Il Corpo Come Linguaggio* (Milan: Giampaolo Prearo Editore, 1974).

19. Lea Vergine, in *Il Corpo Come Linguaggio,* p. 3.

20. Germano Celant, ed., *Art Povera: Conceptual, Actual or Impossible Art?* (London: Studio Vista, 1969), p. 225.

21. Michel Foucault, *The Order of Things* (New York: Random House, 1970), pp. 320–321.

22. Husserl, quoted by Vergine, in *Il Corpo,* p. 21 (cf. Edmund Husserl, *Cartesian Meditations* (The Hague: Martinus Nijhoff, 1977), p. 97.

23. Ibid., p. 5.

24. Judith Barry and Sandy Flitterman, "Textual Strategies—The Politics of Art Making," *Screen* 21, no. 2 (summer 1980): 37–38.

25. Ulrike Rosenbach, *Korpersprache* (Frankfurt: Haus am Waldsee, 1975). As regards the hermeneutic image, for instance in *Salto Mortale,* Rosenbach poses on a swing (posing the theme of the enigma) and aims the video camera at the ceiling where two different representations of woman have been posted: a photograph of the Palestinian commando, Leila Khaled, and a reproduction of a painting by Lockner of a Madonna and child. Then she swings below them, showing first one image, then the other, on the video monitor (formulating the enigma as a question) "which is the true one?" The answer is delayed, she continues to swing. Then she stops, suspended between the two possibilities (leaving the spectator in suspense). Finally, she turns upside down, revealing her own image on the monitor—filmed in a mirror below with the light and camera concealed under her skirt. Thus she proposes an answer: reject existing models, trust yourself, "discover the true feminine structure behind the facade erected by patriarchal thinking" (the enigma resolved). See also catalogue for the exhibition feministische kunst internationaal (The Hague: Haags Gemeentemeseum, 1979), pp. 98–99, 103–104.

26. See Beverly Brown and Parveen Adams, "The Feminine Body and Feminist Politics," *m/f,* no. 3 (1979): 35–50.

27. Vergine, *Il Corpo,* p. 1.

28. Cf. Benjamin Buchloh, "Figures of Authority, Ciphers of Regression: Notes on the Return of Representation in European Painting," *October,* no. 16 (spring 1981): 39–68. He takes the view that representational art forms are historically coincident with periods of economic recession and political conservatism.

29. See Hubert Damisch, "Eight Theses For (or Against?) a Semiology of Painting," *Enclitic* 3, no. 1 (spring 1979): 1–15.

30. See Roland Barthes, "Rhetoric of the Image," in *Image-Music-Text,* trans. Stephen Heath (New York: Hill and Wang, 1977).

31. Raymond Bellour, "The Unattainable Text," *Screen* 16, no. 3 (autumn 1975): 21–22.

32. Damisch, "Eight Theses," pp. 14–15.

33. Michel Foucault, *The Archaeology of Knowledge,* trans. A. M. Sheridan Smith (New York: Pantheon Books, 1972), p. 100.

Beyond the Purloined Image[1]

Roland Barthes has said that those who fail to reread are obliged to read the same story everywhere. Perhaps by a similar default, we are obliged to see the same exhibition time and time again.

Considering that, when I was asked to curate yet another "women's show," I saw it instead as an opportunity to go beyond, exactly to "reread" the biological canon of feminist commitment and situate the question of gender within a wider network of social and aesthetic debates. Specifically, I wanted to show how recent developments in photographic practice, initiated in London, had gone beyond the more reductive quotational tactics of their New York equivalents, precisely by extending a feminist theory of *the subject* to a critique of artistic authorship.

I am not, however, exploring "the truth" of my intentions here in order to create a unitary *author* for the exhibition/text. Beyond its title, there is no explanation; there is, rather, a set of intentions, a group of diverse statements, a practice of selection and collaboration that could be called a *discursive event*. Inasmuch as a fragment of this event concerns the naming of it, I should say that my thematic emphasis is an attempt not simply to purloin but to rework and extend the notion of appropriation. It is one that has been used, predominantly by New York critics, to describe the work of artists who take their images from the so-called mass media and re-present them "in visual quotation marks."[2] Their aim in doing this (the part that interests me) is to contest the ownership of the image and dispel the aura of genius, madness, originality, and maleness that surrounds the *artist-auteur.*

Like their American counterparts in a show such as The Stolen Image and Its Uses, the artists in Beyond the Purloined Image refused to retreat

Catalogue, *Beyond the Purloined Image,* Riverside Studios, London, 1983. Cover design by Marie Yates.

Details, (above) Karen Knorr,
Marie Yates, Susan Trangmar, Judith
Crowle; (below) Olivier Richon,
Ray Barrie, Yve Lomax.

into the esoteric realms of pre- or postmodernism.[3] They are passionately, but critically, committed to the contemporary world; yet they are not content merely to pilfer its cultural estate. Instead, they are exploring its boundaries, deconstructing its center, proposing the decolonization of its visual codes and of language itself. They are adapting what I would call a strategy of *depropriation*.[4] Point of view and frame, use of caption and narrative sequence: all are subject to investigation as Peter Wollen has emphasized in "Photography and Aesthetics." "This is not simply a 'de-construction,' but rather a process of 're-production' which involves a disorientation and reorientation of the spectator in which new signifieds are superimposed disturbingly on the memories/anticipations of old presuppositions."[5]

Mitra Tabrizian for instance takes the concept of "documentary" and turns it inside out by exposing the fabricated reality of the subjects she photographs—designers, photographers, agents, executives. In *Governmentality,* she unmasks not only the codes of the magazine image but also the function of advertising as an institution. In contrast, Karen Knorr appropriates the lush genre of traditional portraiture and transforms it into what she calls "nonportraiture," that is, an acid commentary on the manners, gestures, and social values of a particular class, in this case, those who frequent *Gentlemen's Clubs.* For both artists, the problem of "politics" is posed rather than prescribed, as Victor Burgin advocates—"new forms of politicization within the institutions of art (and) photography must begin with the recognition that meaning is perpetually displaced from the image to the discursive formations which cross and contain it. . . ."[6] Olivier Richon, too, takes a similar stance, imbricating the discourses of science, politics, technique, and literature in a series of *tableux-comme-critiques* he calls *The Proper Names.* Richon purloins the pages of collectors' catalogues and academic books on Orientalist painting and uses them as backdrops for a Sybergergian restaging (a method of front projection) of the European colonialist's exotic spectacle of antiquity. His ironic *mise-en-scène* calls into question the representation of origins, as well as commenting on the origin of representation in the psychoanalytic sense of the term—"The etymon—the proper meaning, the origin of Names—is *oriri:* to (a)rise; Orient and Origin are then just a point on the western horizon, where the sun rises, East of the dividing line. It is a technicolor sunrise, a postcard, a card which comes after . . .

Thus it is the representation of origins, of the orient, which constructs the memory of it; representation never gives access to a primary vision but to a constant secondary revision."

Judith Crowle's revisions of the past are startling and direct. She confiscates stereotyped pictures of men and women from the photography annuals of the 1930s and then subjects these historicized images to a further distortion by using a mirror. Crowle is not "making strange" as an end in itself, but as a means of effectively shattering our traditional view of sexual roles. Ray Barrie embarks on a parallel enterprise, but uses radically diverse sources such as grafiti, advertisements, holiday snaps, and popular literature to map out the still uncharted terrain of male sexuality. His aim is not to locate a fixed site on that route, but rather to observe the constantly shifting landscape of fantasy and reminiscence that shapes our sexual identities; the implicit reference is Freud—". . . but we shall, of course, willingly agree that the majority of men are also far behind the masculine ideal and that all human individuals, as a result of their bisexual disposition and of cross-inheritance, combine in themselves both masculine and feminine characteristics, so that pure masculinity and femininity remain theoretical constructions of uncertain content."[7]

In a piece entitled *Screen Memories,* we trace the man's desire for status, for property; his fear of punishment, his fantasized revenge, and finally the absurdity of this vicious phallocentric cycle. Barrie makes a pointed comment: "Men are obsessed with femininity. Consequently, they have seen feminist theory merely as a means of unravelling that 'enigma.' Feminism also offers clues to understanding how masculinity is formed; but this has generally been resisted since it would require us to deal instead with the absurdity of the phallus (Men never tire of looking up the proverbial skirt, but they don't like being caught with their pants down)."

Marie Yates also pursues "the subject" of sexual difference, but in the occupied territory of language. She deploys a complex juxtaposition of jewel-like images or icons, symbols and indexical signs to engage us in a multilayered reading of her *Dream of Personal Life*. Visually, the work is unified by the technique of montage, but then fragmented into a series of objects. Similarly, there is the unifying pull of the narrative toward some resolution; but this is again refused, revealed to be "fictitious," in order to open rather than close the text. Seeing her work reminds me of Jane Gallop's provocative metaphor: "The notions of integrity and closure in a text (or image) are like that of virginity in a body. They assume that if one does not respect the boundaries between inside and outside, one is 'breaking and entering,' violating a property."[8] In a sense, Yates is "asking for it," that is, a reading which repositions, even deletes, the author herself.

The repositioning of spectator and author alike is a persistent undertaking in the work of Yve Lomax and Susan Trangmar as well. Lomax borrows the rhetoric of film noir to manufacture a "plot" between a mysterious fragment of media melodrama and another equally ambiguous personal interlude. But there is a crucial difference—she breaks the story line, opens the ring of identification, and pushes a "third term" onto the stage in the guise of "lack," that is, a space between the two images which queries the photographs' assumed finitude, rather than solving the enigma of the subject's identity. Describing the work, aptly titled *Open Rings and Partial Lines,* she says "I have attempted to bring into play the basic assumptions of the classical model of communication, i.e. subject/object, sender/message/receiver. In short, to open up these assumptions and not to take them for granted. So . . . in the work I have attempted to produce an assemblage where a 'middle' or 'third' term neither unifies nor fragments or divides, which in turn calls into question the position of the two sides as two sides. It is the play of the neither/nor which excites me."

Trangmar's refusal of logic, her "excess," so to speak, takes another form. She pillages, literally shreds a seemingly infinite reserve of simulated media images and repetitious written phrases, and transforms them into a monumental continuum of sensations which is generally called collage. In this case, it is more like an archaic, yet poetic recycling of the visual debris that exudes from a technologically engorged social body. Trangmar makes this probing remark: "Everywhere we seek the image's reality; we turn the camera movement into a prayer and seek the passion between black and white. If we take technology as an extended or detachable part of a human whole, if we take the lines of communication and knowledge as instruments or media along which the human whole may be projected or represented, then will we not always be returned to lack?"

In summary, but certainly not in conclusion, it is evident that the artists who are engaged in a depropriative practice take their cue from Brecht and Godard, rather than the situationists. They are concerned with the image but not consumed by the spectacle; critical, but not moralistic; obsessed with pleasure, but with the kind to which Barthes referred when he wrote "knowledge is delicious." Moreover, and crucially, *depropriationists* are not afraid to pose the question of subjectivity and of sexuality together with, across, or even against the "allegorical" imperatives of a politically correct art. The depropriative text is heterogeneous, disruptive, open, pleasurable, *and* political. Finally, it also goes (almost) without saying that the artists' intentions reach far beyond the curatorial confiscation of their imaged effects. So let us "proceed analytically," as Brecht suggested, and "transform finished works into unfinished works." In this way, we will make *meaning* possible and our pleasure in it unpurloined.

Notes

"Beyond the Purloined Image," extended version of the catalogue introduction, published in *Block,* no. 9 (1983): 68–72.

1. The title of an exhibition of photographic work by Ray Barrie, Judith Crowle, Karen Knorr, Yve Lomax, Olivier Richon, Mitra Tabrizian, Susan Trangmar, and Marie Yates, which I curated for Riverside Studios, London, August 3–29, 1983.

2. See, for instance, Douglas Crimp, "The Photographic Activity of Post-Modernism," October 15 (1980); also Benjamin Buchloh, "Allegorical Procedures: Appropriation and Montage in Contemporary Art," *Art Forum* (September 1982), and Kate Linker, "On Richard Prince's Photographs," *Arts Magazine* (November 1982).

3. The Stolen Image and Its Uses included work by Vicky Alexander, Silvia Kolbowski, Barbara Kruger, Sherrie Levine, and Richard Prince. It was curated by Abigail Solomon-Godeau for Light Work/Community Darkrooms, Syracuse, N.Y., March 16–April 15, 1983.

4. Stephen Heath uses the term *depropriation* to describe the film practice of Straub, Oshima, and Godard in "Lessons from Brecht," *Screen* (summer 1974).

5. Peter Wollen, "Photography and Aesthetics," *Readings and Writings* (London: Verso, 1982).

6. Victor Burgin, "Photography, Phantasy, Function," *Thinking Photography* (London: Macmillan, 1982).

7. Sigmund Freud, "Some Psychological Consequences of the Anatomical Distinction Between the Sexes" (1925), *Collected Papers,* vol. 5.

8. Jane Gallop, *Feminism and Psychoanalysis* (London: Macmillan, 1982).

On Representation, Sexuality, and Sameness: Reflections on the Difference Show

I want to discuss not difference but "sameness," that is, strategic sameness, a sense of political identity; always tentative, temporary, contradictory but historically motivated and ultimately just as significant in the cultural sphere as it is in any other.[1] The importance of the Difference show, for me, is that it establishes, in spite of the diversity of the work included, a certain unity, an alliance that refuses to play out the postmodernist scenario for this genre of group/theme show, namely, pluralism. Instead, the exhibition takes up, via Kate Linker's curatorship, a position within that plurality of styles and argues for an art practice which responds to social as well as aesthetic imperatives in the process of rejecting the so-called avant-garde of the seventies. It also refuses the modernist definition of art according to media and creates identity across those categories on the basis of shared ideas.

In this respect, the film and video contribution is central. The exhibition's focus is, in fact, the product of two histories, one in fine art and the other in film. For example, the critique of authorship and concern for social purpose (Hans Haacke) combined with the introduction of psychoanalytic theory and the emphasis on spectatorship (Jean-Luc Godard) has produced the visual hybrid characteristic of more recent static work (Barbara Kruger, Silvia Kolbowski, Marie Yates, Yve Lomax). Here, at the most obvious level, there is a similarity of purpose in which narrative, or at least seriality breaks down modernism's holy paradigm: the single, essentially expressive and preferably nondiscursive picture (the kind that proliferates, for example, in the exhibition Zeitgeist). The importance of any didactic emphasis in the

*Difference: On Representation
and Sexuality,* New Museum of
Contemporary Art, New York, 1984,
installation view, foreground, Silvia
Kolbowski, *Model Pleasure,* 1982–84.

context of exhibiting, which is fundamentally part of the entertainment business, should not be underestimated. I maintain then that underlying the controversial response to the Difference show, particularly in New York where it was extensively reviewed, is a certain fear of sameness which illicits, primarily, three responses.

First, the look of sameness: conceptual, dull, difficult, out-of-date, not new, and different; such arguments, based on the notion that one historical style displaces another, are always precarious because the scene shifts so quickly. For instance, an article in a recent issue of a leading art magazine states that the eighties are over and the craze for pictures is already subsiding. There is, however, another objection related to this but more insidious, which says, basically, "It's not English," meaning the Germans and Italians paint and the English make objects. Promoting an often regressive national-ism has been the European art market's solution to the economic slump of the 1970s. On the contrary, one of the Difference exhibition's strengths in bringing together British and North American artists has been to consoli-date the history of critical work on sexuality. But I am also thinking of its contribution to a wider context, one defined by Hal Foster in *The Anti-Aesthetic* as cross-disciplinary practices, engaged in a politic or rooted in a vernacular, that form the basis for a "postmodernism of resistance."[2]

Second, theoretical disagreements that either emphasize the institution, museum, or gallery as a primary target for debate or insist upon an equal rights strategy such as the promotion of all women artists: these are, at best, refusals of feminism and its political implications in the 1980s. At worst, they are invocations, not for difference, but for being different: my position, my work—a policy of nonalignment disguised as integrity.

What I call the exhibition's sameness is precisely the fact that it does not flaunt a plurality of styles, theoretical positions, or national peculiarities. Nor does it reduce sexuality to a diversity of sexual practices or to a sex war, that is, to a struggle between real men and women which could only be resolved by separation, assertions of difference, or, perhaps, a women's show. Instead, the Difference exhibition focuses on the construction of our sexual identities as men and women, always remembering it does this in ways which are specific to visual representations or imaged discourse, not literal debate. In this sense the show embraces, reworks, or at least invites a psychoanalytic redefinition of masculinity and femininity. For both Freud and Lacan, the concept of bisexuality is crucial to understanding the tentative nature of sexual positioning, to understanding the drives in terms of aims and objects rather than predetermined sexual instincts. By emphasizing also the polymorphous perversity of the drives, the way is opened for a reconsideration of notions of perversion and repression which do not simply reinforce conventional definitions of active/male, passive/female. But, most importantly, such an emphasis raises the question of homosexual object choice. And this is the basis of the third objection: that the exhibition does not adequately address *this* difference.

Here, in another way, the exhibition provokes a fear of sameness, fear of the loss of sexual identity and, consequently, of social division and political cause. This, I believe, is a very productive moment in the debate around the issues the exhibition claims to deal with. The argument seems to evolve very schematically in the following way. Initially, around the most recent term in this debate—masculinity. It is said that there is an attempt in certain work (Victor Burgin, Jeff Wall) to create a literal symmetry with the feminine term, suggesting, for instance, that if "the woman" doesn't exist, then neither does "the man," refusing the universal fact and identifying with the fictitious other. Such an assimilation of the privileged into the ranks of "the oppressed" is short-circuited because the oppressed cannot be homogenized in a strategic sense, as a class, any more than "the other" can be defined, in linguistic terms, as a specific category. In another way, too, it is suggested that when men concern themselves with male fantasy or with solving the enigma of femininity it may just be another excuse for looking at women. Some work, however (Ray Barrie, Stuart Marshall), does address the relevant problem of power relations between and among men, exploring what Lacan has called "the fraud of the phallus." But more often, the defense against sameness is to make the issue of masculinity synonymous with homosexuality. Clearly this strategy is also reductive, but I think there is more at stake here than just redefining the feminine term. In the process of reestablishing a social and political identity based on sexual choice, the argument succeeds in transcending the usual dichotomy of men/women. At one

Ray Barrie, *Master-Pieces,* 1981, 6
units, 30 × 30 ins. each, color
autone photographs.

level, it demands analyses of the effects—medical, legal, and so on—of the heterosexual imperative. At another level, it asks what it means to transgress that imperative in relation to theorizing subjectivity itself. Why, for instance, is female homosexuality the repressed term in that analysis? Does this reconstitute the enigma? A symptomatic example: if the first love object is the mother and she is assumed to be a real woman, rather than a primordial object, then one explanation might be the "naturalness" of the woman's desire for another woman, and that perversion might better describe her sexual relationship with a man. But this is obviously problematic since, conversely, it would be implying that a man's sexual relationship with a woman is primary and his desire for men "perverse." What I am suggesting is that feminism may have privileged the relation to the mother's body in a way which did more than explain a different relation to castration; it also asserted our difference from men. Perhaps in the process we made the mother too real, too close, and consequently blamed her for too much.

Although the exhibition does not provide an answer to the third objection, I am suggesting that the way it frames the questions of sexuality and representation allows us to rethink, rather than repeat, the feminist arguments on which that issue is founded. In this sense, the show's strategic sameness makes present and meaningful what is often only a rhetorical plea for a postmodernism of resistance.

Notes

"On Representation, Sexuality and Sameness: Reflections on the 'Difference' Show," *Screen* 28, no. 1 (1987). Paper presented at the symposium Sexual Identity, The New School for Social Research, New York, 1984.

1. Exhibition: Difference: On Representation and Sexuality. Kate Linker, guest curator, Jane Weinstock, guest curator, film and video. The New Museum of Contemporary Art, New York, December 8, 1984–February 10, 1985, The Renaissance Society at the University of Chicago, March 3–April 7, 1985, Institute of Contemporary Arts, London, July 19–September 1, 1985.

Artists: Max Almy, Ray Barrie, Judith Barry, Raymond Bellour, Dara Birnbaum, Victor Burgin, Theresa Cha, Cecilia Condit, Jean-Luc Godard, Hans Haacke, Mary

Kelly, Silvia Kolbowski, Barbara Kruger, Sherrie Levine, Yve Lomax, Stuart Marshall, Martha Rosler, Philippe Venault, Jeff Wall, Marie Yates.

Catalogue essays by: Craig Owens, Lisa Tickner, Jacqueline Rose, Peter Wollen, Jane Weinstock.

2. Hal Foster, ed. *The Anti-Aesthetic: Essays on Postmodern Culture* (Port Townsend, WA: Bay Press, 1983).

Desiring Images/Imaging Desire

"In this matter of the visible," writes Lacan, "everything is a trap."[1] The field of vision is ordered by the function of images, at one level, quite simply by linking a surface to a geometric point by means of a path of light, but, at another level, this function seems more like a labyrinth. Since the fascination in looking is founded on separation from what is seen, the field of vision is also, and most appropriately, the field of desire. Here the viewer enters the realm of lost objects, of vanishing points determined, not by geometry, but by what is real for the subject, points linked, not to a surface, but to a place—the unconscious—and not by means of light, but by the laws of primary process.

In the matter of images of women then, it would seem that everything is doubly labyrinthine. Desire is embodied in the image which is equated with the woman who is reduced to the body which in turn is seen as the site of sexuality and the locus of desire . . . a familiar elision, almost irresistible it would seem, judging from the outcome of so many conference panels and special issues devoted to this theme. Nevertheless, it is a dangerous and circuitous logic that obscures a certain progress, a progression of strategies, of definitions made possible within feminist theory by the pressure of political imperatives to formulate the problem of images of women as a question: how to change them? The legacy is not a through route, but a disentangling of paths that shows more clearly their points of intersection and draws attention to the fact that it is not obligatory to start over again at the beginning.

Discourses on the body and on sexuality, for instance, do not necessarily coincide. Within the modernist paradigm, it is not the sexual body but the phenomenological (Husserlian) body that takes precedence, what belongs to me, my body, the body of the self-possessing subject whose guarantee of artistic truth is grounded in actual experience, often deploying the painful state as a signature for that ephemeral object. Thus, the contribution of feminists in the field of performance has been, exactly, to pose the question of sexuality across the body in a way which focuses on the construction of the sexed subject and at the same time problematizes the notion of the artist/auteur. The body is decentered, radically split, positioned—not simply my body, but his body, her body. Here, no third term emerges to salvage a transcendental sameness for aesthetic reflection. Yet these artists continue to counterpose a visible form and a hidden content, excavating a different order of truth—the truth of the woman, her original feminine identity. Although the body is not perceived as the repository of this truth, it is seen as a hermeneutic image; the enigma of femininity is formulated as a problem of imagistic misrepresentation which is subsequently resolved by discovering a true identity behind the patriarchal facade.

The enigma, however, only seems to encapsulate the difficulty of sexuality itself, and what emerges is more in the order of an underlying contradiction than an essential content. The woman artist sees her experience as a woman particularly in terms of the feminine position, that is, as the object of the look. But she must also account for the feeling she experiences as the artist, occupying what could be called the masculine position, as the subject of the look. The former she defines as the socially prescribed position of the woman, one to be questioned, exorcized, or overthrown, while the implication of the latter—that there can be only one position with regard to active looking, a masculine one—cannot be acknowledged. It is construed instead as a kind of psychic truth, a natural, instinctual, preexistent, and possibly unrepresentable femininity. Often the ambivalence of the feminist text seems to repudiate its claims to essentialism; it testifies instead to what extent masculine and feminine identities are never finally fixed, but are continually negotiated through representations. This crisis of positionality, this instability of meaning revolves around the phallus as the term which marks the sexual division of the subject in language. Significantly, Lacan describes the woman's relation to the phallic term as a disguise, a masquerade.[2] In being the phallus for the other, she actively takes up a passive aim, becomes a picture of herself, erects a facade. Behind the facade, finally, there is no true woman to be discovered. Yet there is a dilemma: the impossibility of being at once both subject and object of desire.

Clearly, one (so-called postfeminist) response to this impasse has been to adopt a strategy of disavowal. It appears in the guise of a familiar visual metaphor: the androgyne. She *is* a picture, an expressionistic composite of looks and gestures which flaunts the uncertainty of sexual positioning. She refuses the lack, but remains the object of the look. In a sense, the fetishistic implications of not knowing merely enhance the lure of the picture, effectively taming the gaze, rather than provoking a deconstruction. Another (and perhaps more politically motivated) tactic has been to assume self-consciously the patriarchal facade, to make it an almost abrasive and cynical act of affirmation. By producing a representation of femininity in excess of conventional codes, it shatters the narcissistic structure which would return the woman's image to her as a moment of completion. This can induce the alienating effect of a misrecognition, but the question persists: how can she represent herself as a subject of desire?

The (neo-) feminist alternative has been to refuse the literal figuration of the woman's body, creating significance out of its absence. But this does not signal a new form of iconoclasm. The artist does not protest against the lure of the picture. In another way, however, her practice could be said to be blasphemous insofar as she seeks to appropriate the gaze behind it (the place of gods, auteurs, and evil eyes). In her field of vision femininity is not seen as a pregiven entity, but as the mapping-out of sexual difference within a definite terrain, a moment of discourse, a fragment of history. With regard to the spectator, it is a tactic of reversal which attempts to produce the woman, through a different form of identification with the image, as the subject of the look.

A further consequence of this reversal is that it queries the tendency of psychoanalytic theory to complement the division of the visual field into sexually prescribed positions by rhyming repression/perversion, hysteria/obsession, body/word . . . with the heterosexual couplet seer/seen. Yet, this division does not seem to be sustained in Freud's work itself. According to Freud, sexual identity is said to be an outcome of the precarious passage called the Oedipus complex, a passage which is in a certain sense completed by the acceptance of symbolic castration. But castration is also inscribed at the level of the imaginary, that is, in fantasy, and this is where the fetishistic scenario originates and is continually replayed. The child's recognition of difference between the mother and the father is above all an admission that the mother does not have the phallus. In this case, seeing is not necessarily believing, for what is at stake for the child is really the question of his or her own relation to having or being. Hence the fetishist, conventionally assumed to be male, postpones that moment of recognition, although certainly he has made the passage—he knows the difference, but denies it. In terms of representation, this denial is associated with a definite iconography of pornographic images where the man is reassured by the woman's possession of some form of phallic substitute or, alternatively, by the shape, the complete arrangement, of her body.

The question of masculine perversions is an important one. But it would be a mistake to confine women to the realm of repression, excluding the possibility, for example, of female fetishism. For the woman, insofar as the outcome of the Oedipal moment has involved at some point a heterosexual object choice (that is, she has identified with her mother and has taken her father as a love object), it will also postpone the recognition of lack in view of the promise of having the child. In having the child, in a sense she has the phallus. So the loss of the child is the loss of that symbolic plenitude—more exactly the ability to represent lack.[3]

When Freud describes castration fears for the woman, this imaginary scenario takes the form of losing her loved objects, especially her children; the child is going to grow up, leave her, reject her, perhaps die. In order to delay, disavow the separation that she has already in a way acknowledged, the woman tends to fetishize the child by dressing him up, by continuing to feed him no matter how old he gets, or simply by having another little one. So perhaps in place of the more familiar notion of pornography, it is possible to talk about the mother's memorabilia—the way she saves things: the first shoes, photographs, locks of hair, or school reports. A trace, a gift, a fragment of narrative, all of these can be seen as transitional objects, not in Winnicott's sense, as surrogates, but in Lacan's terms, as emblems of desire. The feminist text proceeds from this site, not in order to valorize the potential fetishism of the woman, but to create a critical distance from it, something which has not been possible until now, because it has not been generally acknowledged. Here the problem of images of women can be reformulated as a different question: how is a radical, critical *and* pleasurable positioning of the woman as spectator to be done?

Desire is caused not by objects but in the unconscious, according to the peculiar structure of fantasy. Desire is repetitious; it resists normalization, ignores biology, disperses the body. Certainly, desire is not synonymous with images of desirable women, yet what does it mean, exactly, to say that feminists have refused the image of the woman? First, this implies a refusal to reduce the concept of the image to one of resemblance, to figuration, or even to the general category of the iconic sign. It suggests that the image, as it is organized in the space called the picture, can refer to a heterogeneous system of signs—indexical, iconic, and symbolic. And thus, that it is possible to invoke the nonspecular, the sensory, the somatic, in the visual field; to invoke, especially, the register of the invocatory drives (which, according to Lacan, are on the same level as the scopic drives, but closer to the experience of the unconscious), through *writing*. Second, it should be said that this is not a hybrid version of the hieroglyph masquerading as a heterogeneity of signs. The object is not to return the feminine to a domain of prelinguistic utterance but rather to mobilize a system of imaged discourse capable of refuting a certain form of culturally overdetermined scopophilia. But why? Would this release the female spectator from her hysterical identification with the male voyeur?

Again, the implications of suggesting that women have a privileged relation to narcissism or that fetishism is an exclusively male perversion should be reconsidered. Surely, the link between narcissism and fetishism is castration. For both the man and the woman, this is the condition for access to the symbolic, to language, to culture; there can be no privileged relation to madness. Yet there *is* difference. There is still that irritating asymmetry of the Oedipal moment. There is Freud's continual emphasis on the importance of the girl's attachment to her mother. And there is Dora.[4] What did she find so fascinating in the picture of the Sistine Madonna? Perhaps, above all, it was the possibility of seeing the woman as subject of desire without transgressing the socially acceptable definition of her as the mother: to have the child as phallus; to be the phallic mother; to have the pleasure of the child's body; to have the pleasure of the maternal body experienced through

Mary Kelly, working on *Interim*,
1985. Photo: Ray Barrie.

it. Perhaps, in the figure of the Madonna, there was a duplication of identification and desire that only the body of another woman could sustain.

For both the man and the woman, the maternal body lines the seductive
surface of the image, but the body he sees is not the same one she is looking
at. The woman's relation to the mother's body is a constant source of anxiety. Montrelay claims that this relation is often only censored rather than
repressed. Consequently, the woman clings to a precocious femininity, an
archaic oral-anal organization of the drives which bars her access to sublimated pleasure (phallic *jouissance*).[5] Similarly, with regard to the artistic text,
and if pleasure is understood in Barthes's sense of the term as a loss of pre-
conceived identity rather than an instance of repletion, then it is possible
to produce a different form of pleasure for the woman by representing a
specific loss—the loss of her imagined closeness to the mother's body. A
critical, perhaps disturbing sense of separation is effected through the visualization of exactly that which was assumed to be outside of seeing: precocious, unspeakable, unrepresentable. In the scopic register, she is no longer
at the level of concentricity, of repetitious demand, but of desire. As Lacan
points out, even the eye itself belongs to this archaic structure, since it functions in the field of vision as a lost object.[6] Thus, the same movement which
determines the subject's appearance in language, that is, symbolic castration,
also introduces the gaze. And the domain of imaged discourse.

Until now the woman as spectator has been pinned to the surface of the
picture, trapped in the path of light that leads her back to the features of
the veiled face. It is important to acknowledge that the masquerade has
always been internalized, linked to a particular organization of the drives,
represented through a diversity of aims and objects, but, at the same time,
it is important to avoid being lured into looking for a psychic truth beneath
the veil. To see this picture critically, the viewer should be neither too close
nor too far away.

Notes

"Desiring Images/Imaging Desire," *Wedge,* no. 6 (winter 1984). Reprinted in *In-
stabili: la question du sujet* (Montreal: La Galerie Powerhouse et Artexte, 1990), pp.
24–28.

1. Jacques Lacan, "The Line and Light," in *The Four Fundamental Concepts,* ed. M. Masud, trans. R. Khan (London: Hogarth Press, 1977), p. 93.

2. See Jacques Lacan, "The Significance of the Phallus" (1958), in *Feminine Sexuality,* eds. Juliet Mitchell and Jacqueline Rose (London: Macmillan Press, 1982).

3. See Sigmund Freud, "The Dissolution of the Oedipus Complex" (1924), standard edition, vol. 19, trans. James Strachey (London: Hogarth Press, 1968).

4. See Sigmund Freud, "Fragment of an Analysis of a Case of Hysteria" (1901), standard edition, vol. 7, trans. James Strachey (London: Hogarth Press, 1968).

5. Michèle Montrelay, "Inquiry into Femininity," *m/f*, no. 1 (1978): 86–99.

6. Jacques Lacan, "What Is a Picture," in *The Four Fundamental Concepts,* p. 118.

IV Invisible Bodies

Re-Presenting the Body

"Corpus" concerns the body—how it is shaped socially and psychically in the interim moment of aging. Importantly, though, it does this in the specific form of an exhibition.[1] As such, the work involves a process of simultaneously visualizing and theorizing, which, in a way, resists interpretation. In the context of this discussion, then, what I would like to do is take up some of the questions that give perspective to an underlying argument, stressing of course that this is not an explanation, but a parallel discourse, something unsettled, hopefully exceeded, by the art itself.

At one level, the conversational mode of the short stories in "Corpus" appears to represent, quite simply, the familiar view of women's experience. Yet, in relation to the image panels, titles, and triptych structure of the sections, this has recourse to another order of experience, a political as well as personal history, grounded in the ongoing debates of what is still called, but now more tentatively, the women's movement. "Corpus" is the first part of a larger project, *Interim,* which is still in progress. Through *Interim*'s themes (body, money, history, power), many issues which have preoccupied feminists in the past decade are recovered and reworked. First, regarding the project as a whole, the politics of psychoanalysis; following the Foucauldian imperative to place it historically among the discourses that define and regulate the realm of sexuality, can it now be said to have become another orthodoxy? Second, in Part I, the problem of hysteria—a focal point in theory—but clinically speaking, does it still exist? Third, what is the status, or fate perhaps, of the body and of the image in a visual art practice informed by psychoanalysis and feminism?

Mary Kelly, *Interim,* Part I: "Corpus,"
1984–85, installation view, Henry
McNeil Gallery, Philadelphia,
1988, photolaminate, silkscreen, and
acrylic on plexiglass, 6 of 30 panels,
4 × 3 feet each.

Detail, "Corpus."

Extase

"Corpus" makes explicit reference to Charcot's now famous photographs of female hysterics by using the titles of "the passionate attitudes" (*Menacé, Appel, Supplication, Erotisme,* and *Extase*) to announce the work's five sections.[2] Citing the attitudes provided a means of linking popular discourses of the body with those of psychoanalysis as well as placing psychoanalysis itself within a historical context by referring to the founding moment of Freud's theory. Charcot's study, which was the first to observe and distinguish the category of nonorganic nervous disorders, placed emphasis, almost exclusively, on the *visible* symptom. In the process, madness became a spectacle: the theater of hysterics, a play dedicated to the production of unreason as a tangible event. Above all, what I found so significant is that it was a theater in which women enacted the stages of the hysteric crisis and that it was the young women in particular who posed in the passionate attitudes. No doubt, there were male hysterics, but it seems that they were not photographed. At least, it is uncertain, since the figures posed in what could be called "less passionate" attitudes, such as *Irony, Repugnance,* or *Terror,* are older, "unattractive," or sexually ambiguous in appearance. The important point here is that Freud, who began the *Studies in Hysteria* while working with Charcot, shifted the analyst's attention from looking to *listening*. With this, he introduced the linguistic moment into the analysis of psychic disorder. In effect, the body was dispersed, made invisible, with the invention of the "talking cure."

"Corpus" takes up some of the implications of that shift, very schematically, as follows. In the first case, what could be called the "modern" world view, which Freud represents in contrast to Charcot, language becomes central in a way that makes the visual take on a kind of compensatory value (the unrepresentable, the monstrous, even the sublime). Freud in fact calls Charcot a "*visuel*," says he is not a reflective man, not a thinker, that he has the nature of an artist.[3] Thus the visible disorder, expelled from the theater, reappears in the nonpsychiatric discourse of the artist who becomes the prototype for madness. The recovery of unreason is orchestrated through the socially acceptable form of art. More relevant still, at the present time, the body—that repressed object of the medical gaze—returns in the spectacle of contemporary advertising where women's bodies, posed in an infinite variety of passionate attitudes, are all pervasive. The scale, for instance,

J.M. Charcot, "Attitudes passionelles," (Planche XXIII, Extase), *Nouvelle Iconographie Photographie de la Salpêtrière,* vol. 2, Paris, 1878.

"Obsession," Calvin Klein, *Vogue* (United States), March 1985. Photo: Bruce Weber.

of the panels for "Corpus" is based on the dimensions of a small hoarding (or billboard). On that stage, in place of Charcot's figures, emblematic articles of clothing pose, not only as the objects of medical scrutiny, but also as items for commercial exchange or subjects of romantic fantasy. Clearly, there is not *one* body, there are many. Moreover, discourses of the body are not synonymous with images of women. But images of women *are* overdetermined by anatomical referents and by a certain repetitious form of hysterical posturing. So, once again, this spectacle requires a critical shift, within the space of the picture, from looking to listening.

The second point concerns the psychoanalytic concept of hysteria. In theory and to some extent in clinical practice, hysteria, defined in relation to the conversion symptom (the bodily symptom as the formation of a substitute for the repressed wish), has disappeared. Parveen Adams has pointed out that there are two concepts of symptom and two concepts of hysteria in Freud's writings. The first appears in the 1890s, and is evident in the *Interpretation of Dreams;* the second emerges after 1926 with the work on femininity and the pre-Oedipal phase.[4] By that time, both symptom and hysteria are being redefined by the implications of Freud's emphasis on identification and bisexuality. (Dora's cough, for example, is not a substitute but a means of identification with her father, which in turn is linked to the repressed desire for Frau K.) At the same time, this emphasis seems to be shifting the whole field of psychoanalysis away from its preoccupation with woman—*her* repressed sexuality, *her* hysterical symptom—and toward the more encompassing, but also more illusive question of the subject—*its* sexed identity. Here, what interests me is that hysteria continues to have a metaphorical significance. Lacan, for instance, speaks of psychoanalysis as the "hystericization of discourse," posing analysis against mastery and hysteria against knowledge. More importantly, for those expelled, not from Charcot's theater, but from Lacan's *école freudienne*—I am thinking in particular of Luce Irigaray—the hysteric exposes the institution's fundamental misogyny; woman founds the theory of psychoanalysis and sustains it by facilitating the exchange of ideas between male theorists. Thus hysteria, marginalized in one realm, becomes central in another—feminist theory. For Irigaray, the hysteric signifies the exclusion of women from discourse; for Monique Plaza—the revolt against patriarchy; for Michèle Montrelay—

the blind spot of psychoanalysis; for Jacqueline Rose—the problem of sexual difference; and for the film collective of *Dora*—the analyst's symptom and therefore the basis for feminism's critique of Freud.

My work is also deeply implicated in this trajectory, compelled to fill in, or perhaps I should say widen, the gaps in the Freudian thesis. I have often thought of dedicating *Interim* to Dora's mother—the woman who never made Freud's acquaintance. He assumed she had housewife's psychosis. Too old for analysis? Too old to be noticed? Precisely in her invisibility, she underlines the dilemma for the older woman of representing her femininity, her sexuality, her desire when she is no longer seen to be desirable. She can neither look forward, as the young girl does, to being a woman, that is, having the fantasized body of maturity, nor can she return to the ideal moment of maternity—ideal in that it allows her to occupy the position of the actively desiring subject without transgressing the socially acceptable definition of the woman as mother. She is looking back at something lost, acknowledging perhaps that "being a woman" was only a brief moment in her life.

In *Post-Partum Document,* which explores the implications of the mother-child relationship, I asked what the woman fears losing beyond the pleasure of the infant's body and concluded that it is the closeness to the mother's body she experiences in being "like her."[5] Now, in *Interim,* I am asking how the woman can reconstitute her narcissistic aim and consequently her pleasure, her desire, outside of that maternal relation. In Part I, the stories begin with the decision not to have a child and then continue to explore other forms of identification around which the feminine/masculine terms revolve. Effectively, "Corpus" reiterates the hysteric's question: am I a man or am I a woman? And significantly, with the loss of maternal identity, a different order of fear emerges, one which reveals the importance of the repressed pre-Oedipal identification with the father—the desire to be "like him," but the fear of being the *same,* that is, of being "like a man."

At this point, I am prompted to ask, is there no outcome of the Oedipus complex for the girl which is without neurotic consequences? Does, for instance, as Catherine Millot suggests in "The Feminine Super-ego," the pre-Oedipal identification with the father always entail a regressive transference of the demand for the phallus from him to the pre-Oedipal, hence phallic mother?[6] Is it inconceivable that the "masculinity complex" be considered, in some sense at least, as a resolution of the conflict? It does, after all, necessitate the internalization of demand and the setting up of a superego. This process can lead to inhibition and anxiety, as Millot indicates, but at the same time it makes possible what is generally referred to as a profession, or less mundanely, the kind of sublimated pleasure associated with creative work. Notably, it is for this manifestation of "virility" that women propose to make themselves lovable. As Millot points out, "the object of desire—and not the object of love—is feminine."

I find this an intriguing distinction, one which imposes a less obvious, but nevertheless pertinent question. Is the boy's resolution of the Oedipal drama really as unproblematic as has been assumed? Could Millot's distinctions regarding the masculinity complex for women be usefully taken up in relation to men? For example, does the woman who fantasizes the possession of a penis parallel the man who acts out its absence (transvestism)? Is the woman who masquerades as the feminine type, who disguises the lack of a lack, but makes no demand on her sexual partner, comparable to the man who "does what he's gotta do" (the male "display," Lacan calls it), although he senses the fraud and, in fact, has no sexual desire for a woman? Furthermore, taking up what lies on the cusp of the complex—the woman's desire for the child as phallus and the man's desire to give her this "gift," and what lies outside it—the failure to internalize demand which results in Don Juan's (or Juanita's) continual search for "something better," all of this begins to give substance to the Lacanian view that there are as many forms of identification as there are demands. For both men and women, demand constructs a rather fragile relation to being and having. No one has the phallus, of course, but women seem reticent to let men (that is, the man they want to love) relinquish it.

This reticence has implications for feminism too. In failing to consider both sides of the Oedipal story, perhaps the mother has become too real, too close, and consequently has been blamed for too much. What I am suggesting is that the relation to the mother's body has been privileged in a way that does more than explain a different relation to castration for women; it asserts their difference from men. For instance, it is said that men, if they do experience anxiety over aging, transpose it into another mode, a metalanguage; while women articulate it in terms of corporeality—pain, feeling of deformation, or transformation of features, organs, limbs—or literally embody it, "beyond words" is the familiar phrase. Michèle Montrelay describes this symptomatically as the woman who never lets up trying to be her sex. Theoretically she elaborates it as a form of "precocious femininity," that is, an archaic organization of the drives that bars the woman's access to sublimated pleasure. Although I have some reservations about her thesis as a whole, one of her observations is absolutely central to *Interim*'s discursive schema. "The adult woman," she says, "is one who reconstructs her sexuality in a field that goes beyond sex." This is, of course, crucial for the older woman. It is also here, encapsulated in this statement, that I glimpse the social and political relevance of psychoanalysis for feminism, one which goes beyond the meanings of orthodoxy.

The confessional, the speaking of symptoms or, as Montrelay suggests, "saying all," bypasses masculine censure because it transgresses a psychic organization which binds the feminine to passivity and silence. Specifically, the interpretation of sexuality, in the sense pertaining to the analysts' words, does not explain but structures; as Montrelay insists *"it makes sexuality pass into discourse."*[7] Pleasure is no longer derived from femininity as such, but from the signifier, in other words, by the repression of precocity that it brings about. She gives the example of jokes and of "writing." Also, in a political sense, I think this indicates the importance for women of theoretical and creative work, especially work on sexuality itself.

Returning to "Corpus," my emphasis on the shift from looking to listening is not simply a theoretical point, it is also an artistic strategy. Its aim, first with regard to images of women, is to release the so-called female spectator from her hysterical identification with the male voyeur. What I mean is that, for both men and women, to be pleasurably involved in looking is to be positioned actively as subject of that look, to enter the realm of objects and to desire them. At the same time, the woman, not exclusively, but more emphatically, is caught in a self-reflexive web of identifications—Am I like that? Was I like that? Would I like to be like that? Should I be like that? She is no longer surveying the image but her own reflection in it, hoping to catch a glimpse of herself as others see her. Desire then appears to have no object since satisfaction takes the form of identification itself.

Possibly as a defense against the "masculinity" assumed in looking, she is trying on the "mask(s) of womanliness" as Joan Riviere described it in her seminal article;[8] yet there never is, never could be a perfect fit.

Alternatively, by placing the "enigma" of femininity on the surface of the picture rather than behind it, perhaps the process can be reversed. If she identifies, not with the literal figure of the woman, but with her effects, that is, the masquerade, then what she enjoys will be her distance from the alienation or anxiety this usually produces. For the older woman, inevitably, "the image grates," the mask fails, and the options are limited—either madness or laughter. This is why the work does not adopt the tactic of the "open text." Instead, it pushes the closure of traditional narrative to the point of parody. The fairy tale endings in a sense resemble Montrelay's notion of the joke. Rather than reflect the spectator's fantasy, they repress it, creating an empty space where laughter is possible when the repressed returns in the guise of something else. In this case, it is something absurd that shatters the autobiographical trompe l'oeil by revealing the function of the brush stroke, the character; it is only a picture, only a story, only a mimicry of the woman's disguise—playing it out on the "body" of the text.

To represent a motive for one's fear, such as getting older or feeling unattractive, is not anxiety in clinical terms—that would imply the impossibility of rational thought, a "blockage." Hence the scriptovisual method I have been describing is a conscious representation invoking an imaginary loss. A representation can only take on unconscious significance when it no longer refers to anything other than its form, not as an attribute of stylistic formalism, but as the precondition for any meaning. Here, significance is contingent upon the affect of the child's first experience of objects as extensions of the mother's body. For me, writing is also simply this—a texture of speaking, listening, touching; a means of visualizing exactly that which is assumed to be outside of seeing, unrepresentable, unsaid. Although it is wildly speculative, I would like to think that a work of art could instigate a different kind of pleasure for the woman in seeing herself, one that is linked to the loss of a feminine identity formed in anxious proximity to the maternal body. In this sense, the work refers not so much to the anatomical fact or even to the perceptual entity as to the body of fantasy, the dispersed body of desire. Recalling Lacan's description of erotogenic zones as the gaze, the phoneme, the nothing, I am tempted to describe the space of the installation as an instance of "gathering" rather than a condition of reading or viewing from a fixed vantage point. Finally, the textual emphasis is more than an effort to create significance out of the *absence* of the woman's image as representational or iconic sign; it is an attempt to alter the implication of her *presence* in the spectacle of practices and histories that determine the postmodern condition of art.

Notes

"Re-Presenting the Body: On *Interim,* Part I," *Psychoanalysis and Cultural Theory,* ed. James C. Donald (New York: St. Martin's Press; and London and Basingstoke: Macmillan, 1991), pp. 59–67. Reprinted with permission of St. Martin's Press, Incorporated. Paper presented at conference of the same name, Institute of Contemporary Art, London, 1987.

1. See Mary Kelly, *Interim,* Part I, catalogue, Fruitmarket Gallery, Edinburgh; Riverside Studios, London; Kettle's Yard Gallery, Cambridge, 1986.

2. J. M. Charcot, *Nouvelle Iconographie Photographique de la Salpêtrière,* volume II, Paris, 1878.

3. Sigmund Freud, "Charcot," standard edition, vol. 3, trans. James Strachey (London: Hogarth Press, 1968).

4. Parveen Adams, "Symptoms and Hysteria," *Oxford Literary Review* 8, nos. 1–2 (1986).

5. Mary Kelly, *Post-Partum Document* (London and Boston: Routledge and Kegan Paul, 1983).

6. Catherine Millot, "The Feminine Super-ego," *m/f,* no. 10 (1985): 21–38.

7. Michèle Montrelay, "Inquiry into Femininity," *m/f,* no. 1 (1978).

8. Joan Riviere, "Womanliness as Masquerade" (1929), reprinted in *Formations of Fantasy,* eds. Victor Burgin, James Donald, and Cora Kaplan (London and New York: Methuen, 1986).

The Smell of Money: Mary Kelly in Conversation with Emily Apter

Emily Apter: In a preface written for the book of your earlier work, *Post-Partum Document,* you explicitly stated that one of your principal concerns was to see whether some notion of female fetishism could be worked out according to the theoretical parameters of the installation. Emphasizing in the classic Freudian schema of male fetishism the strategic compensation of projected phallic loss through prosthetic substitutions, you then went on to discern a comparable (though different) female fetishism in the maternal reliquary, designed to ward off the fear of an impending "empty nest." *Post-Partum Document* "documents" the museological mania of the maternal collector/fetishist with a gently ironic sympathy. "First words set out in type, stained liners, hand imprints, comforter fragments, drawings, writings, or even the plants and insects that were his gifts"—these are displayed through an affectionate but rigorously formal taxonomy. A similar archival or ethnographic impulse is discernible in the "Pecunia" section of *Interim*. Could you describe the shifts and continuities in your treatment of female fetishism between the earlier and later work?

Mary Kelly: First, there is a continuity in general between the two projects which is established by the visual similarities of serial imagery and also by the way that I approach the subject matter. I would describe this, similarly, as ethnographic, that is, the artist as participant observer, recording the "rituals" of maternity or aging. One of the most important shifts, however, would concern the notion of female fetishism (although I would hesitate to use the term now). It was a central theme in *Post-Partum Document,* but only one of many in *Interim,* which layers several discourses within and across the different sections.

The woman's relation to the child is the classic example (but not acknowledged as such by Freud) of the trajectory of fetishism for the woman. The mother's memorabilia—the way she saves the lock of hair, the tooth, or school reports—signals a disavowal of the lack inscribed by separation from the child. In order to convey this sense of loss, and the subsequent "prosthetic substitution," I used found objects and arranged them in a parody of conventional museum display. But *Interim* does not use the "real thing," because it is an invocation of the fetish already once removed, a "representation." In "Corpus," the photo laminate and not the actual clothing enfolds an absent body; the simulated bar graph of "Potestas" also masquerades as minimal sculpture, a mediated version of the greeting card shapes the visual framework for "Pecunia."[2] All my material comes from popular sources or, more exactly, what has been called "the everyday." Sentimentality is foregrounded in a way that seems either to justify or to reiterate your comparison of my work with the preoccupations of Jeanne, the maternal protagonist in Guy de Maupassant's novel *Une Vie*. It is a self-indulgent replay of lost moments (the vanishing real, according to Lacan). Perhaps *Interim* illustrates the collector/fetishist you speak of, but I would like to distinguish this from the inverse, the fetishist/collector of *Post-Partum Document*. The maternal reliquary is in some sense esoteric. As is the case with "male" fetishism, it reveals an ambivalent but nevertheless passionate relation to her object a. This is closer to the clinical definition of the term fetish. There is a difference in the kind of object cathexis involved here; insofar as the mother (or woman as spectator in the position of the mother) cathects the trace, she places herself in the real. That is, she refuses the recognition of lack, perhaps only momentarily, in view of the artwork. But it is also important to remember that in psychoanalytic practice this "perversion" would pertain to specific forms of this refusal, something which this visualization can only mimic.

In "Pecunia," the spectator (in the position of the older, postreproductive woman) senses a loss that is more overtly "presentified" in the "collection" of cards or the story's references to domestic objects. She is constituted in a relation of lack. But I think that here the castrating instance, so to speak, is also invoking something more fundamental or archaic. The woman's relation to her "things" is one of inaccessibility. The object is already lost, her desire repressed, because it is her own mother as signifier of The Real Other and not the child-as-phallus that figures as the lost object.

Actually, the two works, taken in their entirety, are not so schematically divided. For instance, as *Post-Partum Document* progresses from appropriated words and gestures to fabricated markings in section six, the fetishist does, in a sense, become a collector. And in *Pecunia,* when the narrative describes, say, the woman's addiction to the "smell of palest blue," the collector clearly slips into the place of the fetishist. So there is always an imbrication of the two terms, but defined in different relations to the representation of feminine sexuality.

EA: You have invoked Michèle Montrelay's notions of "concentricity" and "precocious femininity" to describe the woman's autoconstruction as the phallus (fetish) of the Other's other, her regression to primal fantasies about where the child comes from, her "fix" on the child (or refusal to displace her/him). Could you clarify these terms and arguments as they relate to *Pecunia?* How do they allow us to revise the notion of female fetishism such that it may be defined as:

1. (not) not feminine narcissism
2. (not) not masqueraded castration anxiety
3. (not) not obsessional neurosis.

MK: The reason I said that the term "female fetishism" no longer seems appropriate to me is that I would prefer to think about the way the category "woman" is constructed, to look at the various psychic identities that correspond to different moments (subjective, not chronological) in our lives. If fantasy is the instrument of desire, that is, the means by which the sexual drive is represented in terms of aims and objects, then we could speak of the fantasy of the "young" woman as profoundly narcissistic. She is the phallus; the whole body is phallicized, presented as the imaginary object of the Other's gaze. Fetishism in this case would concern the internalization of the split between being and having. Insofar as she is both subject and object of desire, she takes her own body, a part of it, and fetishizes it; that is to say, it constitutes a libidinal attachment that is the exclusive condition for sexual satisfaction. The "masculine" position is acknowledged or acted out, hence "perverse." On the other hand, the consequence of repressing this position is generally associated with the symptoms that define hysteria.

For the reproductive woman, or "mother," the child is the imaginary object, once a part of her, that comes to her as someone other than herself that she can love, as Freud says, with a "healthy" object love. Ironically, from the beginning, she is occupying the masculine position, that is, the position of the actively desiring subject. The child is the phallus for her. Fetishism here pertains to the separation and the inevitable loss of the child-as-phallus. Her imaginary object is maintained either analytically (feeding) or narcissistically (dressing), that is, by forming the child's functions (feces) or effects (clothes) into substitutes that can be controlled. Just as the fetishist described by Joan Copjec "knows what the other wants," the mother wants the child to be what-she-wants-it-to-be and believes the child wants to be it. Perhaps, when the mother's memorabilia is eroticized not as emblems of desire but as her "piece of reality," we can speak of maternal perversity.

However, what the woman fears losing, beyond the pleasure of the child's body, is the closeness to her mother's body which she experiences in "being like her." According to Michèle Montrelay, it is the fantasy of "having the first object" that produces neurotic anxiety (not necessarily fetishism). This perverse relation to the mother's body is the result of what Montrelay has theorized as "censorship" rather than repression. It allows the woman to retain a "concentric" or archaic oral, anal organization of the drives, but at the same time, it disallows her access to sublimated pleasure.[3]

For the "older" woman there are various substitutes for the child, including philanthropy and pets—I know someone who is sending a birthday card to a friend's dog and who calls her cat "Baby"—as well as the contents and arrangement of the home, and especially her "collection" of precious (but not always valuable) things. She seems to slip along the equation phallus = child in the opposite direction, phallus = feces, suggesting a certain archaizing of the drives. Possibly, in this instance, fetishism represents a fixation of libidinal cathexis with regard to particular objects which she loves as she loved her child or her lover once loved her. (I am thinking of Kienholz,

Edward Kienholz, *The Wait,* 1964–65, Tableau 6 feet and 8 ins. 12 feet and 4 ins. × 6 feet and 6 ins. Gift of The Howard and Jean Lipman Foundation. Collection Whitney Museum of American Art, New York.

Elizabeth Cohen, *Attraction,* 1992,
painted wood, cloth, glass,
hypodermic needle, 74 × 38 × 165
ins. Photo: Stan Schnier.

who evokes this sensibility in his famous tableau, *The Wait*.) Often the pre-occupation with taste, texture, smell, and the eroticization of bodily processes indicates a specific form of perversity, that is, coprophilia.

The repression of this perverse relation to the body produces, on the one hand, the real and imaginary illnesses identified with hypochondria and, on the other, the excessive order, cleanliness, attention to detail that signals coprophobia. (Here, I might compare *The Wait* with a work like Elizabeth Cohen's *Attraction*, which provokes a strong sense of this psychic inversion.) In "Character and Anal Eroticism," Freud defines it as a "reaction-formation against what is unclean and disturbing and should not be part of the body."[4]

EA: In the same essay Freud also linked coprophilia to the love of (filthy) lucre:

> Wherever the archaic way of thinking has prevailed or still prevails, in the old civilizations, in myths, fairy tales, superstition, in unconscious thinking, in dreams and in neuroses, money has been brought into the closest connection with filth.[5]

Just as this passage from Freud functioned as a significant intertext for Sandor Ferenczi's essay "The Ontogenesis of the Interest in Money," so Ferenczi's essay became a particularly important catalyst for you in the production of "Pecunia." Following Freud, Ferenczi speaks of childish anal retention in terms of the desire to hoard "dejecta" as so many "savings" for the future.[6] "Civilization," of course, prohibits the accumulation of excrement itself but sanctions its sanitized substitutes—sand, putty, rubber, and later, money. Ferenczi calls these material samples of deodorized and dehydrated filth "copro-symbols." Your work has always seemed to evince a fascination with copro-symbols.

MK: Well, not exactly. According to Ferenczi, money, specifically, is the supreme copro-symbol, but in "Pecunia" the woman's relation to money is shown to be problematic. She is configured with money only insofar as she herself is an object of exchange (i.e., the phallus for the other). As the narrative suggests, she signs the check "without conviction." Her signature fades, something fails at the point of entering into that system of exchange as subject of desire. Perhaps it is the difference between what Ferenczi called "intrinsic value" and "measurable value." In general (but by no means exclusively), the former characterizes the woman's relationship to things. Men, for instance, have collections—stamps, cars, art, and so on—that add up in financial terms, while women collect items of sentimental worth. In "Mater," you may recall the "red Porsche" that features in the classified ad. It has no meaning for the mother except as signifier of someone else's desire. The last panel says, "She only wanted them to be happy." So I would say that the proximity for the woman of her mother's body, its affective force, constitutes a certain block or failure in the process of repression, and coprophilia is the symptomatic consequence. At another level though, you could say that the artwork is the sanitized version of this symptomology, and in that sense, like money, could be called a copro-symbol.

EA: The ensuing observation is part of my own response to the last two questions posed. In the "Conju" section of "Pecunia," the housewife cleans, throwing away tickets, receipts, and lists, "removing the sallow wreath encrusted on the toilet bowl," and dreaming in the flashy cipher (readily traceable to Freud's famous Glanz auf der Nase) of polished oak floors, scalloped tiles, a porcelain sink. All these controlled and sparkling surfaces recall the passion for Meissen porcelain afflicting Bruce Chatwin's fictional character Utz. Utz suffers from Porzellankrankheit ("porcelain sickness"), much as "Pecunia"'s allegorical spouse suffers from housewife's psychosis. Utz reminds us that the word porcelain derives etymologically from porcella ("little pig"), referring to the resemblance of a pig's back to the upper surface of the Venus shell. Of course, now thoughts turn to Botticelli's *Venus* rising out of her shell. Perhaps "Pecunia" similarly enshrines the goddess of love in a temple bedecked with hygienic appliances. The housewife's garden is, after all, blessed with an "insipid cupid pissing in a seashell."

MK: "Conju" is the most striking example of what I would call the coprophobic Imaginary. The wife's sublime (inaccessible) thing is invoked by the repeated phrase, "it could be perfect." In another case she is "sur-

Mary Kelly, *Interim,* Part II: "Pecunia,"
1989, screenprint on galvanized
steel, 16 × 16½ × 11½ ins.
Collection Vancouver Art Gallery.

Detail, "Pecunia."

rounded by an arc of abstinent light," her clean house provoking the consummate ecstasy of a Saint Teresa. This, however, is not perverse. It is the reaction against the repression of anal eroticism and the subsequent formation of what Freud called the "anal character," notably the obsessional tendency that he ungraciously dubbed "housewife's psychosis."

EA: How does this coprophilic or coprophobic "archaizing of the drives" erupt into your figuration of the bourgeois woman inscribed within the claustrophobic socius of the family?

MK: The "bourgeois" woman, as you say, is not really represented in "Pecunia." None of the characters have financial security in that sense. Their problems with money are real, but their symptomatic relation to them is a consequence, perhaps, of this archaizing of the drives. "Filia" is a key series in this regard. The daughter was not brought up to think of herself as a breadwinner but nevertheless finds herself supporting both spouse and child. It should also be noted how frequent this is now. The claustrophobic, single-income, wife-at-home family does not exist and perhaps, as Marx maintained so long ago, never did, except for a minority.

In "Filia" the reaction of one character upon spending the last of her savings is, "he doesn't love me." This "irrationality" points to a psychic structure which underpins the social/sexual division which has produced this startling statistic: women own less than 1 percent of the world's wealth.

For both the boy and the girl, Freud maintains that anal eroticism provides a narcissistic pleasure in something that was once a part of the body, namely, feces. And for both, there is the contiguous belief that babies are produced in the same way. Then, during the phallic phase, the boy's penis is also seen to be detachable in fantasy, and Freud suggests that for the girl the clitoris assumes a similar function. He points out that castration constitutes a threat to this narcissistic integrity of the body, but whereas it ends the Oedipus complex for the boy, it only initiates it for the girl along the lines of the now-infamous equation penis = baby. Since pregnancy is infrequent and late, the wish is deferred but intensely cathected and, I would suggest, intimately linked to the tendency to coprophilia in women. The association of fecal production with reproduction persists and underlines the significance of menses in adolescence. For the boy, involvement in reproduction is conceptualized as loss and sublimated as the "father's gift" at a much earlier stage. Because the penis is his stake in the representation of lack, you could say he has already entered into an abstract system of exchange—phallus = gift = money, status, and so on—an infinite and interminable sliding of the signified, as Lacan insists. But the woman identifies with the child as someone who was once a part of her. She has waited for the phallus to be given to her, never completely decathecting the eroticism of the anal stage and never effectively repressing the maternal body. Her achievements are tentative or temporary, that is to say, in addition to the project of mothering. So, when the children grow up, and especially with the onset of menopause, a certain representation of the feminine body (Montrelay's concentric, oral, anal schema) is posed as the woman's stake in representation. Phallocentricity here becomes the route to sublimated pleasure. This is true even if the woman has chosen not to have a child, because at this moment she realizes, this is really it!

So what makes this delayed Oedipal passage finally possible? Clearly it happens for most women. I think it has something to do with the girl's pre-Oedipal relation to the father. The familiar emphasis is on the symbolic dimension of the paternal metaphor. For instance, the child is given the father's name, the mother invokes it, the ego internalizes it, and the Law prevails. But what is the man's relationship to paternity beyond (or before) giving the name? Julia Kristeva suggests that there are two forms of primary identification—one projective (maternal) and the other introjective (paternal). The latter concerns a libidinal object, which is taken into the self already constituted as a phallic ideal. So, the father is both body and name, desire and meaning. Perhaps the equation money = filth should be prefaced with another, feces = body of the father. The main point here is that for the girl it is the remaking of this imaginary father, that is, taking his place or creating it within language, which defines "sublimational possibility." The phallocentric organization of the drives constitutes a kind of precondition for this. On the other hand, a denial of the imaginary father seems to be psychically linked to anal sadism. For women, this is usually expressed as a reaction which takes the form of overprotectiveness and sentimentality. Remaking the imaginary father is, I think, also instrumental in undoing a certain anxiety for women which is attached to the unconscious fear of being "like a man." And this I believe is the crisis for the older woman who, in "Filia," is described in the position of the father's precocious child in the final place which says, "Someday she wanted to write a book."

EA: In taking up in your logo Ferenczi's suppression of the "non" in "Pecunia non olet," you seem to be emphasizing the repression of anal eroticism within capitalism, its preference for *argent sec,* the "dry" (paper) currency that has come to replace primitive barter and, for that matter, the stickiness of real coins, within the sphere of global financial transactions. In alluding to the lurking threat of dirt's eternal return, you seem to be implying that capitalism, once demystified and desublimated, "stinks," even though it no longer "smells."

Do Freud and Marx converge in "Pecunia" through fantasms of commodified desire, or do you see the psychoanalytic and materialist fetish as anchored in definitions of value (libidinal surinvestment versus exchange value) so fundamentally separate that they ultimately fail to reward any effort at discursive cross-contamination?

MK: In *The History of Sexuality,* when Michel Foucault defines the process of "desublimation" as one that channels rather than represses sexuality, he does not mean that sexuality is repressed for economic reasons but that it is controlled through circuits of the economy. The family, for instance, does not restrain sexuality but provides a support for it. In "Pecunia," the four sections—"Mater," "Conju," "Soror," "Filia"—survey "forms of alliance" as Foucault described concerns of kinship, names, possession, and so on. Each section represents a set of social relations that the woman is designated to fulfill (or not): the agencies of mother, daughter, sister, wife. More important, because these relationships are "saturated with desire," I am trying to trace the way a psychic economy is ciphered through them. In other words, as Foucault insists, the alliance is linked to the economy not only as a contract for the transmission of wealth but also through a body that produces and consumes. So, the logo "Pecunia non olet" refers both to the materialist fetish—trademark, seal of authority, insignia of desire—and to the psychoanalytic fetish, that is, to the specific history of that discourse, to definitions of the perverse subject. Ferenczi is the obvious reference here. Although Foucault was neither a Freudian nor a Marxist, his works perhaps provide the conditions of existence for a cross-contamination of the two discourses.

EA: Could you elaborate on how parts of "Pecunia" define a "perverse" subject?

MK: In its representation of the woman as perverse, "Soror" is important not only because the character transgresses the heterosexual imperative ("She wanted her and she wanted all of her clothes") but mostly because it questions the psychoanalytic injunction to define the feminine on the side of repression by mocking the conventions of so-called perversity. This mockery may be heard in the phrase, "She decided to put on her chain bracelet, lace anklets, and the like and live complexly a little longer."

EA: Soror's bric-a-bracomania (her fondness for kitsch objets d'art) poses another question concerning the aesthetic and class tensions surrounding the "high" representation of "low" art. How would you compare your work to that, say, of Jeff Koons? (I am thinking specifically here of his large-scale porcelain model of Michael Jackson and pet.) Does it contain a politics of bad taste?

MK: Yes, but the difference between my work and the tendency Koons represents concerns the degree of formal mediation, the conditions of exhibition, and the question of audience. Koons appropriates the low-art genre of one class for the amusement and consumption of another. This audience, more privileged in the economic sense, is consequently able to appreciate the criticality of his displacement. Perhaps the differences between the two types of audiences would take us back to Ferenczi's distinction between two types of collections, one based on intrinsic and the other on measurable value. *Interim* recuperates a stigmatized popular culture of sentimentality, but the approach is ethnographic and inclusive, that is, the audience for the work is included as the subject of it and the subjectivity the work parodies does not exclude my own.

Formally, the dimensions and typography ironically restate the style and humor of generic greeting cards but do not literally reproduce them. The galvanized steel invokes, but does not simulate, the look of sentiment. And in terms of presentation, there is an emphasis on intratextuality or cross-referencing among the sections rather than the perception of discrete objects.

EA: Ferenczi implies that the sensual deprivation induced by odorless capital is compensated by for a surcharge of visual or aural pleasure. Art, as visual pleasure, in this sense trades on money's lack. Ferenczi argues: "The eye takes pleasure at the sight of their [the coins'] luster and color, the ear at the metallic clink, the sense of touch at play with the round smooth disks, only the sense of smell comes away empty." Do you see "Pecunia" as embodying this inverse ratio between visual pleasure and odorless capital?

MK: The surcharge of visual and aural pleasure . . . you could say the luster of the galvanized surface and the metallic clink of the steel . . . has another function. For the woman as spectator, the invocatory and olfactory residue is shaped, metaphorically, into a material presence. So possibly the archaic, coprophilic (or phobic) imaginary is thrown into relief so to speak, as a sort of trompe l'oeil. In this sense, the work trades on woman's lack, that is, femininity masquerading as lack. "Sending it up" is at the same time setting it at a distance. By taking herself out of circulation she, the spectator, is no longer the object of exchange but the subject or author of the transaction.

EA: Hal Foster's discussion of Dutch still lifes—historic loci of mediation between the gilded dazzle of the commodity and the transparently shining value of the artistic "masterpiece"—seems relevant here.[8] In your reading of "Pecunia," is the spectator's "glance" the vehicle for (critically) eliding the gleam of the domestic icon with the embossed finish of the work's galvanized steel surfaces?

MK: Well, I would like to say . . . eliding the gleam of your polished statement with my desire for the perfect viewer . . . Yes.

Notes

"The Smell of Money: Mary Kelly in Conversation with Emily Apter," published in *Fetishism as Cultural Discourse,* eds. Emily Apter and William Pietz (Ithaca: Cornell University Press, 1993), pp. 348–362. Used by permission of Cornell University Press.

1. Mary Kelly, *Post-Partum Document* (London and Boston: Routledge and Kegan Paul, 1983), xvi.

2. For the texts of "Pecunia" (published separately), see Mary Kelly, *Pecunia Non Olet* (New York: Top Stories, 1989).

3. Michèle Montreley, *L'ombre et le nom: Sur la feminite* (Paris: Minuit, 1977), in particular, the section titled "Recherches sur la feminite," 57–81. For an English translation, see "Inquiry into Femininity," trans. Parveen Adams, *m/f,* no. 1 (1978): 83–101.

4. Sigmund Freud, "Character and Anal Eroticism" (1909), in standard edition, vol. 9, trans. James Strachey (London: Hogarth Press, 1968), p. 172.

5. Ibid., p. 174.

6. Sandor Ferenczi, "The Ontogenesis of the Interest in Money," in *First Contributions to Psycho-analysis,* trans. Ernest Jones (London: Hogarth Press, 1952), p. 321.

7. Ibid., p. 327.

8. Hal Foster, "The Art of Fetishism: Notes on Dutch Still Life," *Fetishism as Cultural Discourse,* pp. 251–265.

(P)age 49: On the Subject of History

Page 49 is referred to in the "Historia" section of the exhibition *Interim*. It is central to the visual exegesis of the installation and to the argument I am about to make here, but it does not, in fact, exist.[1] Let me explain. "Historia" takes the form of minimal sculptures that resemble four large books. Stainless steel pages unfold to display a montage of image/text screened onto oxide panels. Mimicking the galleys of a generic newspaper or magazine layout, they imply, not the finished work of an heroic narrative, but the metaphor of making history. On the left, the upper register repeats the fragmented image of an unknown suffragette. Part cliché, part memento mori, she replaces Charcot's hysteric with the spectacle of women in the political theater of the 1900s. Below, the metonym VIVA traverses the pages, prompting the viewer to complete a phrase, remember a moment, an event, or an incident of the 1960s. On the right, in the first column, the narrative begins with an emotive reference to 1968, but the meaning of this reference changes for the different speakers who describe themselves respectively as twenty-seven, twenty, fourteen, and three in that historic year. The second column appears as a quote insert, but does not refer to the original story. Instead it elaborates the subjective reflection of the first speaker throughout. In the third column, a slapstick send-up of the older generation breaks abruptly with the nostalgia of the quote sequence. Furthermore, it is presented without a beginning or an end, simply continued from or on the next (p)age, (the page numbers 40–49 are the approximate ages, in 1990, of the women who were active in 1968), and 49, of course, never comes. So, in effect, the absent page projects the narrative into the imaginary space of the spectator. The space of reading, not literally but figuratively in a field of associations, is always to be continued in the present. What interests me, above all, is that I, too, am included in that space, and it is from there, on page 49, where I am situated as another reader rather than a privileged interpreter of the text, that I have asked myself the most important questions concerning the implications of the piece.

First, what view of history is proposed here? From the perspective of page 49, I see two distinct concepts of history being negotiated in *Interim*. One is genealogical, that is, constructive in the sense of description and analysis which applies specifically to Part II: "Historia," where the past is constituted as a narrative with definitive inclusions and exclusions. The other, archaeological in the sense of layered discontinuities, is viewed across the work as a whole—its separate sections, different themes, diverse media—which posits a history without chronology, positions, or answers. This is not a linear history, not, for example, Fredric Jameson's periodization of the 1960s where "the new social and political categories—(the colonized, race, marginality, gender and the like)" appear bracketed in an infinite and indecipherable series, one eclipsing the other without consolidation until the classic Marxist paradigm of class can reestablish a totality.[2] My inclination is more toward Julia Kristeva's nonlinear schema—she calls it "monumental time"—in which the different moments of feminism—legal (discourse of equality), cultural (representations of sexuality/identity), ethical (potentialities of difference)—would be seen as parallel discourses rather than transitional phases.[3] There would not be a continual displacement of marginal discourses *and the like* by a master narrative, but an accumulation of knowledges about the social. This is also why I would maintain that there is no such thing as feminist art. There is only an art informed by different feminisms. If a work of art subscribes to a particular ideology uncritically, then it risks reinventing a social totality that disallows the others to emerge from their bracketed identities as the new subjects of history.

This leads to my second question: what is meant by identity in *Interim?* Reading between the lines of the fictive page, I find a distinction unfolding in the work between identification as a psychically determined process on the one hand and identity as a social and political voice on the other. For instance, Part I: "Corpus" focuses on the woman's narcissistic identification with an image, a psychic process that underlines the difficulty of femininity

Mary Kelly, *Interim,* Part III:
"Historia," 1989, silkscreen, oxidized
steel, stainless steel on wood base,
4 sections 61 × 36 × 29 ins. each.
Collection Mackenzie Art Gallery,
Regina. Photo: Courtesy Postmasters
Gallery, New York.

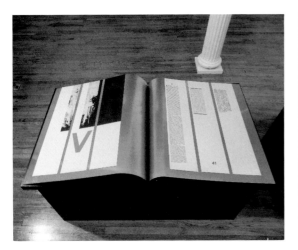 

and points to the hysteric's dilemma. Identity is never fixed, yet it is, in a sense, framed, as the work suggests, by posing or repositioning the garments which act as surrogates for the mimetic body within discursive systems such as medicine, fashion, or romantic fiction. By alluding to the look of familiar greeting cards, Part II: "Pecunia" presents the woman, her things, and the artwork itself as commodity, fetish, gift. In fantasy, there would seem to be as many forms of identification as there are objects of desire. But, because the family is the privileged term of this *mise-en-scène,* desire is, in a way, circumscribed for the woman by the social agency she fulfills (or does not) as mother, daughter, sister, wife; and identity is designated as a consequence of that exchange. Similarly, in Part IV: "Potestas," there is a diagrammatic representation of the woman's social status, her statistical identity so to speak, in the form of a bar graph; but there is also the description of a more ambivalent relation to power in the elliptical narratives that cut across it.

In writing the stories for "Corpus," "Pecunia," and "Potestas," I used the first- or the third-person singular. But, in Part III: "Historia," when the characters give their accounts of the different phases of feminism, they often slip into the first-person plural. There is something evidenced at the level

of primary identification which is already constitutive of a collective or political rather than personal identity: what I might call the function of the
nous, playing on Lacan's reference to the *je.* In his exposition of the mirror
stage, the infant's jubilant assumption of an image precipitates the formation
of the *moi,* an ideal ego which in turn gives way to the social function of
the I. The subject emerges as an effect of language. And the ego, no longer
replete in itself, embarks on the Imaginary's course of setting up Ideals elsewhere.[4] Significantly, this fictitious but necessary structure is the basis for all
secondary identifications and perhaps also underpins the uncertain destiny
of *we.* If a collective identity is formed by replaying the initial moment of
gestalt as an image of political empowerment or totalization, then, at the
same time it produces the alienating effect of a fundamental misrecognition
(the feeling of imperfect fit we experience even at the height of our most
passionate support for a campaign). But, following the imaginary trajectory
of page 49, what does this communal enunciation signify within the specific
context of emerging feminism in the 1960s? And, how do we represent our
history now?

Arrest of a suffragette, London, 1905, artist's source material for "Historia." Courtesy Bettman Archive.

The political identity of the early movement was founded on the notion that women were radically other: excluded from language, barred access to pleasure. Lacan summed it up with the notorious proposition: "The woman does not exist." In order to come into being, to exist, as it were, a transcendental expression of association was required: "We are all alike." But, it was the unconscious dimension of this assertion, the desire to identify with someone who was like us, which more fully explained the powerful emotive force of slogans such as: "Women of the world unite." Unbarring, appropriating the universal term for woman was the precondition for the existence of a movement, its moment of imaginary capture. In the arena of political organization, the effect was to disavow hierarchy, deny conflict, and assume mastery in the guise of our collective bodies, our symbiotic selves.

One of the quotation inserts in "Historia" describes the ecstasy of a collaborative writing project. In a mode suggestive of hysterical identification, the group, seized by the discourse of the Other—the woman who writes well—claims her work as their own. Another insert, in which a young woman organizer is referring to working-class women at a union meeting, begins, "They looked indescribably tired, in a way anonymous, perhaps middle-aged or appeared to be even if they weren't." First, the Other is projected as a figure of abjection, that is, not like us. Yet, when one of the women starts to move in time with the music in the background, the narrator is overwhelmed by feelings of empathy. Interjecting the Other as an image of herself, the quote ends, "And like us she loved to dance."

Again, the account of a meeting in 1970 between representatives of the women's movement and an official delegation of women from Vietnam, initially, revolves around terms signifying separation and distance: "The room was cold, they looked at us it seemed without expression." Only when the Vietnamese women begin to talk about their personal experiences of the war is it possible for the group of feminists to identify with them. The Other is constructed as victim and through a vicarious relation to their suffering, incorporated as the same. Narcissistic overidentification is central, in my view, to both the pleasure and the problem of identity formation. For instance, by erasing difference in the field of the racial or ethnic Other, on the basis of gender the white feminists have avoided the objectification of the Vietnamese women, but at the same time, symptomatically they have

Symposium, *On the Subject of History,* held in conjunction with the exhibition *Interim,* New York, 1990, Laura Mulvey and Mary Kelly.

On the Subject of History, New York, 1990. Symposium panelists Isaac Julien, Griselda Pollock, Parveen Adams, Emily Apter, and Hal Foster.

obliterated their autonomy and, effectively, their power. I say symptomatically, not only because what is repressed, that is, differences among women, will return in another form, but also because in the unconscious, unity, that is, the Real (community of women), must be endlessly reconstituted by desire as a lost object. In the final quote insert, the narrator reflects nostalgically on the significance of the last issue of a magazine which has represented her particular tendency and generation within the women's movement. "I remember thinking that it marked the end of an important era. There was a sense of loss; loss of collective voice, of body politic, and, in a way, of pleasure, I mean the pleasure of identity formed in the company of other women."

Here, the formation of political identity reveals, I believe, something similar to the psychic structuring of nationality. Slavoj Žižek has observed that our enjoyment as a nation, our "thing" as he calls it, is conceived as inaccessible to the Other and at the same time threatened.[5] The unity of feminism is not threatened by men but by a different generation of women who "don't understand"—postfeminists and others. Our enjoyment as a movement is stolen, displaced by the new social, racial, ethnic, and sexual politics of the present. The mythology of feminism, *our* history, comes into being at the moment it is left behind. But this is not the same thing as writing/thinking the histories of feminisms, nor is the impossibility of unity a cause for strategic pessimism. And this returns me to the imperative of page 49.

The slapstick fiction of the series "Continued on the Next Page" cuts across the reality effect of the biographical narratives and the nostalgia of the quote inserts by sending up the way one generation of feminists denies the activism of another. Implicitly, then, the missing page would argue against a privileged or ideal moment of feminist politics; but it would not necessarily relegate feminist theory, the discourse of psychoanalysis for instance, to the realm of orthodoxy. Rather, it would be seen to have continued relevance within the specific sites of struggle which "Historia" traces through the 1970s. Moreover, I think, the alienating effect of the absent ending might suggest that another kind of misrecognition reminiscent of the mirror phase, structures not only the formation of political identity, but also its dissolution. The image of unity is always threatened by division and disarray. At the same time, this instance of ambivalence is generative, creating the condition of possibility for questioning and repositioning and forming not simply new, but instrumental subjects of a certain age.

Notes

(P)age 49: On the Subject of History," published in *New Feminist Criticism,* ed. Katy Deepwell (Manchester: Manchester University Press, 1995). First presented at the symposium held in conjunction with the exhibition *Interim,* Vancouver Art Gallery, 1990.

1. Mary Kelly, *Interim,* exhibition and catalogue, New Museum of Contemporary Art, New York, 1990.

2. Fredric Jameson, "Periodizing the 60s," in *The 60s without Apology* (Minneapolis: University of Minnesota Press, 1984), pp. 178–209.

3. Julia Kristeva, "Women's Time," in *Feminist Theory: A Critique of Ideology,* trans. Alice Jardine and Henry Blake (Chicago: University of Chicago Press, 1982), pp. 31–53.

4. Jacques Lacan, "The Mirror Stage as Formative of the Function of the I," in *Ecrits,* trans. Alan Sheridan (London: Tavistock, 1977), pp. 1–7.

5. Slavoj Žižek, "Eastern Europe's Republic of Gilead," *New Left Review* (1990): 50–62, 189.

That Obscure Subject of Desire: An Interview with Mary Kelly by Hal Foster

Hal Foster: The conceptual structure of *Interim* is delineated in its section titles: "Corpus," "Pecunia," "Historia," and "Potestas." As well as your inquiry into psychoanalysis, they suggest different discourses—Marxist, Foucauldian—even different disciplines—anthropology, history. Why these four terms, and in this relationship?

Mary Kelly: In the five years before I began the production of *Interim,* I developed an archive of informal conversations with women on the subject of aging, and these were the recurring themes. There is obviously a Foucauldian methodology implied in the notion of archive. I wanted to know how the various themes of this interim moment in a woman's life were constituted as discourses and, more ambitiously, I wanted to look at the formation of these discourses within the historical field of feminism. So, I guess "Corpus" recapitulates the debates of the 1970s, which resulted in a move away from an emphasis on positive images to a psychoanalytically informed concern with spectatorship. Then, "Historia" provides an overview and reflects a preoccupation of the early 1980s with the question of "agency," or—from a political perspective—the problem of deciphering the relationship between social and psychic moments of oppression. "Pecunia" revives the topic of commodity fetishism—woman-as-consumer, and all that—which originated in the 1960s, but it transforms it into a question of her desire. This reflects my interest in the psychoanalytic concept of fetishism and its implications for women. And "Potestas," I think, acts again as an overview by placing questions of money, property, or position in a

Mary Kelly, *Interim,* 1984–89
installation view, New Museum of
Contemporary Art, New York, 1990.

wider context. It parodies a kind of biological, sociological, even psychological, binarism in Western culture—a schema of difference which perpetuates sexual or social division. What I wanted to look at, in particular, was the way power reproduces this division in language—in visual representation. I hope this section takes the debate into the 1990s by reassessing what we have or, as it seems, what we haven't achieved in terms of empowerment.

Foster: Visually, *Interim* is a complex work, not only in its play of image and text, but in its repertoire of sign systems. You make references to popular culture, though not in the guise of catatonic representations of commodity images. Instead, you engage the different discursivities of everyday forms. "Corpus" alludes to fashion images, medical diagrams, romance fiction, and its plexiglass panels have the scale of small billboards; "Pecunia" plays on the language of classified ads, genres of personal fiction, and the kinds of riddles and puns found in greeting cards (these also seem to have suggested the size and display of its galvanized steel units). What other languages of everyday life are figured in *Interim,* especially in "Historia" and "Potestas"?

Kelly: You've covered "Corpus" and "Pecunia" so, to continue, "Historia" refers to generic newspaper or magazine layouts—galleys, pasteups . . . the metaphor of "making history." It takes the form of very large stainless steel pages, with images and texts screened on oxide panels. Laura Trippi suggested a reference to Kiefer which was interesting because it is precisely the heroic notion of a nation which I'm contesting here, with this critical history of an oppositional movement. Perhaps it's my version of his *Women of the Revolution.* "Potestas" is an extended pun on the sociological jargon of measurement. Its three-dimensional graph may be comic in its familiarity at one level—actually, at first glance it probably looks like minimal sculpture—but on another, it refers to the graph in a Derridian sense, a visual parallel to the schema of phonemic oppositions, as well as a trope for sexual difference.

Foster: In *Post-Partum Document,* you visualized and analyzed the mother-child relationship. In *Interim,* you address a particular stage in the lives of

Interim, Part IV: "Potestas," 1989, etching, brass, and mild steel, 14 units, 100 × 114 × 2 ins. overall dimensions. Collection Helsinki City Art Museum.

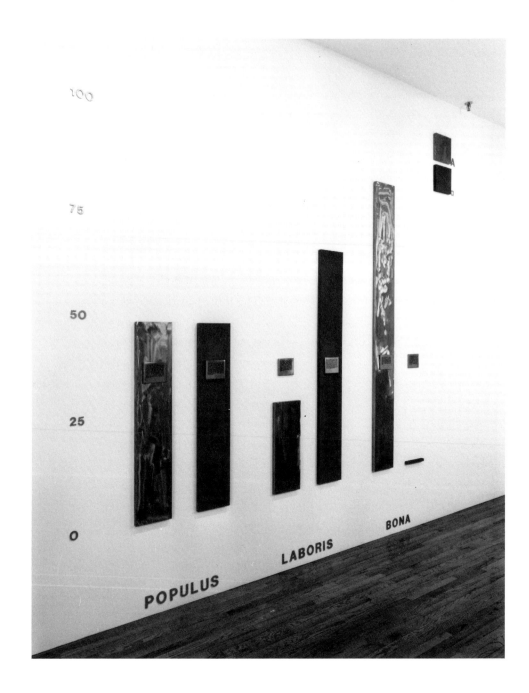

women, a stage beyond reproduction, and putatively beyond desire (the given positions of femininity, you suggest), when the aging process comes to the fore. There is, then, a return to the body here, as announced directly in "Corpus," and, indeed, the posing of the apparel in its image panels refers to the "passionate attitudes" of hysteria defined by J. M. Charcot. Now, in a 1987 text on *Interim,* you implied that the female body was elided in the shift from the visual theater of Charcot to the talking cure of Freud, a shift from looking to listening which marked the beginning of psychoanalysis. Was the female body elided again in the critical focus on the patriarchal unconscious in feminist discourse of the 1970s? In *Interim,* do you relate this moment of elision to the foundational one of psychoanalysis? And, if *Interim* is involved in a return to the body, how are we to think of this?

Kelly: First, it's primarily within the medical discourse that the visible body was eclipsed, as you say, by new sciences like biophysics. But Freud's own discovery of the unconscious can be included in that process, too. I would say that in our time, the repressed—that is, the biological body—has returned as spectacle in the form of advertising. This is the new theater where the hysterical posturing of women proliferates. In both *Post-Partum Document* and *Interim,* I've problematized the image of the woman not to promote a new form of iconoclasm but to make the spectator turn from looking to listening. I wanted to give a voice to the woman, to represent her as the subject of the gaze. And, second, *Interim* proposes not one body but many bodies, shaped within a lot of different discourses. It doesn't refer to an anatomical fact or to a perceptual entity, but to the dispersed body of desire. I think of Lacan's description of erotogenic zones as including the phoneme, the gaze, the nothing, and, in this sense, I feel that the installation should be an event where the viewer gathers a kind of corporeal presence from the rhythm or repetition of images, rather than viewing the work from the fixed vantage point of traditional perspective. Finally, people often say that the body as a visual image is absent in my work. I would argue against such a limited definition of image. The visual field, after all, includes not only the register of iconic signs, but the index and symbol, as well. This heterogeneity of the sign—Norman Bryson calls it the "aniconic image"—is crucial for me because it can have the effect of displacing the female spectator's "hysterical" identification with the male voyeur. So, writing for me is obviously more than what is said. It's also a means of invoking the texture of speaking, listening, touching—Lacan suggests that the invocatory drives are, in a sense, closer to the unconscious—a way of visualizing, not valorizing, what is assumed to be outside of seeing. This is done in order to distance the spectator from the anxious proximity of her body—ultimately, the mother's body—the body too close to see, which is linked at the level of the unconscious to an archaic organization of drives and which bars the woman's access to sublimated pleasure.

Foster: The primary focus of feminist-psychoanalytical film practice and theory in the last decade has been on the question of feminine spectatorship. Theoretically, this has suggested a move away from questions of voyeurism and fetishism, the staples of the patriarchal unconscious, toward questions of hysteria, masochism, and melodrama. Your work has been associated with a related trajectory in art practice and theory. In particular, what is your aim in this archaeological recovery of hysteria? Why is it theoretically important at a time when it is clinically almost nonexistent? Incidentally, the surrealists were also interested—though obviously in a different way—in hysteria; Breton and Aragon called it "the greatest poetic discovery of the end of the nineteenth century."

Kelly: Well, it's exactly the continuing romance of hysteria that interests me. Lacan—who was, at one time, very close to the surrealists—talked about psychoanalysis as the "hystericization of discourse," and posed analysis against mastery, and hysteria against knowledge. And then, there are the women who were expelled, not from Charcot's theater, but from Lacan's *école freudienne*—I'm thinking here of Luce Irigaray. For them, the hysteric exposes the institution's fundamental misogyny; that is, woman founds the theory of psychoanalysis and sustains it by making the exchange of ideas among male theorists possible. So, hysteria, marginalized in one domain, becomes central in another . . . which is, of course, feminist theory. Just to give you some examples besides Irigaray: someone like Monique Plaza says hysteria is the revolt against patriarchy; Michèle Montrelay calls it the blind spot of psychoanalysis; Jacqueline Rose points to the problem of sexual difference; and Dora's film collective claims that the hysteric reveals the analyst's symptom and so becomes, in effect, the basis for a critique of Freud. I don't think *Interim* is an archaeological attempt to recover the hysteric-as-poet or dissident, but to see her more as a theoretical symptom within contemporary work.

Foster: In *Interim,* as in *Post-Partum Document,* you point to gaps or soft spots in psychoanalysis—if these are not too problematic as metaphors—and yet you are generally perceived to be devoted to the work of Freud and Lacan. How would you characterize your negotiation of their theories?

Kelly: Devoted would not be the appropriate term as far as I'm concerned. I have a rather mercenary attitude toward these texts and use their insights—usually into male fantasy—to articulate their "lack" . . . problematic metaphor intended . . . of ability to deal with feminine sexuality. Their work on fetishism is a prime example. Also, I don't rely on Freud and Lacan exclusively. In "Corpus," the central thesis revolves around Montrelay's work on the feminine body and Millot's paper, "The Feminine Super-ego." "Pecunia's" logo, "Pecunia Olet," is taken from Ferenczi's work of the same title on the psychoanalysis of money. And Kristeva's influence seems to me evident everywhere.

Foster: In different ways and to different degrees in "Corpus" and "Pecunia," as in the *Document,* the feminine is located in the positions of mother, wife, sister, and daughter. ("Mater," "Conju," "Soror," and "Filia" are, in fact, the section titles of "Pecunia.") These positions are no more separable in your work than they are in social life, yet you seem to privilege the maternal term. Could you comment on this dominance in relation to your theoretical interests?

Kelly: Certainly *Post-Partum Document* is a work that deals explicitly with the mother-child relationship. In a way, maternal femininity seems almost synonymous with the notion of womanliness. It's what I'd call the "ideal moment," in that the woman, in relation to her child, is constituted as the actively desiring subject, without transgressing the socially accepted definition of her as "mother." But this poses an immediate contradiction. Maternity is not passive and consequently not "feminine." Also, what happens when the child grows up? Is "being a woman" just a brief moment in her life? Clearly, there is a fundamental instability in the category woman, which "Corpus" takes up in exchanges between men and women and among women themselves in the narratives. In a way, I suppose they repeat the hysteric's question: Am I a man or am I a woman? Even when the figure of the mother appears, for example, in "Extase," she is seen to be masquerading; the happy family is really a farce. In "Pecunia," I've decentered the maternal paradigm quite noticeably with the sections' titles. The emphasis here is on the whole set of social relations implicated in the designations: mother, daughter, sister, wife. I was thinking of the way Foucault describes the family as conveying "the law through the deployment of sexuality" and "the economy of pleasure through the regime of alliance"—or kinship. The stories in "Pecunia" caricature the pathologies he describes as being the outcome of this interchange: nervous woman, frigid wife, precocious child, and perverse adult. The latter is especially important because, in terms of object choice, it cuts across the heterosexual assumption—something I felt wasn't clear enough in "Corpus." So, in response to the famous or infamous Lacanian question, "What does woman want?" "Pecunia" might be asking its own question: Are there as many forms of identification as there are demands? But the problem for women—and the one that emerges as the crisis when maternal identity is lost or threatened—is the fragility of the primary identification . . . not with the mother, but the father. Kristeva has suggested that it's the remaking of this imaginary father of the pre-Oedipal phase—being able to take his place within language—that's the basis of "sublimational possibility." The last narrative in the "Filia" sequence signifies exactly that failure to identify with the paternal figure in the woman's symptomatic ambivalence about her economic independence.

Foster: In "Corpus" and "Pecunia," there are more references to the signs of class than in *Post-Partum Document* (though they are certainly there, too). Is this taken further in "Historia" and "Potestas"?

Kelly: Yes, I think so. "Historia," for example, is concerned with social and political, rather than personal, identity. I mean, there are personal accounts of the historical phases of feminism, but the privileged term of enunciation in these narratives is *we*. I wanted to find out how this collective form of address is constituted, how "we" represent "our" histories. This collectivity isn't the seamless entity invoked in slogans like, "Women of the world unite!" The work cuts across this utopian formulation—perhaps a bit too cynically in the slapstick conversations of the "Continued on the Next Page" series—but I think this is a necessary counterpoint to the "reality effect" of the documentary histories and the "nostalgia" of the quotation sequence. One of the consequences of this juxtaposition, which takes the form of a montage of typefaces, is that it problematizes the unity of feminism as an ideology. Even when the point of intersection in the women's stories—there are four, one in each book—is the discourse of psychoanalysis, the meaning of this discourse takes on a specific character depending on the conjuncture in which it emerges for them as a relevant or determining element in their political practice.

Foster: Are questions of ethnicity, of whiteness, also addressed? Or are they of secondary importance in the different historical conjunctures which *Interim* works through?

Kelly: For me, the question of political identity necessarily entails the problem of ethnicity, but that isn't addressed in my work as tokenism; it's taken up around the trajectories of difference—not only sexual difference, but the way white women erase difference in the field of the social or ethnic "other," and, at the same time, vigilantly insist on it when it comes to the other's "Other" . . . I mean white men. But let's go back a minute to the interest in collective identity of the early women's movement. It was founded on the notion that "woman" is radically "other"; excluded from language, barred access to pleasure: Lacan summed it up: "She does not exist." So, to come into being . . . to exist, as it were . . . seemed to require a transcendent form of identification: "We are all alike." Within the arena of political organization, the effect was to deny conflict, to disavow hierarchy. One of the quotations in "Historia" describes the ecstasy of a collective writing project. Seized by the discourse of the other—the woman who writes well—they claim it as their own. In another quotation, the "social other," the abject, is projected and then internalized when, in a description of working-class women at a union meeting, someone begins, "They looked indescribably tired, in a way anonymous, perhaps middle-aged or appeared to be even if they weren't." That is, not like us. Then, she refers to the music in the background, "the chora," which allows her to transform this feeling into its opposite. The piece ends, "And like us, she loved to dance." There is also a quotation about Vietnamese women which revolves at first around terms like "cold" or "without expression," which signify distance, incomprehension, and difference. It's only when the Vietnamese women talk about their own experience of the war that the white women can identify with their suffering; they're constructed as victims and, I think, for us there is a kind of vicarious overidentification here, which obliterates the political imperative to allow specificity and difference without objectification or hierarchy. Frankly, I don't know how that's done, but perhaps this is a beginning.

Foster: *Interim* concerns the desires and fantasies of feminine subjects. How do you regard masculine viewers of your work? How are they positioned by this work? I mentioned to you once that, particularly in front of "Corpus," I felt like an eavesdropper who was sometimes caught, in a flush of shame—like the voyeur, described by Sartre, who is suddenly seen. You mentioned, in reply, "the fourth look." What did you mean?

Kelly: Women, I mean the psychic consequence of the historical existence of a women's movement, the word of the "other" internalized in the place of the Law and the father. She sees you seeing.

Foster: What do you think about the recent investigations of masculinity? What are the problems of "men in feminism," of "me-too-ism," from your point of view? You mentioned once a problem that fascinates me: the reluctance of women to allow the men they love to give up the phallus. What are the feminist investments in "this Other of the other"?

Kelly: I think it's strategically important to say that men can be, are, and have been, feminists. The critique of masculinity—and by this I don't mean exposés of male fantasies about women, but explorations of the power relations between and among men—is comparable to the issue of ethnicity, that is, the taken-for-grantedness of "whiteness." We can't really progress without the "other" side of both of these coins. Now, as for the second part of your question, I can't really answer it, though perhaps I can clarify or complicate it, as the case may be. When I was ruminating over why there was no outcome to the Oedipus complex for the girl, which wasn't ipso facto neurotic, I began to think that perhaps the boy's resolution of this Oedipal drama wasn't so easy, either. I wondered if it would be possible to take Millot's distinctions regarding the masculinity complex for women, and relate them to men. For example, does the woman who fantasizes the possession of the penis parallel the man who acts out its absence in transvestism? Or, is the woman who masquerades as the feminine type—who disguises the lack of a lack, but really makes no demands on her sexual partner—is she comparable to the man who "does what he's got to do?" I mean, what Lacan calls the "male display"; he seems to sense it's a fraud but, in fact, he has no sexual desire for the woman. And, I suppose, you could also take up the woman's desire for the child-as-phallus, and ask what the man's stake is in giving her this "gift?" It seems to me all of this suggests that, for both men and women, demand constructs a rather tentative relation to being or having this phallic term. Of course, no one has it, but I wondered why women seemed resistant to, as you said, letting men relinquish it. It has a parallel in theory, too, because I feel that when we suggest that women have a privileged relation to the mother's body, we are doing more than explaining a different relation to castration, I think we are asserting our difference from men. This assertion seems to point to a certain fear, a fear that's linked, on the one hand, to the desire to be like "them" and, on the other, to the fear of being the same.

Foster: I am intrigued by a comment of Lynne Tillman's (related by Laura Mulvey in your 1986 *Interim* catalogue) that in the narrative of the mother-child relationship in *Post-Partum Document,* theory occupies the position of the father in the Oedipal triangle—the "term" that the mother both refers the child to and struggles against. Is there any truth in this for you? If so, has the position of theory changed in *Interim?* How so?

Kelly: That's interesting. There's a sense in which I did think of *Post-Partum Document* as a kind of secondary revision, in psychoanalytic terms—that is, a rationalization or working through of a difficult experience. You could say this: that theory, like the "third term" of the Oedipal triangle, was the distancing device that made separation from the child possible, but this is simply an analogy. In another sense, though, you could say that psychoanalysis itself became the "third term" in the feminist debate, and provoked a separation from the mother's body—that is, the utopian community of all women—by providing a vantage from which to look at the tentative, constructed nature of femininity and sexuality. The Lacanian diagrams visually represent this "struggle" with theory, which was specific to that historical moment. Now, the terms of the debate have shifted. They're no longer presented as a confrontation between feminism and psychoanalysis, but as a struggle over definitions of feminism and postmodernism. So, the position of theory in *Interim* has changed; it has been assimilated and integrated into an accessible form in the narratives of each section. The question as I saw it when I started this work was how and to what extent had psychoanalysis become another orthodoxy. It now seems evident to me that the political complications of theorizing sexual difference go way beyond this, but I didn't have a position in advance. It's something I worked through, both visually and theoretically, in the making of *Interim.*

Foster: How do you see this "struggle over definitions of feminism and postmodernism?" What are its positions, stakes, and strategies?

Kelly: I'll give you three disparate but, I hope, related examples. "Historia" repeats the image of an unknown suffragette, part cliché, part memento mori, and invokes, in place of the hysterics in Charcot's theater, the spectacle of women in the political "theater" of the early 1900s. Dora's mother again . . . but the implications, I think, are not simply that Freud dismissed his patient's "real" mother . . . yet another gap. He certainly knew of the existence of the women's movement—you can tell by the tone of his address to women in his paper on femininity, and there's his association with Bertha Pappenheim, who was herself an activist—yet there is a refusal to contaminate the new science of psychoanalysis with the issue of feminism. Jacqueline Rose has written a provocative piece about a similar reticence on the part of theorists of postmodernism in our time—Jameson or Habermas, for instance—to acknowledge a certain debt to feminism. Psychoanalytic concepts are applied to questions of sexuality and representation as if the discourse was always there. No reference is made to a specific political formation or to the women writers who initially disrupted the complacency of the structuralist paradigm. Perhaps, like Freud, they've never made their "acquaintance." In the art world, especially, even in postmodern practices of resistance, there has been a tendency in some cases to "mediate" the issues into collectible artifacts. Even among women artists, there seems to be an attempt to obliterate, or at least disguise, any trace of feminist commitment. Politics, not sex, has become the pornographic referent in the field of vision. I'm not saying that art should espouse a particular ideology, but I feel it would be relevant . . . no necessary . . . in the present context, to try to make work that recaptured the historical dimension and the public ambition of the premodern era. I mean this in terms of extended audiences, and not just larger work. I always think of Géricault working on *The Raft of the Medusa,* although that might seem like a strange example.

Foster: No, it's a good one. We might see it now as official art, another of the great nineteenth-century canvases in the Louvre, but, in fact, *The Raft* was "historical" and "public" precisely because it was contestatory; it was a new kind of history painting which criticized the deadly duplicities of the institutions (political, military, and artistic) of the Restoration regime. The question is, where does one locate analogous critiques today? Granted the restrictive artificiality of terms such as "conceptual" and "feminist" art, one could argue that the contemporary critique of art institutions was initiated by the first and transformed by the second. In what way is a critique of such institutions—specifically the commodity form of the art object, its exhibition value—articulated in your work, particularly in *Interim?*

Kelly: I don't believe there can be feminist art, only art informed by different feminisms. The difference lies in how these filter through the work, which is essentially the difference between an appropriation, or colonization, and a "deappropriation," or decolonization, of images of the Other. In my view, decolonization depends on a specific contextualization of the discursive space that surrounds these *objets d'autres*. For example, *Interim* is not simply concerned with imaging the problem of feminine sexuality, but with the historicization of the debates that formed that question in the first place. For me, this approach seems to demand, almost intrinsically, a rupture in the paradigm of single, rather seamless, artifacts. Since the early 1970s, I've worked almost exclusively in the format of extended projects. Each work is divided into sections (*Interim* has four, *Post-Partum Document,* six) and develops over a number of years. Each section in *Interim* engages with a particular institutional discourse: fiction, fashion, and medicine in "Corpus"; the family in "Pecunia"; the media in "Historia"; and social science in "Potestas." These all interact in specific ways within the institutions of art, the museum especially, which are fundamentally split between the demands of education, on the one hand, and those of entertainment, on the other. So, it seems to me that the way to critique the commodity status of the art object may not necessarily be to reproduce it in, what's assumed to be, the critical space of the installation—perhaps this is what's wrong with "the Levine effect"—but to question the very assumption of a spectator who is "supposed to know," meaning also, supposed to buy. I don't think the diversity of positionalities, of spectatorship, can be addressed by a neo-self-referential art of simulation.

Foster: Since its beginnings in Vasari, art history has been discursively bound up with biography. Your work complicates the notion of biography, of the artist-as-subject, radically. Moreover, your projects—with their conversations, notes, graphs, and the like—involve extensive forays into the social, and you have mentioned to me the model of the artist-as-ethnographer. What are the ramifications of this model in general, and in your practice?

Kelly: I suppose in a way my method of working resembles fieldwork—the participant observer keeping notes, writing up the results—but I was thinking more of the "new ethnography" when I said that. It's characterized by two things: an emphasis on the constraints of institutional power, and an interest in forms of experimental writing. This writing, James Clifford says, acknowledges that "identity is conjunctural not essential." So, if I am the indigenous ethnographer of a particular group of women, observing, as it were, the "rituals" of maternity or aging, I'm also, as Clifford points out, "caught between cultures, inauthentic." In the *Document,* as well as in *Interim,* it's the insistent polyvocality in the writing and in the use of media that somehow expresses this. I can think of other artists who use what I would call an ethnographic strategy—Broodthaers, Baumgarten . . . maybe Rollins, Rosler, or Kolbowski—but I am thinking mainly of someone like Hans Haacke. His projects involve extensive research and deploy diverse visual materials in often brilliant institutional critiques. But I've always been troubled by the univocity, by the assumed authority of an artistic or ethnographic presence outside the text. Here I'm not advocating autobiography, but a kind of dialogistic, textual production, in which the historical inscription of the subject describes more than sexual positioning, it questions a particular relation of power. The significance of this attitude, or "model," as you call it, for me is that it leads to work that solicits a certain degree of active engagement in the critique of subjectivity. As for the ramifications in general, well, they're endless.

Note

"That Obscure Subject of Desire: An Interview with Mary Kelly by Hal Foster," in Mary Kelly, *Interim* (exhibition catalogue), The New Museum of Contemporary Art, New York, 1990, pp. 53–62.

V Gender Hybrids

On Display: Not Enough Gees and Gollies to Describe it

> In the case of display usually on the part of the male animal, or in the case of grimacing swelling by which the animal enters the play of combat in the form of intimidation, the being gives of himself, or receives from the other, something that is like a mask, a double, an envelope, a thrown-off skin, thrown off in order to cover the frame of the shield.
>
> Jacques Lacan, *The Four Fundamental Concepts of Psycho-Analysis*

Grimacing, swelling, and swearing "Cut it off and kill it," a nation entered the play of combat in the specific form of intimidation called Desert Storm. On television, I watched the commentators watching the troops watch the spectacle of annihilation, "More fires down there than I can count," said one, ". . . not enough gees and gollies to describe it," mused another realizing that in some profound sense he couldn't see it, could not see the exact spot where the Scud had landed; the place of death, the space of the unconscious. The momentary flashes of charred bodies on retreating buses appeared almost anamorphic, recalling Lacan's reference to the hidden skull in Holbein's painting. Though, what intrigued me at first was not the blind spot, but the gleam of the shield, that is, the facade of American militarism and what it revealed about the pathological structuring of masculinity.

"There is a certain gesture of virility," claims Adorno, "that calls for suspicion." Freud reminds us that the impetus for such gestures is homophobia. And Theweleit points out this psychic disposition in his analysis of the troop as so many polished components in a totality machine. This machine, he says, expresses a certain type of masculinity, a code among men that consolidates other totalities such as the nation.[1] But unlike the protofascist

Freikorps of the thirties, the American military machine of the nineties has a curious flatness. The display of technology, the shiny surface of the shield, is so replete in itself that it produces the individual soldiers as so many unpolished components, unable to camouflage their human frailty, made vulnerable, ambivalent in relation to their role of mastery.

Writing about the Gulf War, Chomsky maintains that the United States, having failed at diplomacy and also having lost its economic dominance, has one thing left: military strength, in fact, a virtual monopoly of force.[2] Yet, there is a certain irony attached to the projection of force in an international context of increasing demilitarization. For me, it suggests that however hard the soldier, male and female, "bust their butts to get it right," it will always be a botched affair.

"The bravura image emerges, but is in some sense also botched." This is how Bryson describes *Charging Chasseur,* Géricault's depiction of an officer's panic. In full regalia, he should embody the machistic spectacle of the grande armée. Instead, he is about to fall. A chasm opens between the actual image and the internalization of the masculine ideal. As a premonitory picture of Napoleon's demise, it also provides an interesting historical parallel to the current crisis of national identity. In my own work, *Gloria Patri,* that painting prompted me to think about the way the installation could set up a scene of mastery and undo it blatantly through mimicry.[3] "Mimicry," according to Lacan, "reveals something insofar as it is distinct from what might be called an itself that is behind it."[4] I'm not suggesting that there is a hegemonic form of masculinity that can be exposed. Rather, I would say that both masculine and feminine identities are transitive, medicated through a set of masks. But something critical is revealed about the character of masculinity when it is staged by women.

Margaret Thatcher is advised by her publicity agent to lower her voice. Patricia Ireland, the president of NOW, announces, "I'm a hybrid." Alexis Smith changes her name from Patti Ann to Alex—"nice and androgynous," she declares. Elizabeth Murray confesses that she has always thought of herself as an asexual gnome. As an artist, I, too, have definitely not wanted to be signified as "woman." Perhaps, this is not simply a professional strategy, but a symptom, an unconscious structure: a name, a voice, a gesture, a skin thrown off to cover the frame of a shield.

Scud missiles, CNN, January 1992.

Mary Kelly, *Gloria Patri*, 1992,
installation view, Herbert F. Johnson
Museum, Cornell University,
screenprint and etching on polished
aluminum, 31 units 20 × 134 × 2⅜
ins. overall. Photo: Kelly Barrie.

I think the extent to which women have internalized the masculine ideal has been ignored. A certain form of precocious femininity has been exorcised—as indeed it should have been. But at the same time, women have overidentified with the kind of agency ascribed to men. What is problematic about this identification lies in its connection to pathological gestures of virility. Such gestures are historically contingent. The Gulf War makes this point explicit. And for me, it raises an urgent question: when women demand the right to go to the front, to fight, to kill the enemy, or when gay men protest over their exclusion from the ROTC, are these appropriate aims to take up in the name of identity politics?

Until now, feminist theory has been centrally concerned with theorizations of the masquerade, with the critique of the objectification of women and images representing the woman as the object of desire. Certainly, this paradigm can be extended to include the man's relation to the feminine term. Nevertheless, what remains outside this formulation, which is taken for granted but not present to be looked at, is the problem of masculinity and its imbrication with whiteness and power.

This returns me to Géricault's painting and Bryson's comment about how it shows ". . . at least for the military culture of his time, that rank, which invariably positions each figure in the chain of military command, and the sense of masculinity as lack, absence, failure, go together across the suture binding the sexual and political orders."[5] There is an intricate connection between the display and the absence of visible effects. In relation to the sexual aim, Lacan describes it as a travesty. But this is not the same thing as masquerade. Located within the axis of identification rather than desire, the display is a form of intimidation, a defense. Exactly, a shield. This armor, this skeletal thing which doubles, the whole process of doubling, is more about homogenization than difference. When someone puts on a uniform, it is not about being looked at, but about obliteration.

This brings me back to the blind spot on the screen, the stain of blood, bodies, and pandemonium that constitutes the anamorphic image within the battleground. It points to a psychic excess that threatens to break the seal of the protective envelope, to puncture the shield by returning to the subject an image of his/her own abjection. Possibly this accounts for the process of dehumanizing the "other" that functions in the time of war.

Crucially though, the underlying association of the abject with the feminine makes sense of the psychic imperative for women to adopt the display. There is a desire to eradicate the traces of a femininity aligned with uncontrollable, contaminated, formless matter; to expel it like the infant rejecting the mother by vomiting her milk: an archaic projection, a thrown off skin that prefigures the mask, but at the same time threatens to ruin it.

Historically, the woman's story began with the hystericization of her discourse, but it has turned, maybe inevitably, toward the discourse of the master. In the case of display, there is a different way of shielding the body which is not about making it desirable; it is about grimacing, swelling, ". . . letting loose and hitting 'em with all she's got."

Notes

"On Display," 1992, *Whitewalls,* nos. 33–34 (1994).

1. Klaus Theweleit, *Male Fantasies* (Minneapolis: University of Minnesota Press, 1977), p. 155.

2. Noam Chomsky, *U.S. Gulf Policy,* Noospapers Pamphlet Series, Harvard University, 1990, pp. 15–16.

3. *Gloria Patri* is an installation consisting of thirty-one units, silkscreened, etched and polished aluminum, 20′ × 134′ × 2 3/8″ overall. It was shown at the Herbert F. Johnson Museum, Cornell University, March 1992.

4. Jacques Lacan, *Four Fundamental Concepts of Psycho-Analysis* (London: Hogarth Press, 1977), p. 107.

5. Norman Bryson, "Gericault and Masculinity," unpublished paper, 1990, p. 21.

Mary Kelly in Conversation with Margaret Iversen

Margaret Iversen: Recalling that historic exhibition in 1976 here at the ICA, when you showed the first three sections of the *Post-Partum Document*—in what was then the male-dominated arena of conceptual art— alongside works by Dan Graham and others, I wonder how you relate to Conceptualism now, if you still consider yourself in that tradition or critical of it?

Mary Kelly: I don't think what I say here is the last word on the work. I usually insist that I am just another reader of it, but when I look at that historical moment, and especially 1976 when the work was here at the ICA—in a series of programs that Barry Barker organized, including artists like Lawrence Wiener, Dan Graham, Art and Language, Victor Burgin—it seems significant to me now that I used a visual strategy similar to theirs, but tried to turn it around so that it did not refer specifically to the institution of art itself, but elsewhere. That is, questions, debates from outside, were brought in to challenge it. I suppose this is where the confrontation between feminism and Conceptualism arose, and marked a turning point in the art movement, too, where it became something else.

Iversen: You are often referred to as a conceptual artist and also as feminist artist. Is that something that you subscribe to?

Kelly: I think the important way to describe it is to say I am an artist whose work is informed by feminism. The way that many people—not so much now, but in the 1970s particularly—tried to define feminist art forms I think simply reinforces a rather prescriptive ideology. It is more interesting to think that there are many different tendencies, and that a work comes out of a specific history and addresses the questions in a way that is not at all universalizing.

Iversen: How did you come to the concept of your most recent work *Gloria Patri?* Did it grow out of *Interim* or was it prompted by the Persian Gulf War? What was the specific occasion for that work?

Kelly: Both. It was definitely the experience of the Gulf War that motivated me to complete it, but I had been thinking about it for some time before. Maybe I should say something about the organic quality, the project nature of the work, which takes up certain aspects of the earlier questions about conceptual art. First of all, I wasn't interested in producing a discrete object but in realizing a project over an extended period of time. It's a very familiar antiformalist strategy to think of all the ways of getting around the problem of composition, such as series, or system, or chance. But to place emphasis on the "idea" means that there is a real shift in the way that you visualize the piece. What I am aiming at in the installation is to get something which is not about style and not about a gestalt of form, but an accumulated sense of these different visual events that really hits you later, a kind of delayed reaction. I think this also comes from film and my interest in what I call the "narrativization of space." It's not just that I use narrative in the work, I am also interested in the way the spectator can be drawn into the space and involved in the experience of real time. Only secondly am I concerned about the way a conventional narrative can operate in that space. For example, it is not just a literal reading of the text, as there are a lot of other things happening in your peripheral vision, especially in this installation: trophies, for instance, which are slightly out of your eye line when you're reading the shield; and also, way above you, there are other kinds of slogans that you are taking in at the same time. I don't think this is at all like reading something which is in a book. It's only in the context of reading in the installation that the writing has its full effect. For me, there is such an organic relation between visualizing and theorizing that I have a hard time saying what comes first. It's certainly not a matter of defining the theoretical issues in advance and then, say, simply illustrating them. It is more a matter of discovering, in the process of doing the work, what these issues are. So in *Post-Partum Document,* in looking at the question of the mother's desire, the mother's relation to the child, I focused on the construction of femininity as maternal. But it was obvious to me, when I was making this work, that there is so much that is left out: all the other moments in a woman's life, and the question of postreproductive women in particular. This made me look at how a woman would configure her desire—her narcissistic pleasure, or whatever—outside of that maternal relation. By raising a whole range of questions to do with money and power and history, this investigation seemed to have excavated a psychic disposition which was deeply troubled by the idea of being like a man: the hysteric's dilemma could, in fact, be posed, "Am I a woman, or am I a man?" The next step logically would be to examine the construction of masculinity. So in *Gloria Patri* this is what I was concerned with: to look, not at the construction of femininity, but at how masculinity functions for the woman.

Iversen: You seem to be saying that you started with the story that comes last in the series: the woman's story. The exercise scene described in the *Gloria Patri* text illustrates the masculine ideal that the woman adopts. It became evident, then, that this was going to be a question while you were working on *Interim.*

Kelly: Yes, you have just reminded me that there is a certain reversal, not only in this work but in the whole trajectory of my work, that I hadn't really thought about before, in that I started with what is, in a sense, less visible in western culture. Certainly, representations of the mother have been absent since the nineteenth century in any explicit way. What I've ended with is an exploration of what is most visible in terms of, I suppose, a quality of masculine display or a certain form of masculine ideal that this work represents. It's very present, very consuming. But at the same time, it suggests a kind of underside: a repression of the feminine that had been the topic of the works before.

Iversen: There is a documentary aspect to your works: you research them, in an ethnographic way. For *Interim* you interviewed many women and studied women's magazines. Was there any similar empirical research which was important in the making of *Gloria Patri?*

Kelly: What I refer to as the "ethnographic" part of this appears in the etched plaques which have quotation marks on the trophies. It was during the Gulf War that I heard soldiers, both men and women, making their comments on the war and I was very struck with the range, from something incredibly inane like "Gosh, not enough Gees and Gollies to describe this," to something very sinister—"Well, we have to cut it off and kill it." So this constitutes the backdrop—for observation, so to speak.

Iversen: What about previous works of art? I know you have mentioned a painting by Géricault as being pivotal in your thinking about the precariousness of masculinity.

Kelly: Yes, I was thinking specifically of Géricault's *Charging Chasseur*. But this takes me back to some more involved thoughts on the Gulf War: how it was presented as a spectacle on television and the foregrounding of the technology involved. I will get back to Géricault in a minute. I was interested, first of all, to present masculinity as something that becomes pathological predominantly in the historical and cultural context of war: something to which Adorno referred, between the two world wars, when he said there is a certain gesture of virility which should be regarded with suspicion. A more recent writer, Klaus Theweleit, in *Male Fantasies,* describes the protofascist organizations of the thirties and says there is a certain construction of this totality, which he calls the troop machine, made up of soldiers, men who lose their individuality in the process of becoming a kind of hard exoskeleton, poised to confront the other. He also suggests that, as a means of expression, this totality presents itself as straight lines and hardened geometric shapes. As I was thinking about how the work would represent this materiality, well, it had to be polished aluminum. When I saw the prototype for the shield, I knew it was right because the surface practically made me sick, it was so severe. Theweleit goes on to say that the troop

Theodore Géricault, *Charging
Chasseur,* 1812. Courtesy Musée du
Louvre, Paris. Photo: © Réunion des
Musées Nationaux.

machine actually sets the stage for other types of totalities, like the nation. And, of course, the national crisis facing the United States as a military force immediately paralleled for me what Géricault saw in the crisis of the Napoleonic Empire at the time he painted the awkwardly mounted soldiers. Writing about the Gulf War, Noam Chomsky said that the United States no longer had a diplomatic role in the world. It had entered an era of alienation, especially in the Middle East, where it couldn't really use diplomacy in the same way. There was also the problem of its economic position, which was certainly by no means what you could call dominant, although this is a more complex question. So all it had was military force. Now this meant, I thought, that you had a really ironic situation: where the United States was producing this war hysteria filtered through a facade of efficacious militarism and, at the same time, the world in general was entering a period of demilitarization at the end of the Cold War.

So I wanted something that would communicate this facade: everything two inches off the wall—you know, even the trophies had to be "faux"—they couldn't be "in the round." It was very much like the surface of the thing that you see on television: the spectacle that the media presented. It just seemed incredible that all the protest about the war suddenly faded away when they took the vote in the House and in the Senate, then everyone brought out the yellow ribbons and decided they had to back it. You had this instant production of nationality and with it a certain masculine ideal which had already shown itself to be problematic. So if you take that historical stage and you pose against it what I was saying about the soldiers' comments: here they are supposed to be managing this incredibly complex technological machine and all they can say is "Not enough Gees and Gollies to describe it." Then you can see how vulnerable and how human they are. It is nothing like the fascists of the 1930s; it has become a parody. And then you have to add to that another dimension, which is that here we had women for the first time in the military, and they were demanding the right to go to the front, to have the right to kill; and at the same time, gay men were protesting their exclusion from ROTC. But once you have women, or gay men and lesbian women, in the military, it can no longer really function in the homogenous or hegemonic way it once did, because it has already become more heterodox: it's ruined, it's absolutely ruined as an

Mary Kelly, *Gloria Patri,* 1992 detail,
shield, 1 of 5, etched and polished
aluminum, 29 × 24 × 2¼ ins.
Photo: Kelly Barrie.

ideological tool in some sense, and this is what really interested me. To get back to Géricault, I was hoping that when you went into the installation, at first there would be a fascination with this facade of militarism. But then, when you came closer and read the stories, it would be like the soldier falling off his horse, because each story sets up a scene of mastery only to completely undo it. The plot doesn't work, and the spectator's relation to the installation is a bit like that too because you don't expect the stories to be so sympathetic when everything else about the work is a bit forbidding.

Iversen: Also, the stories aren't about war itself.

Kelly: No, they're everyday situations which invoke different kinds of vulnerability, showing the impossibility for the man of living out, as it were, that mode of the masculine.

Iversen: Could we talk a little more about the visual form of the work? You mentioned earlier that you didn't want to be locked into a particular style, or to approach the work in those terms, and that you start out with a certain set of ideas and perhaps some metaphorical connotations that are associated with certain kinds of films and materials.

Kelly: The visual references in *Post-Partum Document* are very personal, because I was dealing with a notion of fetishism for the woman; but with *Interim* I was interested in a certain form of narcissism and an engagement with images from popular culture. So in *Interim* the materials change: for example, deciding to use photo laminates instead of the found objects. To place them in a way that was much more evocative of public space, in scale and in relation to the body, was important. But there are ironic references to certain forms of minimal sculpture, too, in *Interim,* such as the David Smith or Richard Serra "effect" in the "Potestas" section, or in "Historia," when I used the rolled steel pages of the book, I often thought about Kiefer's piece called *Women of the Revolution*. I was determined to write a different sort of history: one that wasn't closed or heroic but rather could be seen as a continuing process, and which was concerned specifically with the history of the women's movement. Even though I draw from popular culture, I think what distinguishes not just my work but that of many British artists who have used images from popular culture is that I never directly appropriate without using what Stephen Heath calls the "strategy of depropriation," something that suggests a decolonization of the image.

In *Gloria Patri,* when I made the montages for the discs which appear in the upper register of the gallery, I had such a great time because I found these pristine military logos and then I got to cut them up. I decided it was going to be restricted to cutting two in half, the minimal slice as I call it, and then exchanging them. I didn't let myself get involved in composing: there is just a simple juxtaposition, but enough to make an ironic comment, I hope.

Iversen: I thought it had the effect of obfuscating the symbols, so that you had to struggle slightly to decipher them, as you would with a cubist painting. Also, because some of the military logos incorporated, say, an eagle or a lion, when collaged in this way they form peculiar hybrid creatures. I thought there might be a reference to them, or back to them, in one of the stories about the distorted reflection.

Kelly: I don't mind if that happens: that makes it productive from the point of view of the spectator. But it certainly is not my intention to make some complex, extremely metaphorical setup there, but to make this intervention evident, and to use the placement of the logos (which is very high up in the gallery space) something to suggest the force of those institutional references. It worked very well at Cornell, because the ceilings were thirty feet high and also because the university itself had so many emblems and logos of a similar type. In the ICA space, it is slightly more domesticated in terms of the architecture that surrounds it.

Iversen: You don't usually include iconic figures, but there are these trophy men who are carrying the letters of the Gloria which reminded me of that marvelous figure in the Rockefeller Center, of Atlas bearing a globe.

Kelly: That's right, they don't make those figures anymore: they come from the 1950s, and I liked them because they were as anachronistic as the whole military project of the United States at that time. Having them carry the letter of Gloria, you could say "What price glory?"

Iversen: What about the lighting? I found that very striking as well. Is it intended to evoke some kind of military scenario?

Kelly: I think it does indirectly, because it contributes to that facade-like spectacle, but when it is projected onto the trophies, the effect is one of casting the letters into a three-dimensional space. Ever since *Post-Partum Document,* when I stopped using the found object, I felt I had to find some way to bring back the quality of the index. It is interesting that you brought up the problem of images, representational images, because I'm often thought of as someone who never uses any. In *Post-Partum Document,* I placed a lot of emphasis on the indexical sign, but in "Historia" and in "Corpus," there are in fact quite a few references to iconic images. What I like to insist on, though, is that it's important not to reduce the image to the iconic sign but to see it as a heterogeneous system of symbol, or icon and index. Obviously, in *Gloria Patri* you do have minimal iconic properties: the trophies for instance, which are the closest you get to some figurative element. But in the logos you have a diagrammatic representation—a hybrid kind of symbol—so against that, against the hardness of that form of visual experience, the indexical quality of the light seemed important to me. Just as it did in "Corpus": something that was contingent on the particular installation. The way the spectators get caught in the light when they go up to the shields, or the kind of reflections that you get from the lighting and from your own reflection in the piece, means that the work can be negotiated in different ways. I think I referred to that earlier: I am not just interested in what you read but in the affective force of what you are experiencing while you are reading it.

Iversen: I just thought I'd say something about actually being in the installation and how I was taken aback: it was a similar experience, but different, to having seen one's own reflection in the "Corpus" series. You see your reflection through and against the text. But here it's something that one immediately wants to resist, so at least as a female spectator you almost want to get out of the way so that your image isn't reflected in that shape. I would now like to move on from the visual elements of the work to your use of language and verbal metaphor. I think you are a very interesting writer, and that one should take care to listen to the puns, the connections, the way the stories are all very carefully composed. If you feel it's appropriate, perhaps you would read one of the stories to us before we talk further.

Kelly: "Ignoring the trail, he'd followed a tributary to the river. Sharp currents gouged their course through ferruginous clay, spalling iron ore from the bank where he stood watching the endless flow of water over the rocks: like a tap left on, he thought. That was ideal. It would trap the insects, flushing them down into still pools. There, the trout would be waiting, and he would be too, with bated breath, a snelled hook number four, and a wet fly. No weights or clips. He'd present the bait naturally, that way it would be carried with the current under the stones to the enemy's intimate entrenchment. They spooked easily and he stalked them with a delicate belligerence. Wading upstream, he stirred the sediment and his expectation swelled. He knew they were there. Sometimes he would catch a glimpse of them: scarlet gills, dark fingermarks on the silver side and a white underbelly. He longed to touch one, to feel it, wet and slippery, struggling, its life in his hands. He could do whatever he wanted: cut it up and eat it, or throw it back. When he pulled a hook through the tender flesh, it felt like the point of a sharp phrase that turned an argument in his favor, or the butt of a joke about big cocks and virgins. Lively but short-lived; a brook trout was fragile and delicious. Still, he would probably release it. Just to touch it, that would be enough. He would be satisfied. When a man touches a fish, he reflected, he touches something far away, something *real*. Nearby something gray and white and beaky watched him or his tackle, which one, he wasn't sure. Four feet high, black plumes behind the eye; a heron, possibly a Great Blue, waited to purloin his catch. Its canny presence moved him to observe the wilderness more keenly. The tangle of berries, the dank air, the soft earth, the scent of pine needles freshly crushed. It was life-sustaining, but at the same time threatening. Instinct poised, he prepared to meet the challenge before him, or after him as the case might be. His crested rival, moving closer, eyed the tuftless dibbler who, looking at himself in a watery reflection, saw the body of a beast and the head of a man at the mercy of his own imagination: then it shuddered and let out a raucous 'grak.'"

Iversen: I read this story as having two parts: the first part is a fantasy of mastery over nature and of an imagined natural hierarchy of the fly, the trout, and then the man. You anticipate what is going to happen when you say he has "bated breath": he is caught in some kind of lure or fascination with an image of the great white fisherman. The mood completely changes when the bird is introduced and the man becomes objectified as a "tuftless dibbler." He then looks at his reflection in the river which is all fragmented. There is also the issue of sadism, was that part of your idea?

Kelly: Yes, there's an implicit heterosexual sadism being played out meta-phorically. Each story has a different function in terms of the fantasy of mas-tery it explores. In contrast to this one, there is another story where the man is witnessing the birth of the child, so it's asking a question about his stake in paternity. Or in the baseball story, it's much more about the man's homoerotic relation to other men, also his loss of control, about his age and his body. But it is overdetermined by his class position, and by what he represents as an unemployed man in a specific social context. Then, proba-bly surprising, the fourth one is about an adolescent boy who listens to Nine Inch Nails (industrial/techno) which locates him in a way as dissatisfied, white, and working class, but his idea of mastery is primarily one that's associated with transgressing his mother's desire. This is interesting when you think about the bad boy/bad girl image in art, too. You know how it's just the other side of the authoritarian coin, because it is only when you're positioned within that ideal—which is constitutive of a certain masculine identity—that you compose yourself either as the law or as breaking it. In a certain sense, the feminine term falls outside of it, not literally but in terms of this negotiation: it's hard to be bad if you have no position from which to make the transgression. The way the characters, in the third and fourth stories, view women makes it logical that in the last story you will think there is every reason why a woman would not want to be a woman: that she would actually try to distance herself from that image of abjection and embrace this notion of mastery, rather sadomasochistically, against herself.

Iversen: We have been circling around some psychoanalytic concepts: we have just raised the issue of abjection. One of the reasons why I wanted the story in front of us is because I think you can get so much out of the stories in themselves, without a whole backlog of psychoanalytic theory. I know because I teach some of your work to undergraduates who don't know anything about psychoanalysis. But it might be interesting to rehearse quickly some of the important psychoanalytic concepts which are in the background of your work, although they are not stated on the surface or even necessary for a comprehension.

First, there is the issue of ego formation and the mirror stage. It's unfortunate that the English term "stage" has the theatrical resonance but doesn't convey the sense of a stadium with the connotation of a competitive arena. I think most of us think of the mirror stage as the necessary illusion of a coherent body image in anticipation of a future coordination. But we tend to forget about the unpleasant aspect of this experience: the way it's linked with an original infantile distress, the fear of the fragmented body, so that in very close proximity there is this shockproof image and this total fear of fragmentation. There is also the way in which narcissistic identification with another, who is perceived as superior, unleashes fraternal rivalry and aggression. Clearly, notions of aggressivity are very important in the context of this work.

But I wanted to suggest to you that perhaps one way of looking at your work as an intervention—I mean you have never been supine in relation to psychoanalytic theory—is that you might be suggesting that Lacan's formulation, the notion of the ego, is in fact a description of a certain masculine pathology of the ego. I brought along what I think is proof positive that this is the case: a passage right at the end of a 1953 article, "Some Reflections on the Ego," which was first published in English, where Lacan talks about Homo Psychologicus and the relation between him and the machines he uses. He says that they are very striking, especially in the case of the motor car: "We get the impression that his relationship to this machine is so very intimate that it is almost as if the two were actually conjoined: its mechanical defects and breakdowns often parallel his neurotic symptoms. Its emotional significance for him comes from the fact that it exteriorizes the protective shell of his ego, as well as the failure of his virility." So masculinity and the structure of the ego are very closely linked.

Kelly: That is exactly what I was interested in: what you could describe as this defensive structure of the ego. But I'm very fascinated by what Lacan *didn't* say, and how you work through the gaps. For example, the quote that you just gave reminded me of another statement on the notion of display which comes from the *Four Fundamental Concepts,* where he says that the "male" animal in this play of combat throws off something like a skin to cover the frame of a shield. Why is it the "male" animal? So much time has been spent thinking about the construction of femininity: using the concept of masquerade to describe a psychic structure for the woman that was aligned to a certain notion of passivity and silence. It was assumed that in making her visible, precisely in being looked at, that she played out this part as "lacking." That is, she disguised the lack of a lack, created desire through that kind of veiling. But isn't it absolutely true that this is the case for men too? If you look at something like bodybuilding, it is not the penis but the body itself that is phallicized, made into something to be looked at rather than "listened to." And you could say that this discussion of masquerade shouldn't be restricted to the discussion of sexual difference, in that explicit sense, because it also has implications with regard to race and class. I re-member.thinking about that in the seventies when the punk movement produced a certain form of subcultural visibility that was about marking the body with a sign of lack, and in terms of "ethnic" identity: who is it that wears the native costume? I recall how on Guatemalan money the women are barebreasted, but the men are in modern dress. Acting out the phantasm of what the other wants you to be—Homi Bhabha talks about this and of course, Fanon, in *Black Skin, White Masks.* Although I would align masquer-ade with the visualization of that position of otherness, I don't think of difference as symmetrical in the sense of self and other. What you have is the heterogeneous nature of difference posed against what is the same or homogeneous. So if we go back to the quote from Lacan and think about another psychic structure, one which involves the notion of display, it seems to suggest at least three things.

The first, you could say, has to do with playing out the part of having the phallus, or the fraud of the phallus, that is, a certain definition of display that concerns the sexual aim. But there's another use of it, which is not implicated in this "sexual travesty," as Lacan calls it, but comes out of his discussion of mimicry. That is the notion of camouflage which, for me, in relation to the military, is irresistible. When someone puts on a uniform, what happens? He loses any visible distinction from the others except as he's positioned in that particular organization. He obliterates difference in order to install himself in this hierarchy, and in fact loses the body totally in order to have a speaking presence, to have authority. It's not just the man in his military uniform, but the businessman in his suit, or the artist in his leather jacket: it is all about what will give you a place from which to speak, at the cost of having a kind of bodily presence. In the installation it is important to me how, at one level, the body seems to have been erased, with this hard shiny metal surface, but then as you negotiate that space, the body reappears and dramatizes that whole relation of absence and presence. Third, there is what Lacan describes as intimidation: not the lure, which is what is effective in devising the masquerade, but this thing that he calls the shield of thrown-off skin that defends us against the vulnerability of visibility and body.

Although this is a little controversial perhaps, I would say that it is impossible to think about that defensive structure of the ego without also thinking about the problem of identification. I know this is an extremely schematic suggestion, but if it's the object of desire and not the object of love that is feminine, then there is something about constituting the subject in terms of this object of desire that is taking place in the whole phantasmatic scene of masquerade. And there is something else taking place on the side, of what I have been calling the display, that concerns how you set up an ideal. It's what you love: what you want to be, not what you want to have. When you talked about the mirror stage, you alluded to the fact that there are two end points: the first is aligned to that aggressive moment of identification, but the later point involves an internalization of the image and the setting up of an ideal. I think it is culturally overdetermined that the ideal will be (for want of a better term) masculine. And my project, in short, is to see what that means for women. Perhaps we have unconsciously incorporated a form of masculinity that is equally problematic, and this crisis of women in the military is just a symptom.

Note

"Mary Kelly in Conversation with Margaret Iversen," *Talking Art,* ICA Documents, 1994, pp. 101–117. Transcript of the seminar held in conjunction with the exhibition, *Gloria Patri,* Institute of Contemporary Art, London, 1993.

Miming the Master: Boy-Things, Bad Girls, and Femmes Vitales

.

When it comes to sexuality and images, the theoretical imagination has been captured for the most part by the lure of masquerade. Work informed by psychoanalytic theory in particular has followed the shiny surface of that concept through the maze of women's objectification, constructions of the feminine and strategies of resistance to prevailing visual codes. More recently, it has illumined the issue of masculinity as well, but the focus remains on what is obviously signifiable of that identity as iconic sign. Falling outside this formulation, taken for granted but not present to be looked at, is the problem of masculinity's imbrication with relations of power. The events of the Persian Gulf War—especially the presence of women in the military (not to mention my own inclination to wear a professional "uniform" of another kind) have prompted me to sidestep the masquerade and take up instead the notion of masculinity as *display*. Finally, in light of Lacan's significant omission of the "female animal" from his discussion of the topic, I have found it a compelling alternative.[1]

Lure

First of all, I should say that when I align masquerade with the feminine term, I simply mean that it functions in that position psychically, that is, in the space of passivity and silence assigned to the object of the look. But this does not imply indifference. The subject *actively* takes up a passive aim, continually negotiating and infringing the limits of this psychic antinomy. The spectacle, in this sense, is not literal. At the level of the unconscious, the masquerade can refer to a gesture, a symptom or a complex system such as masochism. At another level, the masquerade impinges on the cultural order as a mode of conscious acting out; a performance of identity which is bounded, as Emily Apter has suggested, by the tyranny and pleasure of the stereotype.[2] The stereotype produces at once a visual rhetoric of socially specific meanings and a cipher of incalculable unconscious intent. The masquerade effectively maneuvers between the compression of the signified and the endless deferral of the signifier, by articulating the body as a language by making it visible, sometimes subversively so.

Here, I am thinking not only of the *femme fatale,* but of the *homme vital.* In his interrogation of masculinity as masquerade, Norman Bryson refers to an image of Schwarzenegger: "The whole body is phallicized, from marks of inflation, to removal of body hair, to exaggerated dilation of the veins. The masculine imago is contemplated, in other words, by erasing out the actual genital area and passing its characteristics to the body image as a whole via a trope of metonymy: the whole is made to stand in for the part."[3]

No doubt this has become the formulaic method of depicting male virility; nonetheless, it is enacted in the feminine position psychically, in so far as he sees himself from the place of the Other as the "would-be" object of desire. This is evident even when the metonymic trope is replayed with a significant reversal, as it is in the pornographic version of the body builder where the marks of inflation and exaggerated dilation accrue to the missing part. The presence of the penis only enlarges the absence of its symbolic dimension: in being the phallus, he cannot have it. Or, at least, that kind of simultaneity of psychic positionality would provoke a crisis.

Kobena Mercer has explored this ambivalence in his reading of a photograph by Robert Mapplethorpe, *Man in a Polyester Suit.*[4] First, noting the objectifying consequences of framing the open fly, then doing a double take, he acknowledges the empowering fascination of that image for the spectator in the position of a gay black man. Sexuality siphoned through the stereotype of race leaves a curious residue: woman is the body, but the black man, as Frantz Fanon puts it, "is a penis."[5] Both masquerade as being for the Other. His image, though, takes on the disguise of *having* "the real thing." In seeing it, the threat of the phantasmatic phallus fades. Or does it? When sexual and racial difference are condensed into a single metaphor of corporeality and then displaced on to a specific part of the body, that object is

Lyle Ashton Harris, *Constructs #10,*
1989.

endowed with the power of a fetish. By substituting the penis for the missing
phallus, the threat of castration, which in this case, could be said to include
the unconscious imprint of historical retribution for racial injustice, is post-
poned. Moreover, as Fanon has argued, the founding moment of difference,
embedded in the assumption of an image as gestalt of the body, privileges
not only the signifiers of gender, but also those of race.[6] In the fetishist's
scenario of deferment, then, the eroticization and degradation of the racial
as well as sexual other can be played out at the same time. By substituting
something, in this case the penis itself, for another penis of imaginary proportions, the viewer indulges the ambivalent pleasure of controlling or being controlled by his peculiar piece of reality. Yet it is precisely this
invocation of the Real that threatens masculinity with ruin by botching, so
to speak, the notion of difference as symbolic play.

Alessandro Codagnone, video
still from the installation *Mean
Room,* 1994.

Read symptomatically, the desire and disturbance generated by the male
body suggest the difficulty of representing masculinity as masquerade, even
when reworked parodically in an effort to expose the absurdity of sexual
norms. Take for instance *Constructs* by Lyle Ashton Harris or Alessandro
Codagnone's image of a man in boxer shorts, blond wig and heels.[7] There
is a moment of laughter and recognition, yet there is also something else,
something beyond the pleasure of producing gender hybrids, that disturbs
the balance of their athletic bodies, not consciously perceived, but felt: a
sense of vulnerability, of illness and of death. This fear of "weakness," according to the artists, is projected on to what is seen as "feminine" within
the gay community itself, and often denigrated, reinforcing an expression
of the masculine as virile display.

Within a more conventional domain of gendered images as well, masculinity has been construed as the production of tangible might. In the analysis of subcultures, rock music, particularly heavy metal, is cited as exemplary in this regard. Gestures of virility appear to abound—long hair, leather, high energy performance, sutured to the amplified sound of repetitive riffs in four-four time. But it is exactly this appearance of difference that betrays the passive aim: to be what the other wants you to be, as Roland Barthes describes it, "pure object, a spectacle, a clown."[8] To signify a position outside the Law is to become a figure of infinite excess, but definitive lack. This is not to say there is no relation of power involved in seduction, but it is not the same thing as legitimation.

The tendency to link the spectacle of masculinity to representations of the working class seems especially relevant to the distinction I am trying to make between the masquerade as lure and the display as ruse of authority. Stuart Hall, for example, equates the boots, braces, and cropped hair of the Skin Heads with "qualities of hardness, masculinity and working classness."[9] He maintains that language, dress and ritual are symbolic objects that can be made to form a unity. Yet they also reveal an unconscious process that disrupts systematic intent. The subject lies, that is, disguises himself with the clear and visible signs of his otherness. Lack is fundamental, but nevertheless layered with social contingencies. If separation from the means of production is internalized as a demand which cannot be given its object, then what prevents the subject from sliding, unconsciously, into empty want and erasing the historicity of that frustration. Perhaps, nothing. But I think it is also possible that the psychic economy offers the contract of symbolic castration as a way out. By translating demand into desire through the so-called defiles of the phallic signifier, it provides the liminal means of representing not only sexual, but also *social* difference and the possibility of expressing it in the form of class antagonism.

In this instance, the figure of virility is not simply a defense against the feminizing effects of disempowerment, but a strategy, as Michèle Montrelay observes with regard to women, that throws the dimension of castration into relief as trompe l'oeil.[10] "The crazy things, feathers, hats and strange baroque constructions" with which she invokes the sartorial surfeit of the masquerade easily slip into the signifying chains, safety pins, bondage, and hair dye of the Punks. Their visibility, perhaps even more than the Skin

Heads, registers the social conflict explicitly as a seditious sexual trope. Style can evolve into something homologous as Hall suggests, but in my view, when it does, it is no longer style. It becomes invisible, in effect a uniform, and, as such, begins to function more in the manner of display. According to Lacan:

> In the case of display, usually on the part of the male animal or in the case of grimacing swelling by which the animal enters the play of combat in the form of intimidation, the being gives of himself, or receives from the other, something that is like a mask, a double, an envelope, a thrown-off skin, thrown-off in order to cover the frame of a shield.[11]

One of the implications of Lacan's statement, as I see it, is that the psychic trajectories of display and masquerade are not symmetrical. What transforms an expression of virility into a relation of "having" rather than "being" seems to involve a complex disappearing act. This, perhaps, explains why the signs and insignia of domination are so elusive.

Both concepts—masquerade and display—are implicated in the broader discussion of mimicry which, referring to Lacan, is an activity employed in three dimensions: travesty, camouflage, and intimidation.[12] In the first form, which places emphasis on the sexual aim, masculine and feminine identities are mediated through "something like a mask." Revolving around a relation to the phallic term, the masquerade pretends to be "lacking"; *le parade* or virile display professes to be replete. The subject wants to be loved for what he is not, hence the travesty as Lacan sees it: there is no sexual relation.[13] In both instances, the function of the mask is that of a *lure*. But, while the masquerade in all its effects can be attributed in some way to that function, the display cannot. It is also shaped in the dimensions of camouflage and intimidation that give the mask a different force—that of the double, the protective envelope, the thrown-off skin. Thrown-off precisely to cover the vulnerability of being seen.

Camouflage

Lacan describes the effect of mimicry in the strictly technical sense as *camou-flage:* "It is not a question of harmonizing with the background but, against a mottled background, of becoming mottled—exactly like the technique of camouflage practiced in human warfare."[14] The soldiers' appearance is, in fact, strikingly nonmimetic. They do not look like anything: a shapelessness inserting itself into the landscape; nothing in particular becoming mottled in the general scheme of things, hoping to go undetected in the light. This is not a matter of adaptation, as Lacan insists, but a *process of inscription.* In an effort to escape being trapped by the gaze, the subject inscribes himself in the picture in the manner of a "stain." Inevitably he is caught in the field of vision and fractured, split between what he thinks he is and what he shows the Other. Still, there are different ways of becoming a picture: a stain is not a lure. The spectacle lures the Other into looking behind the veil by creating the desire to see something. But the stain tricks him into thinking there is nothing there to see.

"What I am doing is no greater or less than the man who is flying next to me," says Major Marie Rossi to a CNN reporter in January 1992.[15] Standing in the desert dressed in camouflage and becoming mottled against a background of institutionalized male dominance, she insinuates that national defense is sexblind. The first tactic of camouflage is to become invisible, not unseen, but seen to be the same. For the camera she is a shimmering surface in the distance, not quite a picture, but an impression made in advance. She is wearing a uniform; exactly, the parts made uniform, none greater than the whole. To achieve this, her individuating corporeality, *her* body, must be obliterated. Klaus Theweleit writes: "What the troop machine produces is itself as a totality that places the individual soldier in a new set of relations to other bodies: itself as a combination of innumerable identically polished components."[16]

That psychic disruption which *is* sexuality and which the body implies, must be denied. Object choice of any kind is strictly off-limits, but, of course, it is still on their minds. And, the soldier (fe)male is a continual reminder. The prefix signals an alarming addition to the ranks; a remainder of "affect" invading the consummate order of military command.

She is, however, not Private, but Major Rossi. This is the second maneuver of camouflage and the one which links it inextricably to the display; that is, the specific form of visibility conferred by rank. Authority accrues or is diminished according to her place within a coded hierarchy. Power is

Cadets march in formation during a ceremony at the U.S. Air Force Academy, Colorado. Courtesy United States Senate Historical Office, Washington, D.C.

presented through the absence of conspicuous effects. Virility is disembodied, but discernible as gesture, voice, intonation, insinuation, or silence. Theweleit again: "The troop also produces an expression; of determinations, strength, precision; of strict order, of straight lines and rectangles, an expression of battle and of a specific masculinity."[17]

The expression of masculinity as order imposes a curious displacement of desire. What the soldier cathects, above all, is the abstract order of the law itself. And what is repressed returns in similar guise, that is, as a form of linguistic contagion. Judith Butler has observed that, in the military context, an utterance can become the equivalent of an act. To say, "I am homosexual" establishes an identity which in turn is equated with a conduct.[18] The imaginary scene of verbal seduction might express the interlocutor's unconscious wish, but provokes instead a reaction-formation: "perverse" desire can be caught like a disease, transferred through speech. Hence, the juridical solution: Don't ask, don't tell. But renunciation, as Freud points out, preserves the wish by reproducing it as prohibited desire. Similarly, Theweleit suggests that even in peacetime the troop machine has a border to defend, "it compresses inward toward its own interior," which in the current situation means policing the sexual conduct of its components, and "war offers temporarily, an opportunity for discharge."[19] An army paratrooper, having taken her first Iraqi prisoner of war, wrote to her mother from the Persian Gulf describing it as "the most exciting thing since sex I've done."[20]

Furthermore, Theweleit concludes, "The surplus value produced by the troop is a code that consolidates other totality formations between men, such as the nation."[21] The nation, like gender, has a psychic border, and a "display" of nationalism can also fail to cover the frame of a shield that has lost not only its economic metal but also its diplomatic sheen. This seems to have been exactly the case for the United States during the onset of the conflict with Iraq, leaving the president with only one "manly" option—force. Thus, in a case of grimacing, swelling, and swearing "Cut it off and kill it," a nation entered the play of combat in the specific form of intimidation called Desert Storm.

Intimidation

Threatening ejaculations and gestures as thrown-off skins cover the body's vulnerable interior with an imaginary carapace. "The ego," Freud maintains "is first and foremost a bodily ego, it is not merely a surface entity, but is itself the projection of a surface."[22] This is, I think, what Lacan has in mind when he calls display a form of *intimidation:* gestures of virility deployed not only in the service of the sexual aim, but also as the ego's defense against annihilation. From Freud's point of view, within the perception-consciousness system, the ego takes sides with the object to resist the id. However, "the libidinal subject," as Lacan reformulates it, "interacts, not with his environment, but with his orifices."[23] In the schema of narcissistic identification, the ego takes sides against the object and the body's orifices are subjected to control by means of a libidinal cathexis of the body as image. In its earliest formation, then, the imago vacillates wildly between the body as *gestalt* and the *corps morcele.* The drive for self-mastery is continually thwarted by an incoordination that takes on existential proportions. In *Some Reflections on the Ego,* Lacan states:

It is the gap separating man from nature that determines his lack of relationship to nature and begets his narcissistic shield with its nacreous covering on which is painted the world from which he is forever cut off, but this same structure is also the sight where his own milieu is grafted on to him, i.e., the society of his fellow men.[24]

In this formulation, I see a crucial intersection between the ontological question of "man" and the ethical issue of social transformation. Display as a form of intimidation is grounded in the founding moment of the subject as his "narcissistic shield," yet virile display as the specific "sight" of masculinity is "grafted on to him" in the same move. The shield bears the impress of "society," etched on to its phantasmatic surface through the operations of the ego ideal. This I believe, also opens the concept of display to a symptomatic reading, that is, to a definition of the particular pathology of masculinity that prevails in a circumstance like war. Although, I do not mean to say that the historical reality of war is reducible to psychological explanation. Rather my interest resides in the historical overdetermination of the symptom and the problem it poses for feminism at the present time.

To return, then, to Major Rossi, whose literal carapace was a Chinook chopper, it was not invulnerable and her death has become an ignominious testimony to equal access. Metaphorically, it is suggestive of the intimate relationship between man and the machine—"Its mechanical defects and breakdowns often parallel his own neurotic symptoms," observes Lacan. "Its emotional significance for him comes from the fact that it exteriorizes the protective shell of his ego, as well as the failure of his virility."[25] In Major Rossi's case, the failure of virility was not determined by her gender, but by the intimidating display of technology itself. The aura of digitized control, distant from the scene of battle, dehumanized, presented the individual soldier of the Gulf War, unlike the protofascist *Freikorps* of the 1930s, as so many unpolished components in their archaic armor who were made to appear imperfect and ambivalent in relation to the role of mastery.

The military facade throws "strength" into high relief as a defining attribute of masculinity; not simply physical, but moral strength with its emphasis on achievement. Lt. Col. Rhonda Cornum, for example, is described as an Army flight surgeon, helicopter pilot, biochemistry Ph.D., paratrooper, Persian Gulf prisoner of war, Purple Heart recipient, and conservator of heterosexual norms—wife and mother. When captured, she had only one regret: No time to swallow her wedding ring. No weakness there. Two broken arms, a wrecked knee, bullet wounds in her shoulder: war is an occasion to display the self-punishing, self-sacrificing symptoms of a "strong ego" like trophies.[26]

Combat, in a sense, materializes the ego's tendency to build itself up by opposition, displacing its alienation on to the other. Jacqueline Rose points out that ". . . paranoid impulses don't just project onto reality as delusion; they affect reality and become a component of it." And regarding the Gulf War she adds, "the problem for Bush was that, having called up the image of Hussein as utter monstrosity, he had to go to war."[27] While the immediate impact of the conflict may have blurred the distinction between fantasy and reality, the after-effects brought it into focus again. First, there was a certain irony attached to the deployment of force in an international context of increasing demilitarization. Secondly, the escalation of electronically regulated warfare was experienced in fact as a loss of control by soldiers in the field. Finally, the problem of women and gays and lesbians in the military— having called up the image of *that* "utter monstrosity," the institution's hegemonic status would never be the same.

"Sameness" is exactly that intractable quality of authority which places the burden of authentication on the other. The military institution is only the most obvious instance of an all-pervasive, but less conspicuous display of virility. Take, for example, the typical EOE ad encouraging women, minorities, and the disabled to apply: the unspoken term (white able-bodied male) assumes a relation of power in which the infinitely variable and hence vulnerable majority are "feminized."

I would argue finally that display, as a defensive strategy of the ego, attempts to maintain a distance from the objectifying function of the gaze and project instead the idealizing agency of identification. Beyond the specular dimension of the shield, it supports the subject's narcissistic relation to an ideal; how he makes himself lovable in the eyes of the Other, *he* being the appropriate designation here, since, as Catherine Millot points out, it

Lt. Col. Rhonda Cornum speaking at halftime, Army-Navy Game, 1991. Lancer photo: Don Schwartz.

Rules Committee, U.S. House of Representatives. Courtesy United States Senate Historical Office, Washington, D.C.

is the object of desire and not the object of love that is feminine.[28] And the ideal, insofar as it is shaped within the gendered order of the symbolic, is masculine.

Of course, to assume a position of authority does not mean it is internalized as such. At least, for the subject to sustain that illusion of unity, to take his own ego as the ideal, would induce a dysfunctional form of megalomania rather than a discourse of mastery.[29] Even though the conditions of subordination may be socially discernible, their psychic consequences are less certain.

Clearly, a masculine or feminine position is not synonymous with the category man or woman. Indeed, the subject is not commensurate with any fixed identity as such. Behind the mask, what is discovered is not the truth of sexuality but its opacity. Lure or shield, both disclose no more than the specific modes of that failure. Nevertheless, considered in another way, as an enactment of difference within a designated site or status, the display internalizes and encodes the structures of power and dominance as masculine. I am not suggesting there is a hegemonic form of masculinity to be exposed, yet something seems to ruin the act when it is staged by women.

Hybrid

When Homi Bhabha describes hybridity as an effect of uncertainty that afflicts the discourse of power, he is referring specifically to the English book and its colonial appropriation.[30] But I also find the term useful in thinking about the way power is afflicted by the uncertainty of gender when women appropriate the familiar symbols of male authority by adopting the display. This displacement of value from symbol to sign Bhabha says distinguishes the operations of the hybrid from those of the fetish and endows it with a certain legacy of resistance. Yet the fetish is neither good nor bad and the hybrid, in my view, is not always subversive. In particular, the "gender hybrid" can serve to legitimate as well as disrupt the dominant discourse or to institutionalize the marginal and, through a process of disavowal, can be reconfigured as a fetish.

In a display of political authority that has now become a caricature, Margaret Thatcher lowered her voice, tailored her clothes and projected an image of control unparalleled by any of her male counterparts. She inscribed herself into the political picture of the conservative party with a calculated conformity, but the camouflage was less than perfect. "People are more conscious of me being a woman than I am," she complained.[31] The facts of gender, imposed, internalized as an effect of the interpolation: Look, a woman! "Iron Lady," ironic mask, at once revealing and denying an "itself" behind it. "Hybridity," explains Bhabha, "represents that ambivalent 'turn' of the discriminated subject into the terrifying, exorbitant object of paranoid classification."[32] "In practice as sentimental as a Black widow," remarked a BBC commentator, turning Thatcher into a specter of terrifying uncertainty and in a sense, a hybrid; but her exorbitance was neither disruptive nor transformational.[33] Reveling in the Falklands victory, prodding Bush to go to war with Iraq, taking an aggressive stance on capital punishment, she unsettled the feminist assumption that women are not violent. By combining the rationality of law and order with a stereotype of gender, Rose argues that "Thatcher presented a femininity which does not serve to neutralize violence, but allows for its legitimation."[34]

Alternatively, attempting to avoid gender stereotypes when she was questioned by the *New York Times* about her political aims and her sexual orientation, Patricia Ireland, the president of the National Organization for Women said: "I'm a hybrid." Although she probably meant to convey the idea of something "new," I was intrigued by the article's description of the "dichotomy" of her image. At one moment, she was ". . . leading a counter protest outside the abortion clinic . . . jostled and spat upon by Operation Rescue." At another, ". . . every hair in place, she attended a seminar of constitutional lawyers . . . parsing the intricacies of abortion law."[35] What constitutes the effect of uncertainty here is neither the problem of her gender, nor of her object choice, but the problematic of political representation for feminism. The disavowed, jostled, and spat-upon protester reenters the official discourse of jurisprudence parsing intricacies as an advocate of women's rights and *estranges* the basis of its authority, that is, the rules that determine who can speak, about what, and for whom. Her presence, even with every hair in place, marks an absence in the established order of things. And her statement exerts a pressure, not adversarial but solicitous—the desire to be considered.

"As soon as I desire," writes Fanon, "I am asking to be considered."[36] It is the desire not to be desired, not to be "sealed into thingness," but to be recognized that prompts the self-effacing strategy of camouflage. The Sunday *Times* describes an artist "dressed casually in a lavender T-shirt and faded black dungarees, her make-up-less face framed by frizzy gray hair" recalling her desire: "To be a painter meant, I thought that I could never get married or have a family. It was like going into a convent."[37] To paint a picture, first it is necessary to become one; to become mottled, in this case, against the gender-biased background of abstract painting in the 1950s. But it is a familiar insinuation beyond periodization. Desire requires a sacrifice. To be considered, "I turned myself into an asexual gnome," she confessed, writing herself back over, but not exactly *on* the line of what is called the avant-garde—those practices which privilege the sexual economy of masculinity, and moreover, privilege sexuality itself as their central and most subversive theme. An imperfect double, her *horsexe* traced over his *per(e)version;* she attempts to erase difference, while he appropriates hers.

Recall, for example, Andre Breton's encounter with Nadja's visionary madness, Marcel Duchamp's cryptic invention of an alter-ego, Rrose Selavy, or Andy Warhol's Drella, the cross-bred (Dracula-Cinderella) persona of his novel *a.* "The artist" has already positioned *himself* on the side of the heterogeneous and the unsaid, the insane, the outrageous and the perverse, then named it after *her.* To be a "woman artist" and to be signified as such is like a double negative. Of course as Susan Suleiman conjectures, being "doubly marginal" she could conceive of herself as "totally avant-garde."[38] She could trace her passion for the masquerade back to the maternal body; to pleasure which is forbidden, but not perverse. Through the trajectory of the castration complex, the subject is ejected into a domain of symbolic obstacles which inevitably turn around the Name-of-the-Father. Janine Chassequet-Smirgel comments, "The pervert is trying to free himself from the paternal universe."[39] He creates chaos in an effort to erode difference once it is in place. *She,* on the other hand, in making an alliance with the mother, would be returned to the Signifier of the Real Other and to the realm of lost objects. For me, there is an irresistible analogy here, one concerning the fate of work informed by feminism in the recent past.

The Oedipal dramas of art history are staged between fathers and sons across the body of the mother. To resolve the ambivalence of his active and passive wishes, the son is faced with a dilemma: Should he kill the father or seduce him. But what of the daughter? She is also given the father's name which positions her as his potential rival. This event however, takes a significant turn. It has been customary, within many cultures, to assign a forename which displaces the symbolic meaning of the paternal metaphor by changing it into a sign of her difference, her disinheritance. Consequently, among women artists and writers there has been a long and honorable tradition of pseudonyms, initials, and enigmatic agnomina; disguises which, in their curious mimicry, afflict the patronym with uncertainty. In her catalogue an artist writes, "I guess I had the desire to be somebody different, to reinvent myself. I first picked the name Alex arbitrarily from a person in a movie as a nice, androgynous nickname." [40]

Once again, I find the invocation of an "outside sex" symptomatic. Perhaps it is not enough for a woman to internalize her paternal imago in the form of an ego ideal. She must also present a self-image which instates her fully and centrally within the father's jurisdiction. For she cannot break the law, or revise the canon, from a place outside of it. Ingest his name and status first, *then* spit it out. Yet her participation in the totem meal is contingent on a disavowal of the mother. And that is her dilemma.

My interest here is not the clinical picture of that conflict, but in the artistic strategies that "work through" the psychic resistance to, and the specific social imposition of, aesthetic rules. Considered as a discursive system, rather than a history of designated movements, the avant-garde could be said to construct the category of creative subjectivity as essentially transgressive and metaphorically feminine. In this respect, it cuts across the discourses of both modernism and postmodernism, appearing as a divergence from the norm when it poses as oppositional practice, but converging with it on the issue of originality. [41] In fact the notion of transgression constitutes one of the foremost rules of recognition for originality within the institution of fine art; so much so that the creative subject, presumed to be male, could be said to *assume the masquerade of transgressive femininity as a form of virile display*. The same scenario applies to the daughter too, who must not be dutiful, that would let the mask slip, reveal her disguise. The masculine ideal

Zine cover, *Bad Girls,* New Museum of Contemporary Art, New York, 1994.

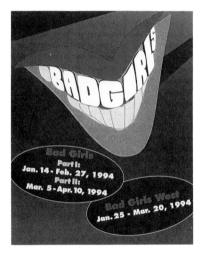

she incorporates effectively returns her own image to her, as in a mirror, inverted. The double fraud of "being-as-having." To pull that off, she must resolve her Oedipal dilemma, then subvert it, create chaos, erode difference, be "perverse": in other words, be "bad."

Grimacing, swelling or "spilling and spewing, exhorting, insulting, cajoling, cheering and cursing" in the words of Marcia Tucker, artists (mostly women and a few good men) entered the play of combat in the form of an exhibition with the appropriate and timely title, Bad Girls.[42] It opened in New York in January 1994 simultaneously with its "independent sister" in Los Angeles, Bad Girls West, the coincidental Bad Girls show in London, and two mainstream films of the same name. The exhibition was complex and extensive and my treatment here will be schematic. But, precisely because of its extent—there were over one hundred participants, and its complexity—there were two sites (one of which divided the presentation of work into Parts I and II, and both included video programs, a zine and souvenirs) the exhibition as a system privileged curatorial authorship in terms of reading, or making sense of, its unwieldy imaged discourse. This is signaled by the genre—it is a theme show, and developed through conventions of presentation such as wall text and other forms of visual or audio aids that signify access to curatorial intention. The exhibition's spatial and temporal organization also emphasizes spectatorial engagement and above all, entertainment. Finally, curatorial intentionality is consolidated in the catalog of which, in contrast to the dispersal of visual events, there is significantly only *one* version and in it, both curators celebrate the undutiful daughter's coming of age. Their stated aim is to appropriate the avant-garde's tradition of transgression for their own. In effect, they have abandoned the discrete camouflage—leather jackets, no makeup, and no-nonsense of artists who hoped to "pass" by denying sexual difference as well as the feminist masquerade that dutifully reassigned it by representing "woman." Instead, they have adopted a form of intimidation, "Bad girls aren't polite, they're aggressive," writes Tucker, "they curse, rant, rave and make fun of and mimic whomever and whatever they want, themselves included."[43]

Mimicry as an artistic strategy can expose the visual codes that constitute the canon to ridicule. Yet, it also discloses the psyche's defensive posture in the act of doubling: the thrown off skin; thrown off to cover the frame of a shield, to protect the artist from the enfeebling effects of her gender. In this intricate rendition of display, *a woman mimics a man who masquerades as a woman to prove his virility.* Or, translated into zine-speak: A girl thing being a boy thing being a girl thing in order to be a bad thing.[44]

As an institutional practice, the exhibition is antitraditional, but not necessarily oppositional. The curators stress that not everyone included in it is a feminist, but they are unconditionally and without exception, "bad." "Not only do these artists disobey explicit commandments enjoined by the fathers and handed down through the mother's complicity," claims Marcia Tanner, "they ignore the entire myth of male hegemony, of paternal lawgivers in art and everywhere else."[45] In this, they have upheld the avant-garde's central and most sacred convention: art as transgression for its own sake. The aim is not simply to subvert the law by proposing a different order, but to *pervert* it by opposing all order, entirely and everywhere.

As the expression of a curatorial desire, the exhibition asks the artist to imagine herself free of the paternal universe, suggesting that she has already shaped herself within it—an identification so complete, a mime so perfect, *he* would want to be like her. "They've freed themselves with such spiritual irreverence, such conviction and assurance, that male artists are now imitating them."[46] Of course, "they," fabricated by the curatorial imagination, are not synonymous with the checklist of artists whose statements and practices never quite concur with the given theme. Probably, the most productive reading takes place in the gap between them.[47] But, what I want to take up, in a more general way, is the implication of the *diatext* (exhibition and catalog combined) as double; that is, the avant-garde imago and its bad girl double. In the gap produced between the historicity of misbehavior and its repetition by the Other, a dislocation, but not a shift, of power is visualized or, more accurately *visualizes.*

The exhibition presents a vertiginous diversity of media and dimensions, but the visual rhetoric collides on a single tact: the joke. It ranges in complexity from parody and appropriation to slapstick, innuendo and pun. Above all, there is one image that, for me, encapsulates this rhetoric and the particular kind of spectatorship the exhibition endorses. It is an untitled, black and white gelatin silver print by Coreen Simpson, conventionally real-

Coreen Simpson, *Untitled,* gelatin
silver print, 1980. Courtesy New
Museum of Contemporary Art,
New York.

ist in that it appears to record a chance event, but unusual in the subject and object positions it constructs. In the photograph, two women divide the frame. One, her more-than-full figure enhanced by a tight knit dress, conjures an image of excess. The other, svelte shape and demure attire, implies restraint. Yet, the picture illicits an instant eruption of laughter because it construes "just the opposite" meaning. The pivotal point of this reversal is the oblique glance of the woman of an exiguous type at the voluminous posterior of the other.[48] She is caught looking, exposed in a moment of shock and disgust; her pretensions, her desire to please, her susceptibility laid bare for all to see. She is out of control, off balance. In fact, she is falling out of the frame and destabilizing its symmetry while the carnivalesque figure takes charge. She is placed firmly in the frame, the light pulling her into the foreground, her stance an expression of composure and confidence. But this does not mean she becomes the object of identification for the viewer. In the background, there is a rather obscure, but crucial outline of a man with his back to the camera, signifying that the male gaze is, in a sense, excluded from the picture. A woman, in the position of spectator, takes his place outside the frame. The joke is told for her pleasure at the expense of both subjects in the photograph—one as an object of ridicule and the other as spectacle. Situated in the masculine pose psychically, she then realigns herself with the image of transgressive femininity. The fact that she chooses the bad girl thing, rather than being assigned to it, is empowering; but the photograph's division of the frame is indicative of the kind of partition the exhibition imposes on its audience. Indeed the resolution of the image, its intelligibility and tendency to closure produces a form of enjoyment specific to the joke: either you get it or you don't. It is significantly different from the prevailing notion of the avant-garde text as the instigation of a difficult pleasure, one in which, as Barthes suggests, the subject struggles with meaning and is lost.[49]

Tucker's interpretation of avant-garde textuality has very little to do with its historical manifestations in art and literature. Linking it instead with Carnival's symbolic inversion, she claims that the role of the avant-garde has been to "turn things upside down."[50] Carnival occasions have always been officially sanctioned by the dominant culture. It is permitted to break the law within its own limits; to turn things upside down for a day. As events

they are extravagant yet self-contained, usually indifferent to an organizational politic, but that does not mean they are without political significance.
Carnival festivities make fun of those of a higher status, Tucker claims,
"bringing them down to size."[51] Hence the exhibition's emphasis on humor
as a tactic of intimidation is undertaken, in the end, as a *display of mastery*.

In contrast, the avant-garde's relation to the law is not one of inversion,
which implies a separation from one order and the naming of another, but
of perversion, that is, the suppression of structure and division. This is not
to say that heterogeneity as an aesthetic stance cannot be institutionalized.
Indeed, it has become a defining feature of "high art." What interests me is
the way the authority of the institutional discourse is unsettled when a will-
ful misreading (such as Tucker's) is mapped on to its surface. The spontaneous objections to the exhibition—there are too many artists, it all looks
alike, why only women—articulate in negative the silent assumptions of
scarcity, originality, and a certain gender, making visible what is present but
not seen because it is taken for granted as the precondition for, and the truth
of, all great art. As Bhabha comments in another context, "the display of
hybridity—its peculiar 'replication'—terrorizes authority with the ruse of
recognition, its mimicry, its mockery."[52] On the one hand the exhibition,
it seems to me, is exactly this, a ruse of recognition. The title itself, Bad
Girls, traced back, written over the "avant-garde" (bad boys known simply
as "good artists") produces a surplus—too visible, too literal, too desiring.
For this reason it results in a deficit, that is to say, the title inscribes a lack
into the insignia of "greatness" by turning transgression into a sign of sexual difference.

At the same time, the uncertainty this project generated in the art world
was not indicative of its reception elsewhere. Within the entertainment sector, it fell into place without a ruffle, largely because the bad girl was mis-
taken for her more familiar and commodifiable double, the *femme vitale*.

Fetish

Infused with desire according to the logic of fantasy, rather than the dictates
of the object, a fetish is said to be both unpredictable and obstinate. Yet,
inevitably its imaginary form is filtered through regimes of visibility which
leave a culturally specific residue on the enchanted thing. In other words,

fetishism's incantation of the sexual crisis is historically inflected. Since the Gulf War, for example, there have been innumerable images of women in uniform, provocatively posed with machine guns or tanks, as well as a prolific genre of thrillers which feature the ingenue murderess. Although what I find most intriguing is the sedate variation on this theme which has been proffered by the fashion trade.

In August 1992, Anne Klein launched *My Uniform*. Double-breasted suit, slicked back hair, the model is composed within a flank of smiling firemen. Their identical white shirts and black ties forge an alliance with the corporate image of men in suits who are remarkably unmemorable and, for exactly that reason, strategically positioned as those for whom the "others" will perform, will explain, will ask to be considered. But their array of shiny buttons and, above all, badges weld another kind of union. They are objects, as Genet phrases it, "in which the quality of males is violently concentrated," not the silent insignia of power, but the specular display of rank.[53] Inserted into *that* picture, her uniform appears to be much more than a stain.

Bhabha maintains that in the fetishistic ritual the object changes, while its meaning remains the same. It must substitute for the missing phallus and register difference at the same time. But with the hybrid object, the semblance of the authoritative symbol is retained while its meaning changes; that is, it comes to signify a certain process of distortion.[54] For instance, the Anne Klein image gives the appearance of retaining some aspects of male authority associated with the uniform—the model's absence of jewelry, of exposed body parts or exaggerated posture. But against the imposing backdrop of emblazoned masculinity, that meaning fades. The distortion of her symbolic presence turns precisely on her absence of rank. Note the Chief Fireman's white cap, it becomes the key signifier of that order from which she is excluded, signaling her return to the site of sexual difference. This displacement is in fact so severe that the ambivalence it generates overturns the significance of her image as a hybrid and becomes once again the fetish for which meaning always remains the same.

What *My Uniform* has in common with the bad girl phenomena—the films by design and the exhibitions by default—is the neutralization of a social conflict that threatens the imperatives of heterosexuality and gender hierarchy. The clothes, gestures, and role playing that dominate the repre-

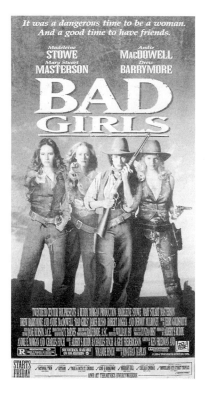

Bad Girls, film poster, 20th Century Fox, 1994.

"My Uniform," © Anne Klein II,
Mirabell, no. 39, August 1992. Photo:
Arthur Elgort.

sentation simply present a new configuration of phallic attributes, at once disguising and reinscribing the women's lack. For the hypothetical male fetishist, the script might be: If women are equal to men, that is, not castrated; then I will be castrated. Yet I can see she is different from the others so I am safe.

To some extent, the demand for equality by women in the military may be regressive, particularly when it is presented as the "right to kill," but in another way, it provides a seductive image of empowerment. After all, when Rhonda Cornum dons the uniform, she does get it right. As George Sand said "to avoid being noticed when dressed as a man, one must already be accustomed to avoiding notice when dressed as a woman."[55] The desire to identify with the masculine imago is incited by the thrill of passing. But the portrayal of Cornum as a hybrid combination of gung-ho militarism and motherhood is also an occasion for ambivalence and, perhaps another scene of disavowal. For the hypothetical female fetishist the script might be: If women are not equal to men, that is castrated, then I am castrated. Yet, I can see she is not like other women, so I am safe.

For the woman, display provides a form of protection against her social subordination, but it is also problematic. In the case of display, not only, as Lacan says, on the part of the male animal, but also the "female animal," entering the play of combat means covering her vulnerability with a peculiar psychic armor, one that separates her, finally, from other women. While a certain form of precocious femininity has been exorcised, and I would not want to revalorize it here, women may have overidentified with the kind of agency ascribed to men. In effect, the internalization of that ideal has supported the unconscious alignment of the feminine with derogation and abjection. In the historical perspective of sexual politics, Joan Riviere's influential observation of the woman's crisis has been reversed.[56] Now it seems that "manliness" is her defense and on her narcissistic shield, the icons of hysterics have been painted over with the emblems of the master. To address that critically would mean acknowledging that one of feminism's monumental paradigms—the masquerade, has shifted.

Notes

1. This article extends, in another way, issues which I originally addressed in the form of an exhibition. See *Gloria Patri* (catalogue), Herbert F. Johnson Museum of Art, Cornell University, and Ezra and Cecile Zilkha Gallery, Wesleyan University, 1992.

2. Emily Apter, "Acting Out Orientalism: Sapphic Theatricality in Turn-of-the-Century Paris," *L'Esprit Createur* (issue on "Orientalism after Orientalism") 34, no. 2 (summer 1994): 102–116.

3. Norman Bryson, "Géricault and 'Masculinity," *Visual Culture: Images and Interpretations,* eds. Norman Bryson, Michael Ann Holly, and Keith Moxey (Hanover and London: Wesleyan Press, 1994), pp. 235–236. Although I agree with Bryson's use of the concept of masquerade to describe the psychological poses of the body builder, I feel it is less appropriate with reference to the paintings by Géricault. For example, the destabilization of the image in *Charging Chasseur* does not imply, as Bryson claims, a failure of the "masculine masquerade." If he describes the military culture of that time as one which positions the male figure in a chain of command, that is, rank, then "failure" here, in my view, pertains to a different, though equally fragile, psychic structure, namely, the *display.* In this article I argue that display involves the internalization of an ideal of masculinity encoded as an authoritative absence, rather than seductive presence, of the body or its visible effects; so when the soldier's display of virility in that sense fails, it turns into a posture which, because it suggests vulnerability, resembles the masquerade, but does not really function in the same way either socially or psychically.

4. Kobena Mercer, "Skin Head Sex Thing: Racial Difference and the Homoerotic Imaginary," *How Do I Look?* ed. Bad Object-Choices (Seattle: Bay Press, 1991).

5. Frantz Fanon, *Black Skin, White Masks* (New York: Grove Press, 1967), p. 170.

6. Ibid., p. 161. In chapter 6, "The Negro and Psychopathology," footnote 25, Fanon interestingly applies Lacan's formulation of the mirror phase to the question of racial difference, the founding moment of which he locates in the pre-Oedipal aggressive stage.

7. Alessandro Codagnone, *Mean-Room,* installation including etched plaques, handwritten text, photography paste-ups, and video. Whitney Museum ISP Open Studio, 1994.

8. Roland Barthes, *Mythologies* (Paladin, 1972).

9. Stuart Hall, *Resistance through Ritual,* eds. J. Clark, S. Hall, T. Jefferson, B. Roberts, Hutchinson, 1976, cited in Dick Hebdige, *Subculture: The Meaning of Style* (New York: Methuen, 1979), pp. 113–114.

10. Michèle Montrelay, "Inquiry into Femininity," (1977), trans. Parveen Adams, *The Woman in Question,* eds. Parveen Adams, Elizabeth Cowie (London and New York: Verso, 1990), p. 264.

11. Jacques Lacan, *The Four Fundamental Concepts of Psycho-Analysis,* trans. Alan Sheridan, ed. Jacques-Alain Miller (London: Hogarth Press, 1977), p. 107.

12. Ibid., p. 99. In defining three types of mimetic activity, Lacan follows Roger Caillois's analysis in *Meduse et Compagnie.* See also Roger Caillois, "Mimicry and Legendary Psychasthenia," *October* 31 (winter 1984).

13. Jacques Lacan, "God and the Jouissance of Woman," *Feminine Sexuality,* eds. Juliet Mitchell and Jacqueline Rose (London: Macmillan, 1982).

14. Lacan, *The Four Fundamental Concepts of Psycho-Analysis,* p. 99.

15. Anna Quindlen, "Women in Combat," *The New York Times,* January 8, 1992.

16. Klaus Theweleit, *Male Fantasies,* volume 2, "Male Bodies: Psychoanalyzing the White Terror," trans. Erica Carter and Chris Turner (Minneapolis: University of Minnesota Press, 1977).

17. Ibid.

18. Judith Butler, lecture and discussion at the Whitney Independent Study Program, New York, March 4, 1994.

19. Theweleit, *Male Fantasies,* p. 155.

20. Linda Bird Francke, "A Different War Story," *The New York Times Book Review,* August 10, 1992.

21. Theweleit, *Male Fantasies,* p. 155.

22. Sigmund Freud, *The Ego and the Id* (1923), standard edition, vol. 19, trans. James Strachey (London: Hogarth Press, 1961), p. 26.

23. Jacques Lacan, "Some Reflections on the Ego," paper read to the British Psycho-Analytical Society, May 2, 1951, published in *The International Journal of Psychoanalysis* (1953): 11.

24. Ibid., p. 14.

25. Ibid., p. 15.

26. Rhonda Cornum, *She Went to War,* the subtitle reads: "The inspiring true story of a mother who went to war, as told to Peter Copeland." (Novato, CA: Presidio

Press, 1992). My emphasis here is on what has been written *about* her, *not* on her own comments, which are thoughtful and at times even critical of the Gulf War.

27. Jacqueline Rose, *Why War?—Psychoanalysis, Politics, and the Return to Melanie Klein* (Oxford: Blackwell, 1993), p. 29.

28. Catherine Millot, "The Feminine Superego" (1984), trans. Ben Brewster, *The Woman in Question,* eds. Parveen Adams and Elizabeth Cowie (London and New York: Verso, 1990), pp. 294–306.

29. See Kaja Silverman's discussion of reflexive masochism in "White Skin, Brown Masks: The Double Mimesis or With Lawrence of Arabia," *Differences* (issue on masculinity) 1, no. 3, (1989).

30. Homi Bhabha, "Signs Taken for Wonders: Questions of Ambivalence and Authority under a Tree Outside Delhi, May 1817," *Race, Writing and Difference,* ed. Henry Louis Gates Jr., (Chicago and London: University of Chicago Press, 1985), p. 174.

31. Kenneth Harris, *Margaret Thatcher Talks to the "Observer,"* published as a separate booklet, January 1979. Cited in Rose, *Why War?,* p. 65.

32. Bhabha, "Signs Taken for Wonders," p. 174.

33. John Nott, interviewed on BBC Panorama, *300 Days,* January 4, 1988. Cited in Rose, *Why War?,* p. 65.

34. Rose, *Why War?—*Psychoanalysis, Politics, and the Return to Melanie Klein, p. 59.

35. Jane Gross, "Does She Speak for Today's Women?" *The New York Times Magazine,* March 1, 1992.

36. Fanon, *Black Skin, White Masks,* p. 218.

37. Deborah Solomon, "Celebrating Paint," *The New York Times Magazine,* March 31, 1991. She is quoting the artist Elizabeth Murray.

38. Susan Suleiman makes this comment in the context of discussing *The Ravishment of Lol V Stein,* by Marguerite Duras, in *Subversive Intent: Gender, Politics and the Avant-garde* (Cambridge, MA: Harvard University Press, 1990), p. 16.

39. J. Chasseguet-Smirgel, "Perversion and the Universal Law," *International Review of Psychoanalysis* 10 (293, 1983): 299.

40. *Alexis Smith,* exhibition brochure/checklist, Whitney Museum of American Art, New York, November 21, 1991–March 1, 1992.

41. My limited concern here is with the critical apparatus that constructs an artist/

author for the work of art and the gender bias that implies. This may sound in some respects similar to Poggioli's emphasis on the psychological "residues" that underpin the ideological "formulas," of the avant-garde, but in my view, this is no more problematic than an historical analysis such as Burger's. See Renato Poggioli, *The Theory of the Avant-garde* (1962), trans. Gerald Fitzgerald (Cambridge, MA: Harvard University Press, 1968), and Peter Burger, *Theory of the Avant-garde* (1974), trans. Michael Shaw (Minneapolis: University of Minnesota Press, 1984). In both accounts, it is not the object the discourse constructs, that is, ideology in first case, (expressed as activism, antagonism, nihilism, and agonism) and the sociopolitical history of the work of art in the second (periodized as the autonomy of art in bourgeois culture of the late eighteenth century, the aestheticism of form as content in the mid- to late nineteenth, and the critique of both suppositions by the historical avant-garde of the early twentieth); but the conclusions they draw from their respective analyses which effectively cancel out any transformative potential for the discourses/practices of the neo-avant-gardes. Hal Foster takes up this point critically in "What's Neo about the Neo-Avant-Garde?", *October* 70 (fall, 1994): 5–32. Yet all the arguments, including Foster's, seem to ignore the fact that authorial subjects are divided—ethnically, socially, sexually—and the effects of these divisions inevitably disrupt in unexpected ways, I think, the relevance of evaluative projects as such.

42. Bad Girls, an exhibition organized by Marcia Tucker at The New Museum of Contemporary Art, New York, Part I: January 14–February 27, 1994, Part II: March 5–April 10, 1994. Bad Girls West, an independent sister exhibition organized by guest curator Marcia Tanner for the UCLA Wight Art Gallery, Los Angeles, January 25–March 20, 1994.

43. Marcia Tucker, "The Attack of The Giant Ninja Mutant Barbies," *Bad Girls* (catalogue) (New York: New Museum of Contemporary Art, and Cambridge, MA: MIT Press, 1994), p. 20.

44. In conversation with zine artist Tammy Rae Carland, Los Angeles, 1994.

45. Marcia Tanner, "Mother Laughed: The Bad Girl's Avant-Garde," *Bad Girls* (catalogue), p. 77.

46. Ibid.

47. Mary Kelly, "Re-Viewing Modernist Criticism," *Art After Modernism: Re-Thinking Representation,* ed. Brian Wallis (New York: The New Museum of Con-

temporary Art and Boston: David R. Godine, 1984). See section on "Exhibition and System," pp. 99–103.

48. Compare Mary Ann Doane's analysis of "Un Regard Oblique" by Robert Doisneau in which the male subject gazes obliquely at the female nude in complicity with the spectator at the expense of the older woman who is centrally framed in the picture and becomes, in that exchange, the butt of the joke. Mary Ann Doane, *Femmes Fatales: Feminism, Film Theory, Psychoanalysis* (New York and London: Routledge, 1991), pp. 28–31.

49. The implication here is that the notion of transgression as a process that disrupts the systematic order of language is the dominant theme within the discourse of avant-gardism and that the institutional question has been in a sense, more marginal. In this respect, Barthes's distinction is exemplary: "Text of pleasure: the text that contents, fills, grants euphoria; the text that comes from culture and does not break with it, is linked to a comfortable practice of reading. Text of bliss: the text imposes a state of loss, the text that discomforts (perhaps to the point of a certain boredom) unsettles the reader's historical, cultural, psychological assumptions, the consistency of his tastes, values, memories, brings to crisis his relation with language." Roland Barthes, *The Pleasure of the Text* (1973), trans. Richard Miller (New York: Noonday Press, 1989), p. 14.

50. Tucker, "The Attack of the Giant Mutant Ninja Barbies," p. 24.

51. Ibid., p. 28. Tucker bases her comments on Peter Stallybrass and Allan White, *The Politics and Poetics of Transgression* (Ithaca: Cornell University Press, 1986).

52. Bhabha, "Signs Taken for Wonders," p. 176.

53. Jean Genet, *The Thief's Journal* (1947), trans. B. Frechtman (Harmondsworth, England: Penguin, 1967).

54. Bhabha, "Signs Taken for Wonders," p. 176.

55. George Sand, *Histoire de Ma Vie* (Paris: Gallimard, 1970). Cited by Jan Matlock in "Masquerading Women, Pathologized Men: Cross-Dressing, Fetishism, and the Theory of Perversion," *Fetishism as Cultural Discourse,* eds. Emily Apter and William Pietz (Ithaca: Cornell University Press, 1993).

56. Joan Riviere, "Womanliness as a Masquerade" (1929), *Formations of Fantasy,* eds. Victor Burgin, James Donald, and Cora Kaplan (London and New York: Methuen, 1986), pp. 35–44.

Index

if she's changed. no
huge leather jacket
e her face, small
ss, emblazoned: liv
onsense baby, if you
I am in debt, no dou
mitted, wishing t
Stunned by the 'ri
ued by every detai
had a presence m
attractive without t
d to have them, kep
y found some that
t stylishly distress
, wore them all th

if she's changed. h
huge leather jacke
ke her face, small
ss, emblazoned: lu
nonsense baby, if yo
I am in debt, no do
nmitted, wishing t
. Stunned by the 're
ued by every deta
had a presence m
attractive without
ad to have them, ke
ly found some that
ut stylishly distres
g, wore them all t